GOURMET *to* GO

GOURMET *to* GO

A Guide to Opening and Operating a Specialty Food Store

ROBERT WEMISCHNER
KAREN KARP

John Wiley & Sons, Inc.

New York • Chichester • Weinheim • Brisbane • Singapore • Toronto

Copyright © 1998 by John Wiley & Sons, Inc.

Library of Congress Cataloging-in-Publication Data

Wemischner, Robert.
    Gourmet to go : a guide to opening and operating a specialty food
store / Robert Wemischner and Karen Karp.
      p.   cm.
    Includes index.
    ISBN 0-471-13939-4 (cloth : alk. paper)
    1. Food industry and trade—United States. 2. Food service—
United States. I. Karp, Karen. II. Title.
HD9005.W45   1997
641.5′14′068—DC21   97-14628

To the memory of my aunts who so many years ago believed in me and spurred me to continue learning and teaching others and myself to appreciate the finer things in life.

R. W.

To my assistants: Johnny Ceballos, Jake Sigmund, and Monica Gelinas, who really go with the flow. To the people who inspire, educate, and support my enthusiasm and well-being: Dick Batten, Anna Herman, Jay Perry, and Elfi Six.

K. K.

~

CONTENTS

~

PREFACE

Is the specialty food business for you? How do you know? Maybe you're a chef who's got the back-of-the-house routines down cold. You've worked your way up the kitchen hierarchy from cook (or dishwasher) to sous chef to executive chef. You're piloting a smoothly running kitchen, staffed by highly motivated cooks, supported by an excellent sous chef, but you're bored with the routine. You need a greater challenge, and you want more creative autonomy. The 60- and 70-hour workweeks are beginning to wear thin. Your salary, albeit a good one, is just not enough. You've been salting away some of that hard-earned pay and your financial reserves are beginning to look healthy. You've been itching to go it alone, to put yourself on the line; you want to offer your quality foods to a larger audience and reap the rewards of doing so. What to do? Open a gourmet food store with an emphasis on prepared foods-to-go in a location that will draw all of the clientele you've been serving in the restaurant where you now work.

Perhaps you're the food and beverage manager for a large hotel chain, honing the financial and managerial skills you learned in hotel school. The bottom line looks good to your boss. You've kept labor and food costs in check. You're a real "people person" who can easily establish a good rapport with the cooks and busboys. Over the last five years, you have worked your way up the corporate ladder from waiter, to dining room manager, to catering supervisor and now to food and beverage manager, but you've reached a plateau. The prospects look less than glittery for any big time promotions in the near future. You've saved a little money and have developed a file of prospective investors during your tenure at the hotel. You're thinking about taking those moneyed individuals at their word—the ones who say to you "Give me a call if you ever decide to open a place of your own."

It may be that the corner deli has been in your family for almost fifty years. Your grandfather began it a few years after he came over from the Old Country. Your father is getting on in years, and you've been taking a more and more active role in running the show. Times have changed, however; people are eating less meat, and higher fat foods are starting to lose their universal appeal. The store needs freshening, and that space next door is ripe for takeover. You've been doing prepared foods for all these years, but you need to take credit for it and expand the line. Pasta salads have supplanted the old macaroni salad and that Italian-style roasted potato salad with olive oil and rosemary has eclipsed the good old-fashioned mayonnaise-laden potato salad of your youth. That space in the corner could display a well-chosen array of wines to go with the rotisserie chicken you've been meaning to add to your offerings. The loan officers at your bank like those mile-high sandwiches you put on the catering trays you send over for their lunch meetings, and they like your steady business even more. Maybe your line of credit can be extended. Why not bring your "friends at the bank" a business plan for expansion along with that next tray of sandwiches and arrange a time to sit down and talk?

You could be a graduate from a prestigious culinary school who worked in restaurants for a few years just after graduating. Then, tired of the highly pressured environment, you were lured away by an upscale supermarket chain to develop recipes and oversee production for their in-store food service department. By now, though, the large, somewhat impersonal, multitiered corporate hierarchy is beginning to chafe. You'd like to be your own boss. You decide to take the plunge.

Maybe you're the proud owner of one of the last family-run grocery stores on the good side of town. Prime meats and high quality produce have been your stock-in-trade. The grandchildren of your first customers are now bringing their children in for that free cookie handed over the bakery counter. Those large chain supermarkets closer to the interstate are expanding their prepared food offerings, though, and you need to compete. Your deli cases need refreshing, and while you're at it, you might as well add a self-serve soup and salad bar. You're not sure which way to go, however, where to put the bulk of your bucks.

With its healthy dynamism, specialty food retailing never stands still. Time and again, it's been shown that those retailers who are slow to respond to change in the retail climate don't make it. It's survival of the fittest, and being fit means being able to cater as deftly to busy two-career couples (with or without kids) as to the single urban professional who simply does not know how to cook, but who is seeking a good, even restaurant-quality, meal at home. Quick, tasty, wholesome, varied, convenient and affordable describe what customers are demanding from their local specialty food retailer. If a retailer's offerings don't fill the bill on at least two of these, then chances are that store won't be around to see the next trend.

With an ever more discerning, well-traveled public looking for alternatives to dining out, the retailer is forced to be on top of the trends—or to set them. Bottom-line-conscious retailers today need to monitor closely the buying patterns of an increasingly diverse population. They have to know what their customers are thinking, what their buying habits are. They have to account for these in their marketing efforts and product mix. The well-informed specialty food retailer also knows that restaurant chefs and cookbook authors influence food trends, and that he or she needs to offer the tools and ingredients to recreate those dining experiences at home. All the same, paying close attention to what these chefs, in particular, and the food media, in general, are saying is only part of the story.

Flash back more than twenty years to Paris in the mid-1970s, and to Robert Wemischner, a future gourmet retailer who wanted to join the many breaking new ground.

Young and innocent, I entered the world of gourmet food retailing dazzled by what I had seen, tasted, and experienced in Paris in the mid-1970s. Fauchon . . . Hediard . . . Dalloyau . . . Le Comptoir Gourmand of Michel Guerard . . . Lenotre . . . all places whose form and content set a standard of perfection that I longed to duplicate (more on those and other touchstone temples of gastronomy later). Theirs was a world of sparkling foods, high priced, pristinely presented, sold by helpful but unobtrusive counter clerks who knew their clientele and knew their product line from the inside out, who were confident in recommending the makings of a no-work-for-the-host takeout meal. In the store of my dreams, all of the foods were neatly and attractively wrapped and complete down to the extra leakproof containers of sauce and dressing, all with precise and detailed preprinted instructions for reheating and serving. Spoiled by the best, fired up with enthusiasm, I sought to recreate a bit of the spirit, if not the letter, of Fauchon's magic on this side of the Atlantic. Why not start at the top? I thought. Well, things did not turn out quite the way I planned. (They seldom do in the retail business.)

First of all, finding the prime ingredients to replicate the jewels in Fauchon's display cases proved to be difficult—and finding the customers for them was even harder. I was willing but the public wasn't quite ready. Compromises needed to be made. Although dreams die hard, good businesspersons quickly learn that in the specialty food trade, as in all retailing, it is essential to be flexible with your dream. Foie gras and salmon in sorrel sauce would have to wait while the customers become used to Chinese chicken salad and vegetable pâté. In my reconfigured dream, I would (and did) introduce the public slowly to new foods, never bombarding them with too much novelty; if you lead cannily and carefully, the customers will follow. Generous sampling and much talking and romancing (through store signage and printed newsletters) proved key. Over time, I found that once customers gained confidence in my foods, they were receptive to anything I sold them. It didn't take long to turn "What's that? Is it good?" into "If *you* sell it, then it just *has* to be good." Initially resistant customers became willing and venturesome.

A few of the hard-won lessons: Realize that packaging (and, of course, contents) are vital. Provide good service, because it's paramount. Know your customers, address them by name, and never insult them by adopting a know-it-all attitude. Be sure all your staff do the same. And never forget that customers who are willing to pay a high price for convenience and quality also seek the status that comes with serving such special foods. Being the first on their well-manicured block to try my foods was a privilege they would gladly pay for. In summer, my customers played a game of one-upsmanship, vying to see who could bring the most tasteful and most beautifully presented picnic to the outdoor music festival. Did I care that *they* took all the credit for preparing the foods themselves? Of course not. They bought a completely new concept or, rather, an old concept redesigned, repackaged. They spread the word, which in the 1970s helped the business grow, which in turn advanced the concept of gourmet to go in the hands of independents, which spawned supermarket and hypermarket clones of the concept (1980s to the present) . . . and from there the rest is history.

Are there any sure-fire strategies to success in the specialty food industry? Can opening a business be reduced to a formula with a finite number of steps and variables? Probably not. If you follow the logical sequence of steps presented in this book, dotting all of your I's and crossing all of your T's, will you succeed? It depends. As in any other industry, there are the "overnight" success stories about owners who had no right to succeed, given the rules they broke along the way, and yet who beat the odds and succeeded in a big way. Was it "luck"? Maybe. Was it "timing"? Maybe. Was it "location"? Maybe. Was it the force of their personality? Probably several of these and more. You can't plan for such success.

But if there is one constant that we have heard time and again from owners of specialty food stores, both large and small, independent and chain-affiliated, it's this: Give the customers a good reason to integrate a new habit into their lifestyle (i.e., to become your repeat customer) and you will gain a loyal following. Whether you are freeing up a customer's time in a frenetic, overcommitted routine, or offering convenience (easy-in, easy-out), you have to key into your customer's habits and eating patterns to be successful. And you have to do it every time. No misses allowed. A customer may forgive you once and be bought off with a refund and free replacement for the foods they didn't like; two lapses and you've lost them to the competition.

Once they have established time in their lives for you, however, and as you continue to provide reasons for them to come back for more of your products and services (with variety, cyclical menus grounded with an unchanging basic menu of offerings), then you've got them hooked. Furthermore, they will spread the word for you. Bar none, the best advertisement is one happy customer telling his or her friend about you. Be sure to acknowledge that referral by offering something special to the individual you have to thank for sending you a new customer.

From retailers who are marketing their product line to shop-at-home customers on the Internet to stores that offer a full line of organic produce and chemical-free poultry, the specialty food retailing industry is going in many directions at once.

Savvy retailers soon learn that, to be successful, they need to look over their shoulders constantly for the next trend; they must find a way to fit new products and services onto an already crowded plate. Acting on trends without missing a beat and taking creative risks to stay hot every moment of every business day is really the name of the game. As in all retailing, of course, convenience and consistency of quality run neck and neck in importance with service.

Any way you look at it, opening a business is a risk. In today's retailing and economic climate, challenges are bigger, stakes are higher, risk are greater, but rewards for success and opportunities to succeed are just as big. In this book we will communicate just how competitive and serious the business of specialty food retailing is today. We will provide you with a comprehensive overview of the industry, the market, the tools to get you to the point of being able to make a commitment to go ahead, a thorough outline for your business plan, checklists for the most important planning stages, anecdotes and recommendations from the top players in the industry, and tips and insights into the intangibles of what makes good businesses good. You will have a better chance of success by being well-armed and taking all the right precautions through careful preopening research and development. You will see that, for success, it is not just information and organization but ample funding that will give your new business a fighting chance to ripen, develop, and succeed. Guided by this text and the accumulated wisdom of sage retailers who've paved the way, and fueled by your own enterprising spirit and imagination, dream big, plan carefully and proceed with confidence to success.

ACKNOWLEDGMENTS

We gratefully acknowledge all the shop owners and other professionals around the country who agreed to be interviewed and share their secrets and stories with us. It is their spirit and passion for bringing good food to the marketplace that not only sets an example in specialty food retailing today but also paves the way for future entrepreneurs.

Robert Wemischner
Karen Karp

GOURMET *to* GO

CHAPTER ONE

INTRODUCTION AND HISTORY OF THE SPECIALTY FOOD BUSINESS

On the face of it, it's a simple enough transaction. You enter a well-stocked, attractive gourmet food store any time of day, are entranced by a seductive array of freshly prepared foods, encounter helpful and knowledgeable service, and proceed to purchase dinner for four, from a perfectly seasoned soup to a glistening crisp tart for dessert. Exit thanking the counterperson (whom you are not surprised to learn is the owner) for his or her courteous help. Take the foods home (no leaky packages). Heat as directed, devour all with relish, and be eager to get back to the store as soon as possible to try something new or buy more of the same for a repeat performance.

Sound easy? Well, it isn't. Many unseen hands and many unaccounted-for hours of work and attention to detail went into creating that picture and the process of maintaining that level of perfection is never-ending; vigilance to detail cannot flag. How often is the reverse the case? Instead of the above, picture this: you enter a neighborhood gourmet retail shop and find that the display cases look picked over or unclean, the garnishes are wilted, and the glass is spattered with food. You come to be enticed and the selection is limited. Sauced foods look congealed and unappealing—sold without a clue for the neophyte about how to reheat properly. (Should the foods be covered? Should they be heated quickly or slowly, microwave or conventional oven, and for how long and at what temperature?) The salads are either overdressed and oversalted or dessicated, with that day-old macerated look. Desserts seem to be dry around the edges. Even worse, the

1

sales staff is unknowledgeable about the products being offered, or they're simply not interested in filling you in on the details of the product's preparation, or they're bored, distracted, or just plain put-upon to serve you in the first place.

What could have been done to remedy the situation? In general, all of these negative first impressions could have been avoided had management run a tighter show, marketed their wares more effectively (leading to more sales, and therefore fresher products), and offered a line of products with broader appeal. As for the personnel, store management needed to be there to greet customers as they entered the store. They should have instituted an in-depth training and mentoring program. The crucial tasks of displaying and selling, not just dispensing, the foods must be entrusted to individuals who are right for the job. Despite training, staff must be hired on that basis—it's easier to begin with the right people than to try later to mold the wrong individuals to do the job.

In a field as dynamic as specialty food retailing, it's helpful to know about where the business came from in order to predict where it may be going.

A SHORT HISTORY OF SPECIALTY FOOD RETAILING: SO MUCH IN SO LITTLE TIME

The specialty food industry has come a long way since 1948 when an enterprising young salesman named Morris Kushner first introduced a line of then-exotic delicacies into select supermarkets and groceries. From its tentative beginnings to its vibrant, complex personality today, this dynamic industry has continued to mirror the changing interests and tastes of the American public.

It's difficult to pinpoint specific events, stores, or people who were trend-setters, whose influence could be called more significant than that of other events, stores, or people. In its infancy as a product category, specialty food usually meant imported and ethnic food. Back in the 1950s, according to John Roberts, Executive Director of the National Association for the Specialty Food Trade (NASFT), "Specialty food meant the exotic (caviar, foie gras, truffles and smoked salmon), ethnic (imported pasta, lingonberries, olive oil) and novelties (chocolate-covered anything) and a handful of regional American concoctions."

According to Kushner, who became the 1973 Fancy Food Show Chairman and instituted the first Product Awards, with the return of American soldiers from Europe after World War II, "the American palate was slowly becoming more sophisticated." The returning GIs were hungry for many of the foods they had come to know in France, Italy, Germany, and Austria. With America a prosperous nation, interest in all things European was running high, and the influx of Europeans who migrated to the United States at about the same time only increased the demand for foreign foods. Imported foods started to make their way to grocery stores in the major metropolitan areas, where they were enjoyed by Americans and foreign-born nationals alike. These foods served as the core of the specialty food product lines at the time.

It was way back in 1953 when a young trade show organizer named Charles Snitow formed an alliance with some of the first specialty food importers and distributors. Out of that alliance sprang the first trade show held in New York under the aegis of the newly formed NASFT. The trade expositions (aka "Fancy Food Shows") were an indication that America was beginning to embrace imported food specialties in a big way. They've only gotten bigger ever since.

A Wider World

Historically, the 1960s saw an explosion of tourism as Americans took advantage of a strong dollar and traveled to Europe, bringing back with them a taste for some of the foods they experienced abroad, for things exotic and foreign. The American market opened up to the world's cuisines. In response to demand, specialty food vendors sought out and imported everything from canned French escargots to German pickles. Emboldened by their success with these products, specialty food purveyors widened their net and began importing delicacies from other parts of the world. The list has not yet stopped growing.

A Complex of Factors

It's difficult to say how the specialty food store, as we now know it, began. What's clear, however, is that its antecedents sprang or mushroomed from a variety of beginnings with many influences, both domestic and foreign. It's equally difficult to track how many specialty food stores or businesses there are even now, let alone how many there were two, ten, or twenty years ago. Multiple theories about the business's true origins abound. In fact, there is no agreement about whether there is a discernible starting point. A few factors stand out, however, factors that seem to be benchmarks for the industry as we know it: Following World War II, the cultural influences already mentioned were joined by dramatic advances in food technology, better transportation systems, growing industrialization, and increasingly widespread use of chemical fertilizers and genetic plant engineering. The changes in food production led to the homogenization nationwide of foods that reached the plates of Americans. As a result, regional foods, previously limited to their areas of origin and therefore prized, were available all over the country. Seasonality was usurped by marketing and the manipulation of Mother Nature. Television, radio, and highway billboards advertised "new," "convenient" foods, and fast foods were fast being adopted as replacements for what forward-thinking Americans had always known, cooked, and eaten.

At about the same time, corner groceries, often family owned for many generations, were being replaced by small supermarkets. With access to larger amounts of capital and endowed with more space, these new markets could stock their shelves with a larger array of brands. The smaller stores lacked space to carry such selections even if they could afford to buy them. The few national brands that had existed prior to 1940 were faced with new competition as small regional manufacturers grew rapidly into national companies, thanks to burgeoning technology.

With more people working longer hours, convenience in general became an important factor in foods bought for home cooking. In the early 1970s, the microwave oven emerged as an indispensable tool in many kitchens. Soon, more vegetables were sold frozen or canned than fresh, bread came wrapped in multicolored plastic bags from a factory far away, and individual parts of chicken could be bought, without bones and already cut up! The average American began to lose "intimate" contact with food, and regional diversity was fast becoming a thing of the past. Here's where the backlash came in, backlash that led to the growth of the independent, often creatively conceived and stylish specialty food store.

The concept of modernization was everywhere and the more that technology advanced, the more eager the American public was to embrace it. This mentality has persisted for some fifty years now, with only small pockets of people advocating a return to, or maintenance of, the "personal" in food production, merchandising, and consumption. The first, very vocal group of these food purists were the hippies of the late 1960s. Their "back to the roots" and back-to-nature mentality sparked the natural, vegetarian, and organic food sectors of the industry. When the hippies "matured" and began to desire material goods or send their kids to college, their ethical beliefs were turned into successful entrepreneurial ventures—Tom's of Maine, Celestial Seasonings, Ben & Jerry's, Trader Joe's, among others.

Recent immigrants also contributed to the development of the specialty food market. With little seed money and just a bare-thread connection to others from their country, these enterprising individuals not only had a desire to connect to their homeland but also saw a viable market in importing nostalgic food favorites. They opened small stores selling, at first, ethnic packaged foods. Later they augmented their offerings with prepared foods and staples like milk, eggs, and butter—selling the latter to draw in customers. They usually began their businesses in neighborhoods where their ethnicity dominated, thus being able to operate during the period of learning English. Later, as their market share and customer base expanded, they moved to other neighborhoods, often leading the way for others who would move and begin new businesses there. European immigrants, especially Italians, not only brought their native foods but also imported elements of style such as fine marble, brass, and mirrors to decorate their stores, the decor being utilized to enhance the foods sold. These first stabs at sprucing up the image of the ethnic store gained them customers from crossover markets. Individuals from outside the ethnic group, and even outside the neighborhood, began to shop in these stores. Slowly, after first buying familiar items like pasta and parmesan, these customers were seduced by the less familiar and the chancy, such as extra virgin olive oil and sun-dried tomatoes. Here's where the industry took a giant leap.

CONVENIENCE REIGNS

At the same time, however, food and packaging technology kept advancing with convenience as a driving force in marketing and merchandising new products and services (i.e., TV dinners, drive-ins, Instant Breakfast, Cup-a-Soup). Soon the need for convenience, the desire for the exotic, and the memory of a home-cooked meal converged in the niche that became the specialty food store as we know it today: Stores evolved into places where educated consumers could buy a variety of things of superior quality to cook at home. "Fresh" and "imported" became synonymous with high quality. In the larger stores one could usually find an array of merchandise including prime produce, meats, and cheeses. Sections of shelf-stable items usually included a range of packaged goods such as imported pasta, rice, preserves, olives, dried legumes, and canned vegetables. Convenience items such as pasta sauces and sliced deli meats were also beginning to appear alongside hearth-baked bread and other bakery goods. To cap things off, imported and domestically produced bottled beverages and whole bean coffee and whole leaf teas were beginning to emerge in a category all their own. When starting out, many of the pioneering stores specialized in one area, often beginning with a focus on cheese or charcuterie. Over time they enlarged the scope of their product line, for the convenience of their patrons, and to capture as much of the market as possible.

IS BIGGER BETTER?

home cooking

During the same period, supermarkets got larger and larger, with the personalized touch so highly valued in small stores giving way to faceless checkout clerks and nameless people behind the counters. Discerning consumers hungered for a more soul-satisfying way of learning about and shopping for food, one with a human touch. In the 70s and early 80s, as the total population grew, this market sector grew proportionately; the specialty food industry and specialty food stores, particularly in urban markets, began to flourish. Meanwhile, with the American standard of living on the rise, the taste for exotic foods remained unabated. You could almost see a kind of "culinary imperialism" at work among this part of society who wished to consume and acquire as many new and fancy ideas and products as possible. For specialty food, the 1970s were the first boom years. Today, sophisticated palates exist outside of major urban areas and the nature of specialty food retailing is again changing. Things seem to have come full circle with a new generation of large supermarket chains catering to their customers' desire for "fine," imported, organic, vegetarian, and prepared foods, all previously found only in the specialty food store.

A NATIONAL TREND

Although in the 60s and early 70s, attention focused on the East Coast, especially the New York metropolitan area, the earliest evolved of the country's melting pots, specialty foods continued to make inroads in other parts of the country. Fancy Foods shows were held in places as far afield as San Francisco, New Orleans, Chicago, and Las Vegas, signaling the growing national interest in specialty foods. Americans were better educated, more well-traveled, becoming entranced by the cuisines of other countries and increasingly concerned about the healthfulness of their diets. More and more women were entering the workforce, abandoning the traditional homemaker role, with the result that two-income families were becoming more common. More disposable income, coupled with less time to spend it, drove the need for foods that were more convenient to use but still delicious—and healthful. Here again, the specialty food industry mirrored America's taste for innovation, and specialty food stores were faster than traditional supermarkets to respond to this growing demand, to offer prepared foods as well as the ingredients to cook well at home.

YANKEE INGENUITY WITH OLD WORLD FLAIR

The emphasis in specialty foods, however, was still Eurocentric, as the industry moved into the 1970s. A few American-produced items were beginning to elbow their way onto the shelves of markets all over the country. American producers started to see the need to tailor foreign foods to suit the American palate and introduced product lines which often recast European specialties into an American idiom, suited to American tastes.

At the same time, food enthusiasts (not yet called "foodies") were becoming more adventurous in their eating habits and responded by embracing all manner of imported and ethnic food products. These consumers were also increasingly more conscious about the healthfulness of what they were eating. Taking their place beside imported foods, these new specialty foods were homegrown and domestically produced. According to John Roberts, Executive Director of NASFT: "[Just as] the introduction of most high-quality European items drove the industry's growth during the 1960s and early 1970s, . . . by the early 80s, domestic companies had discovered that real volume and distinction lay in producing high-quality goods in product categories unique to the American market. . . ."

Americans were seeking new taste sensations, both in restaurant and in specialty food stores. Restaurants become a new form of theater and their chefs became its stars. Eating out became a national pastime, until it became too expensive and consumers turned to entertaining at home. Cooking as a recreational pursuit gained in popularity. This led to more frequent entertaining at home, which, in turn, spawned a whole new cottage industry, reflected in the number of specialty food stores opening in major cities around the country. In 1978 the Silver Palate, a 165-sq-ft specialty food store, opened on New York's Upper West Side. It led the way, selling prepared food and convenience to a highly paid, urban professional clientele, long on money but short on time. From its tiny storefront, the Silver Palate made an impact far greater than its size would indicate. With its success, and with a tradition of venerable and elegant prepared food stores in Europe as models, many highly individualized gourmet takeouts appeared in major cities around the country. With the availability of high-quality prepared foods, cooks could be hosts at their own parties, often supplementing their own culinary efforts with foods purchased at area take-out stores.

Well-educated and well-off "Yuppies" (young urban professionals) became a target audience for "gourmet" foods in the 80s, while working parents and two-income families became the rule rather than the exception, further catalyzing the industry. Prepared or easy-to-prepare food items came to monopolize the product lines of many specialty food vendors. While Americans were becoming more knowledgeable about ethnic cuisine, they also showed interest in returning to American "comfort foods," a trend that led specialty food retailers to reinvent the classic dishes of an earlier time. In addition, with the dollar being devalued abroad, new manufacturers and vendors sprang up across the land, with the result that fully half of what were considered specialty foods were American made. At the same time, however, interest in foods from parts of the world other than Europe (Asia, Mexico, the Middle East, India, and elsewhere) began to influence the breadth of offerings on specialty foods purveyors' shelves and in their refrigerated cases. Although in the early 80s, the country was thrown into a tailspin by a serious recession, "the specialty food industry was not significantly hurt," according to Kushner. Tighter money may have meant indulging less frequently in luxury foods, but it certainly did not eliminate the demand for them altogether. In the late 80s, increased interest in healthful foods and environment-friendly packaging, coupled with growing awareness of ethnic cuisines, propelled the industry to respond with products boasting detailed nutritional analysis and recyclable packaging. Chefs were becoming celebrities and spokespersons (through cookbooks, the media, and television appearances), often developing retail lines inspired by their restaurant creations. Cooking in restaurants where chefs appropriated ingredients from all of the world's pantries also influenced the way people wanted to eat at home. Hence the increased demand for ever more exotic ingredients filled the shelves of many specialty food stores.

Entering the 90s, despite economic turmoil, specialty foods continued to grow. Prepared foods gained ground with more and more people wishing to beat rising restaurant prices but still eat well at home—with little or no effort. Supermarkets got on the prepared foods bandwagon, and the independent specialty food retailer has had to compete in an increasingly segmented market. Personalized service, exciting presentation, and consistency of quality have all continued to gain in importance in retaining old customers and reaching out to new ones. Previously the sole province of antiseptic health food stores, health-conscious foods with an emphasis on organically grown prime ingredients are going mainstream, just as traditional supermarket chains are embracing broader and deeper assortments of specialty foods in their product array (with in-store bakers, cafés and full-service restaurants ever more on the horizon).

What's next? Some of the same and some of the startlingly different. Trends often come from unexpected places. The store you open and operate may spawn the next trend. Who knows?

SPECIALTY FOOD STORES AS THE NEW AGORA

As supermarkets grow bigger, offering a more comprehensive selection of specialty and prepared foods, "foodies" (as the trend-conscious cooks and eaters of the top few percent of the population have come to be called) have created a demand for ever more specialized specialty food stores. Cholesterol and dietary concerns aside, cheese stores and premium ice cream shops have become vigorous in many markets. Coffeehouses and spicy food vendors, among other specialists, are springing up all over the suburban landscape, prepared to satisfy the needs of an increasingly food-interested public.

Hungering for personalized attention, consumers in ever greater numbers are shopping in the smaller, more specialized stores—and not only for the food. In addition to having their palates charmed, these customers enjoy interacting with a food seller who is knowledgeable about the store's offerings. Being greeted by name upon entering a store and receiving service with a smile satisfies a basic human need. Stemming from their ethnic food store origins, specialty food stores provide a way for people to interact with their neighbors, a refreshing antidote to the anonymity that characterizes the larger chain stores. They satisfy the need for one-on-one human transactions in a world where we talk more to our computers and answering machines than to our fellow man. In effect, the story has gone full circle, from the early ethnic-flavored Mom-and-Pop delis in big city melting pots (where the second generation owner often served several generations of a family) to suburban gourmets to go (either single unit or part of a larger chain), serving the needs of today's customers who demand good food, coupled with convenience, good value, and good service.

Nowadays the picture for growth is bright with all kinds of operators getting into the act—from convenience stores to prepared foods specialists, health food stores to hypermarkets and discounters, all eager to share a piece of the increasing pie. The customer base has widened considerably from those days when new immigrants and the "carriage trade" were the main sources of clientele for specialty foods. In fact, according to the NASFT, even during the "lean" years for the U.S. economy, the specialty food industry valiantly held its own. From 1989–1995, there has been steady growth in the retail dollar value of sales of gourmet and specialty foods, from $22 billion in 1989 to $35 billion in 1995 (*Gourmet News*, March 1996).

In an industry where sales are expected to reach close to $41 billion in 1998 (*Packaged Facts*, 1996), distinctions are becoming blurred. No longer do specialty food retailers stand alone as a distinct entity or have the province of specialty foods all to themselves. Independent as well as chain groceries, gourmet stores, health food emporia, upscale delis and discount megastores are all horning in on each others' turf. Hybrids of the same breed, all of these have two things in common—they are all selling food and providing service.

SPECIAL SEGMENTS OF THE INDUSTRY

In a dynamic industry where definitions are hard to pin down, many variations on the theme of specialty food stores exist. From small-scale Mom-and-Pop specialists to generalists, megastores, and hypermarkets, specialty food retailers run the gamut. The most important player in terms of sheer potential for monopolizing market share is the supermarket. Slowly supermarkets are being reconfigured to accommodate the changing dietary needs and lifestyle of the American public. Supermarkets are acknowledging that what the customers want is a large variety of "meal solutions": quick, healthy, convenient, and affordable, and the prepared foods departments in supermarkets are the area where those needs can best be accommodated.

Product mix is just that—mixed. Supermarkets are "crossing over" to organics and adding more specialty foods to their shelves. Historically slow to cash in on the prepared food trend, progressive supermarket chains are also now going after the upscale take-out food dollar more and more. Their level of commitment can be seen in the number of highly trained chefs they are hiring to helm their prepared foods departments. In fact, as of July 1995 nearly one quarter of supermarket shoppers look to buy a take-out meal for that night's dinner and don't mind paying extra for the convenience of one-stop shopping. ("It's Mealtime—Are Supermarkets on the Menu?"—*FMI*, September 1995) The old-fashioned service deli, with its standard array of cold cuts and salads, doesn't cut it anymore.

Upscale restaurants are opening bakeries and adding take-out arms adjacent to their dining spaces to provide high quality foods to office workers under pressure to eat at their desks. The long business lunch is a thing of the past.

Caterers are expanding into retail outlets to extend their reach and bolster revenues.

Coffee bars and bakeries are beefing up their product mix and adding more foods-to-go as well as eat-in with their lattes and iced blended coffee drinks. These very coffee houses and cafes are going cyber, becoming an office away from the office with multiple computer terminals hooked to on-line services—one more way to keep the customer spending money while they work or communicate on the World Wide Web.

Formerly stodgy health food stores are diversifying by adding more staples and conventional products to their shelves in an effort to keep the customer from going elsewhere to finish their shopping. In the process these very stores are emerging from the natural food niche into the mainstream.

Returning to the site where the incipient specialty food industry began, gourmet-to-go and prepared foods departments are proliferating in some of the most prominent upscale supermarket chains.

In a sense, gourmet foods have come home again. Back where they began, gourmet foods now take up more and more shelf and case space in supermarkets. According to *Packaged Facts*, the gourmet food market will grow to greater than $50 billion by 2001. That translates into a lot of opportunity for retailers if they are ready to seize it, but it's been a long and rocky road to specialty food's current presence in supermarkets. Many supermarket experts are unsure about how to make their stores the choice of discerning shoppers seeking quality foods requiring little or no preparation. By no means is this move toward an emphasis on specialty and prepared foods a universal phenomenon in the supermarket business. Isolated though upscale examples of the more innovative retailers who are making a significant commitment to these offerings range from Wegman's in the Rochester, NY, area to the Harris-Teeter chain in North Carolina with stores in Atlanta, as well to Larry's Markets in Seattle, to name just a few among an elite group.

Beginning back in the 1940s, a small line of gourmet food items appeared on shelves in their own section of the carriage trade grocery store. Now gourmet-to-go and prepared foods are proliferating in some of the most prominent upscale supermarket chains.

SOME NEW DIRECTIONS FOR SUPERMARKETS

In many ways, supermarkets are a sleeping giant when it comes to being the prime source for prepared foods and specialty foods. Bill Pizzico, publisher and editor of *Progressive Grocer*, believes that

> Supermarkets need only to really tune into people's lifestyles. They can then create product lines to convert the customer to think of them first as their one-stop meal planning center that accommodates everyone's needs—from the most traditional to the most radically different. Supermarkets are learning that they need to communicate what they have to offer and how customers can use it in varied combinations. They also have to work hard to change the typical supermarket mentality which says 'if it doesn't move in two weeks, drop the product line.' As with anything new or in this case, newly re-defined, it takes time to convince customers of the high quality of prepared food offerings available in supermarkets. . . . The supermarket industry is a can-do industry peopled with a lot of talent; it can do anything once it decides to.

Thinking "beyond the box," where supermarkets begin to change the way they market to their customers, is just starting. Eatzi's, a prepared foods superstore in Texas, operates as a subsidiary of Brinker International, a large restaurant conglomerate; this is one groundbreaking hybrid that brings prepared foods takeout to a new level. Here the retailer combines the best of two worlds, the restaurant and the retail store, by offering a complete array of restaurant-quality prepared foods, with all necessary accompaniments; the operation is backed by the necessary marketing muscle and merchandising expertise to capture the public's interest. Drawing inspiration from the scenario where the chef comes out of the kitchen to meet and greet the customers in the dining room, Eatzi's chefs go beyond the kitchen to assist customers in making decisions about meal planning. This kind of merchandising puts those with food expertise eye to eye with the customer who will consume what he or she has prepared—certainly not a bad way to gain the customer's confidence in the product and get feedback in the process. This kind of creative operational strategy should be exploited by the independent specialty food retailer as well.

SUPERMARKET IN-STORE FOOD SERVICE: LIMITED SUCCESS . . . SO FAR

Given Americans' propensity for one-stop shopping, it isn't surprising that supermarkets are augmenting their offerings by building full-scale prepared food departments within their stores. What is surprising, however, is their limited success with these ventures. Gourmet to go, however, is a personality-driven business, a concept that often runs counter to the supermarket mentality. As part of a larger corporate structure, most supermarkets operate with layers of management handing down decisions and policies from the top down. One- and two-store operators, and even those with six or eight locations, have proven that in-store food service departments can work and be profitable, but larger multiunit chains have largely failed.

WHY? WHAT CAN THE BIG GUYS LEARN FROM THE LITTLE GUYS?

For starters, these departments require well-trained professionals to run them. Furthermore, these individuals must be empowered to exercise their own initiative in fine-tuning the operations. They must be allowed to "own" their jobs in order to be responsive to the needs of their local clientele. They have to be able to deliver on promises they make to their "regular" customers, which means that they need corporate support to build revenues for their departments, making them into self-contained profit centers coveted by all other department managers in the store. To conserve both profitability and the image of product freshness, managers need to be able to make split-second decisions about moving product from one area of the department to another. As foods in a self-serve prepared entrees section age and reach their "pull dates," they need to be moved to an area such as the deli where persuasive selling by a well-spoken counterperson may save the day. That kind of flexibility is a prerequisite in any specialty food operation, whether large or small, independent or part of a midsize or larger chain. Once again, the retailers' representatives on the selling floor or behind the prepared foods counter must think on their feet at all times.

Management Is Not Always from the Top Down

From salespeople to counter clerks to managers, each member of the staff in a supermarket food service department must be able to communicate effectively to higher levels of management and then must be allowed to respond quickly to changes in consumers' demands (equally true for the independent specialty food retailer).

Chains are learning that they need to micromanage to their neighborhoods in order to compete with the independents whose strength is just that. Larger supermarket chains are finding out that gourmet to go is not a cookie-cutter type of operation. Consider that in 1997 fast-food restaurants (many with drive-up service) accounted for 41% of all food taken out (having slipped from 48% in 1996); restaurants other than fast-food outlets account for 21%; other sources account for 18%, which includes independent gourmet-to-go stores, delis, pizza parlors, coffee shops, convenience stores, and a small percentage of others; the remaining 22%, hardly the lion's share, belongs to the supermarket chains. Note that in a national poll taken by the Food Marketing Institute, in 1997 gourmet-to-go shops and specialty food stores accounted for 7% of the total sources of takeout food, more than double the figure shown for the previous year (from "Trends in the U.S.," Food Marketing Institute and *The Food Marketing Industry Speaks*, 1997). Independent retailers have a niche to fill and are filling it in ever greater numbers. With convenient locations, well-focused product offerings, good service, and careful management, specialty food retailers stand to win and gain greater market share often despite or because of what other segments of the market are doing.

Presently, much of supermarket takeout is poorly presented or maintained. Again, properly trained staffing is key, and knowing your market is essential. According to Marcia Schurer, an industry consultant based in Boulder, Colorado, "They [the customers] will be rushed and hungry, and they'll want to eat so they compromise and buy something they don't really want. And that causes a problem in the way consumers perceive supermarket takeout." Stephan Kouzomis, a food service consultant in Cincinnati, agrees: "Supermarkets haven't had a reputation for good food preparation, and the cooking, the theater, the sampling, are good ways of overcoming that." Schurer continues, "Doing too much is worse than doing nothing at all." She contends that "Variety is wonderful but you can do well with twenty items if they are all fresh and appealingly displayed and you have the turnover. If you don't have the turnover of inventory on a regular basis, you run the risk of displaying food that has lost the freshness appeal."

Supermarkets aren't alone in their need to maintain not only a reasonable variety but also consistently high quality throughout the array. No matter where they are sold or purchased, prepared foods above all must be fresh, be perceived as having good value, be convenient, and increasingly more important nowadays, be healthful.

Prepared Foods Don't Always Sell Themselves

Good selling skills are at the heart of the successful operation of a prepared foods department, whether it be in a supermarket or a smaller specialty food store. Unlike shelf items in the rest of the supermarket where consumers simply fill their shopping carts with much of the same merchandise week in and week out, offerings in a gourmet-to-go department need to be explained. Printed materials, including menu ideas and recipes, often support sales by educating a customer to like and use a particular unfamiliar item. Above all, however, customers need to be romanced, to feel respected and rewarded by the attentions of the sales staff. Without true hands-on involvement of behind-the-counter staff (and management's commitment to back it up), the foods in the deli cases will suffer poor turnover, the quality will decline over time, and the reputation of the department will sink. Once burned by a bad experience, customers will take that part of their business elsewhere, most likely to the neighborhood gourmet-to-go shops or other independently owned specialty food stores, where the owner knows each customer by name. This same owner has a leg up on the chain store competition if he or she stays on top of trends, is responsive to filling special orders, and provides special goods and services geared to the local clientele.

As noted previously, gourmet to go is a personality-driven business, and larger chain operators, with their corporate decision-making structures have largely failed because they lacked the necessary flexibility.

What Can the Independent Retailers Learn from the Big Boys?

What can the independent specialty food retailers learn from those supermarkets that have developed their prepared foods departments into innovative profit centers?

✳Increase Customer Impact by Showing Off Your Store's Wares

Bringing a sense of drama to in-store food service is more and more the way supermarkets are capturing the consumer, seeking both quality and convenience. At the center of this trend are in-store exhibition kitchens with culinary school–trained chefs on display, preparing foods in full view of the customer. The image of freshness and expert preparation is communicated strongly in this way. Customers are always seduced by the show. They are often willing to pay a premium for foods that communicate the message of " restaurant quality, " prepared by cooks in full chef regalia, tall white toques and all. (Of course, it helps for these same customers to be equally impressed when they bring the foods home and eat them. "The proof of the pudding. . . .")

In-store bakeries build sales by bringing their best decorators up front where customers can see deft hands at work in a spotlessly clean kitchen. Supermarket in-store bakeries find that accommodating last minute cake orders helps to win new customers, a lesson that should not be lost on independent retailers as well.

Recognize the Value of Signature Items

Image!

something identifiable whether it be the product (sauce) or "hospitaliano"

Such items (or exclusive product lines or private label merchandise) build a store's image. Many successful retailers will point to a breakthrough item or line that has become their trademark or strong suit in retailing. Whether on the product side (i.e., cheese, wine, prepared foods, unparalleled breadth in variety of shelf-stable items or gift baskets) or on the service side, one item or one bit of extra service should stand out as the calling card that brings customers to your door and keeps them satisfied and loyal. Find it and build your promotional campaigns around it. Many retailers readily have come to understand that it's not always profit that comes first in defining their image. Supermarkets are finding out that they can still maintain an upscale image even while not taking a full markup on selected items (items with higher profit margins can help to make up the difference). You make a statement by offering an extensive array of one line of products, whether shelf-stable or perishable, and that is often more important than getting your full margin on an item. It can create an image for your store that is unique and distinct from the next retailer and will give you the edge on gaining and retaining customers.

Stephan Kouzomis, a consultant we quoted earlier, says that, unless supermarkets address consumers and plug into their lifestyles and hence their needs as consumers, they will not succeed in the prepared foods category. Buck Jones, another supermarket industry consultant and former editor of *Progressive Grocer* magazine's section on Food Service, agrees:

> To be successful in the supermarket food service business, we must develop, build and manage the departments from a food perspective, not from a grocery perspective. Traditionally, the grocery perspective deals with the most economical way to buy, store, transport and display meal ingredients. Systems were built to deliver these ingredients in the most economical and cost-effective manner. The food perspective, on the other hand, starts with analyzing how customers buy and eat food, and then works backward by determining the best way to sell it.

This is where the independent retailer can fill a need and carve out a special niche. Thus arises the golden opportunity for gourmet to go. Specialty food store owners should regard the supermarket, not as a threat to their survival, but rather as a convenient place for shoppers to sample the more popular categories of specialty food (cheeses, imported oils, condiments of all kinds, preserves, premium quality coffees and whole leaf teas, etc.). Once educated, those same consumers will return to the specialists to obtain even more rarefied and unique items that are simply out of the range of a supermarket's line of product offerings.

Specialty food retailers can learn from supermarkets, but they can also learn from other store operators who focus on a narrower range of product. When planning your store, consider keeping your eye on the following:

- *Coffeehouses*—Who could have predicted that the decidedly low-tech coffeehouses of the 1960s would reemerge as the high growth retail phenomena in the 1980s and 90s? In the hands of a few mega coffee companies with penetration into the market nationally, the coffeehouse or coffee bar has been reinvented as a meeting place, refueling stop, and general hangout for people of all ages and demographics. Even those who have no pretensions to espousing anything that smacks of "gourmet" have wholeheartedly embraced the concept of a freshly brewed cup of coffee or espresso based drink. Here again, consistency of quality in the product they are selling is key to success. Tremendous buying power, good merchandising, and a healthy advertising budget have all helped here as well. While paving the way for the Mom-and-Pop coffeehouses, larger chains also make it hard for the little guy to compete. The same is true in specialty food stores with a broader product line.
- *Tea Rooms*—Much less ubiquitous, these retailers often position themselves as an antidote to the fast-paced, "get-'em-in-and-get-'em-out" assembly line type coffee bars. Often updates of the stodgier British-inspired ladies preserves, these retailers are springing up all around the country in many guises and forms and confirm the adage that "everything old is new again."

- *Single Item Specialists*

  Cheese Shops—In the 1970s, when the taste for imported cheeses wasn't threatened by concerns about the intake of fat, and cholesterol was just a word and not a fear, estimates put the number of cheese stores at about 2200. In the health-conscious 1990s that number has dwindled to a mere 200 or so, augmented by the increasing number of supermarkets, discounters, health food chains, liquor, beer and wine stores all getting into the cheese act.

  Caviar Emporia—As a sheer luxury item, caviar can't be topped; for the small percentage of gourmets who indulge in premium quality caviar on a regular basis, there are a few caviar emporia, mainly on each coast, to fuel the indulgence (Petrossian's and Caviarteria in NYC, Aristoff in Los Angeles, etc.).

   Upscale Confectioners— Ranging from stateside outposts of French or Italian confectioners to old-fashioned or refashioned corner candy stores, these could arguably be counted among the specialty food retail ranks.

  Artisanal Bakeries—Also drawing from European models, bread bakers employing ancient methods of sourdough bread production are gaining an ardent audience among the food cognoscenti and represent a mini-trend emulated even by supermarket bakeries.

In the chapters that follow, we deconstruct the history of the industry into standard stages of business development to help you determine what is the most feasible option to explore in your targeted area. We elaborate on some notable operating scenarios to shed light on the minefields of specialty food retailing, paying particular attention to what can go wrong with certain concepts of certain sizes in certain areas, and we will examine possible remedies for problem areas. We show how the necessary steps of business preparation might apply to your concept, how your service plans will be affected by your intended menu, and how merchandising relates to design, to mention just some of the important areas that we consider. Most importantly, we help you assess your personal strengths as a specialty food entrepreneur so that you can identify the opportunities that present you with the greatest potential for success.

CHAPTER TWO

GETTING STARTED: WHAT IS THE INDUSTRY TODAY AND ARE YOU PREPARED TO ENTER IT?

With more consumers juggling work and family, take-out meals versus meals consumed in restaurants have grown from 47% in 1986 to 59% in 1995. With more and more people telecommuting or working at home, restaurants and gourmets-to-go with eat-in facilities are becoming a home away from home for individuals seeking more than just a meal (witness the phenomenal growth of coffee stores and tea salons as meeting places and places for meeting). Dual-income households and higher discretionary incomes resulting from the increasing participation of women in the work force continue to benefit the gourmet and specialty food industry. The increase in the number of single-person households, coupled with longer workdays and workweeks, will also continue to drive the specialty food market. Despite the continued rise in the numbers of cookbooks being published and bought in this country, the number of home-cooked meals Americans eat (and what's more, the number of home-cooked meals American families eat together at home) is on the decline, all of which points to the greater dependence on the take-out meal, all good news for the specialty food retailer.

The growing ethnic diversity of America's population means that ethnic specialties are becoming more important. Greater availability of and familiarity with ethnic foods means a wider acceptance by the general population with the result that salsa now outsells ketchup—just one startling change in the food buying habits of the American public. Foreign travel also contributes to the public's greater willingness to try new ethnic foods. Baby boomers are not only carrying their ethnic food preferences with them into middle age, but they have also laid the groundwork for the next generation to develop similar tastes (*Packaged Facts*, 1996). All these factors play an important part in the composition of product lines in gourmet-to-go stores. To compete, owners and operators need to stay on top of these trends.

WHERE DO YOU FIT IN?

The breed of specialty food store that has become known as gourmet to go has undergone many changes since its early days during the mid-1970s, when it could be considered to have come into its own in this country. The social causes of the 1960s were replaced by the socializing of the late 1970s and 1980s. Hard to pigeon-hole, gourmet to go is truly a mosaic with many differently shaped facets. In a sense, reduced to its essence, the modern gourmet to go is a reinvention of the corner deli, which in many cases had an ethnic slant (Jewish, Italian, German, etc.), offered a small seating area, and, above all, prided itself on personalized service and convenience. Going full circle, the current day gourmet to go sells foods, both shelf stable and perishable prepared, often drawn from many different ethnic cuisines. Service and convenience are no less important nowadays than they were thirty or forty years ago.

What is the profile of the average gourmet to go, and of the people who run them? Other than superficial similarities, the stores themselves are as varied as the people. From the generalist small Mom-and-Pop shops with a few deli cases full of prepared foods, cheeses, and other specialties, to the specialist such as cheese and wine shops, to the gleaming deluxe supermarkets with broad and deep arrays of multiple product lines displayed alongside or in addition to the regular merchandise, gourmet to go is indeed a multifaceted breed. [It was in 1948 when veteran specialty food retailer Morris Kushner introduced a limited line of gourmet foods to the shelves of the fancier (read: upscale) supermarkets, first making gourmet foods available to a wider audience; approximately forty years later they still have a prominent presence in supermarkets, but nowadays are often augmented by elaborate prepared food departments, sushi counters, self-serve coffee bean dispensers, full-scale bakeries, and flower and candy shops, all under one roof.]

There are no neat categories into which fall each and every specimen, and therefore, no neat answers to the question, "Will it succeed?" It comes down to location. What will play well in Manhattan cannot necessarily be replicated in Peoria or L.A. or at any of the points in between.

CATEGORIZING "GOURMET FOODS"

The kinds of foods that may fall logically within the bailiwick of a specialty food retailer are as diverse as the retailers who sell them. In the wide-ranging world of products that specialty food retailing encompasses, one may argue that there are differences to be found among true "gourmet" (items thought to be the exclusive province of upscale, elitist specialty food stores), fraudulent items (good packaging, poor contents), and "transitional" items (products which are appearing with greater regularity on supermarket shelves). In fact, more packaged specialty foods are sold through supermarkets than anywhere else.

Size makes a difference too. Some operations are large, multiunit businesses, ambitious in scope, veritable destinations for shoppers looking for an afternoon out, a culinary adventure. Many of *these* began with one location, were successful, and seized the opportunity to expand into other markets with replications of a proven formula. Other operations are small, compact stores chock full with an array of in-house signature prepared foods, shops that extend their presence through ancillary services, such as catering, corporate gifts, and wholesaling. Other specialty food businesses are anchored to a neighborhood, a resource for serious gourmet cooks. Yet others are a showcase for an established restaurant or catering business, a way of making the production space and staff do double duty, thereby increasing revenues. Such an operation can also be a way of reducing food loss or waste and finding an outlet for excess food production. Take, for example, Gourmet to Go, a 14-year-old chain of specialty food stores and catering operations in St. Louis, whose owner, Barbara Schwartz, touts the advantage of maintaining two separate but interrelated arms of her business. "In addition to doing carryout, we also do corporate catering; we have a large segment of our business devoted to gifts to go for corporate and residential gifting. We also do residential catering. In this way, we can move a tremendous volume of products. We can offer a large selection." She concludes, "You have to have enough variety so people don't get bored; conversely, you need lots of outlets to sell variety to. So it's a win-win situation. We and the customers both are satisfied."

In recent years, restaurants and catering companies have entered the field in record numbers as a way of extending their reach, diversifying, filling in on the downtimes. Conversely, many specialty food stores are beginning to offer eat-in food service (witness the rise of the new, or newly reinvented "café-bakery") in response to a growing demand for a casual, anytime-of-day dining experience. Even hotels, such as those in the Ritz chain, are entering the fray with gourmet-to-go shops in many of their properties drawing from their restaurant kitchens. No matter which operation you use as your model, a common thread runs through all of these variants—the importance of service. Ask any retailer how to retain customers and the answer is, unfailingly, simply "Good service."

Getting to the point where you are ready to serve the public is what the next section of this chapter is about. As a specialty food entrepreneur, you must first assess who you are and what your inherent strengths are as a potential operator. Only then can you combine these with a host of factors to build a successful business.

THE FEASIBILITY STUDY—WILL YOUR CONCEPT FLY AND SHOULD YOU BE THE PILOT?

Feasibility (*n.*) The state of something which is capable of being done, effected, or accomplished; suitability; probability; likelihood
——From *Random House Dictionary of the English Language*, 1967

All of the discussion so far in this book has been about history, trends, concepts, and how the specialty food business has changed over the last forty years. Up until now we have not discussed the people who make the industry tick. It is not entirely due to science, chance, or even ample funding that specialty food businesses have made it in the past, are making it today, or will make it in the future. Like every other business, big or small, in the end, what makes a food business click is the people structure behind it. After your good ideas have finished burning a hole in the creative and adventurous part of your brain, it is time to settle down and look at what it will take, from a capability perspective, to get your specialty food business off the ground. This is called the feasibility stage, and it is the first time you have to be disciplined about getting your thoughts in order so that they can be read and understood objectively.

When you embark on the feasibility study of your business, you will be looking for signs that indicate not only that the business is a good idea from a conceptual and financial perspective, but also that you are the best person to run it. This is done through a series of tasks and surveys, exploring, with broad brushstrokes, the potential for your business.

The first stage of our feasibility study is a simple personality profile, while the second is an exploration into the purpose of your business—what needs will it fill and for whom? Following these steps, we will ask you to explore the market—the economic climate, general demographic areas under consideration, and competition in these areas—for the place where you are thinking of opening your business. Lastly we will guide you to taking a first look at the financial feasibility of your idea. Relax: it isn't scary and it isn't advanced math. It is, instead, a preparation for a later business development phase, namely the business plan. Completing a feasibility study or studies for your proposed business will help keep you from feeling overwhelmed by processes that come later when you write a business plan. The feasibility study will simplify the options or possible directions. Completing it gets you close to knowing the potential success of your business idea so that you can define further how to make the business work and be profitable.

Personality Profile of a Successful Operator—Who Are You?

Here's a preliminary checklist, questions to ask before embarking on the gourmet-to-go venture. Use it to assess your own personality profile.

1. Do I have what it takes to weather the vicissitudes of an often high-pressure, initially low-paying job?
2. Am I thick-skinned and passionate enough to endure the disappointments and rejections inherent in bringing anything new to the public?
3. Am I a good communicator as well as a good listener?
4. Am I a "people person" who will enjoy interacting with customers? Or would I rather be behind the scenes planning, administering, motivating, and training others to take that role? Can I train and inspire others to care about their job and about my business as much as I do and make them see clearly the benefits of doing so? (See number 23 for a variation on this question.)
5. Can I relinquish control and effectively delegate responsibilities to key personnel?
6. Can I see the big picture clearly and tend to the details effectively as well?
7. Am I a creative thinker who thinks on my feet and can solve problems?
8. Can I think with a cool head rather than an irrational, raging heart?
9. Can I dissociate my emotional side from my rational, business-minded self?
10. Am I truly capable of keeping a number of balls up in the air at the same time?
11. Can I answer the door while the phone is ringing?
12. Can I swallow my pride and admit that the customer is right (even when in my heart of hearts, I know it isn't so), firm in the belief that standing behind my products and services is the only way to succeed?

13. Am I prepared to take a risk, realizing that there is no such thing as a sure thing in the retail business?

√ 14. Do I have, or am I willing to seek, professional assistance in drafting my business plan? Am I willing to suspend plans to open my business if a feasibility study indicates that it won't fly, given location, budget, demographics, or any of a number of other factors?

15. What do I expect to get out of my business, other than a decent income for time and effort expended?

16. What "goodies" do I need to keep me engaged in a highly demanding and dynamic business?

17. Will I be able to put the business first, ahead of family, friends, and my own personal pursuit of financial comfort, recreation, and relaxation?

18. Is profit my primary goal?

19. Do I have the requisite enthusiasm for the food *service* profession?

20. What is my passion for food based on? What kinds of foods do I love?

21. Can I write compelling copy for a regular newsletter or descriptions of foods and their background as point of sale pieces that will compel customers to try new things? If I cannot do this (due to lack of ability or time), do I, or will I, have someone in mind on staff who can?

22. How can I communicate my love for high-quality, well-prepared foods to my customers?

23. Do I pledge to listen and interact with customers to give them what they want?

Soul-search long and deep in finding the answers to these questions. You should be able to look yourself in the eye and say an emphatic "Yes" to all of them before proceeding.

Forming a background against which the preceding questions should be asked, the general observations that follow, observations about what it takes to succeed in this demanding, detail-oriented field, should be kept in mind.

1. An owner or manager has the responsibility for directing, controlling, and planning the day-to-day operations of the business.

2. As owner or manager, you will be responsible for making generalizations, evaluations, and decisions based on measurable or verifiable criteria (consistency of food quality, sales, waste or loss, returns, customer complaints).

3. You will also be performing a variety of duties, often changing from one task to another of a different nature, without loss of efficiency, productivity, or composure.

4. You will also be involved in doing and/or supervising repetitive work or the same work according to set procedures, sequences, and pace.
5. You will be a motivator of staff.
6. You will be an allocator of resources.

According to Kathleen Allen, Associate Professor of Entrepreneurial Studies at USC, there are ten truths about successful entrepreneurs:

1. While traditionally business owners were more often male (and married), now they are twice as likely to be women.
2. They express that their wish to go into business for themselves is based on a wish to be independent and take charge of their lives.
3. They are generally very comfortable with ambiguity, chaos, and uncertainty.
4. They are not big risk takers or gamblers, but rather calculated risk takers.
5. They have been fired many times from typical jobs during their past working career.
6. They started "businesses," however small or rudimentary, at a young age.
7. They tend to be opportunistic and innovative but not always creative.
8. They team up with creative people.
9. They put teams together, excel at gathering resources and rely on team synergy to get the job done.
10. Some are bureaucrats, good at setting up structure and managing within structure.

Allen has also found that it's true that some are bored after startup and then move on to open a new business.

On the subject of boredom in business, Carolyn Pesci Peterson, owner of a public relations and marketing company in Houston, has this to say: "Research tells us that to be compelling, a goal has to be at least 10 percent more challenging than what you're currently capable of doing. If it isn't, you run the risk of investing in boredom. If you get bored, your lack of enthusiasm will hinder success of the objective. You know how it is when you just don't feel like doing something one more time. Avoid the malaise by invigorating the work with new spirit—build in new motives, do it different, make it better!" (*The Gourmet Retailer*, June 1996).

Do you recognize yourself in any or all of the truths above? Are you then willing to challenge yourself to do more than you have done in your working career so far? If so, you're probably on the right track if you're considering opening your own business.

But you surely won't be the first person in entrepreneurial history to learn that going with gut feelings is not always the best route to take when it comes to business decisions. A far more objective approach is the way to go. The *feasibility study* is one of the ways to get an objective assessment of your business concept.

Of course, there are no sure things in the world of business; however, starting your career as a business owner with a detailed analysis of the pluses and minuses surrounding your concept and its location stacks the cards in your favor when dollars, time, energy, and commitment are all at stake.

SO JUST WHAT IS A FEASIBILITY STUDY?

A feasibility study is a way of testing the business concept and providing a road map for the entrepreneur. Think of it as an outline of the major highways en route to starting your business. It is designed to help you address the following fundamental questions.

Why, Where, What, When, and How

Why?   *Why* open the business you have in mind? Included in this should be answers to the following:
1. Will you be—
    (a) Creating demand for a set of goods and services that is currently unmet?
    (b) Or meeting an already established demand for the kinds of products and services you intend to offer?
    If the answer is b, then how is the public currently served? Is there a need for yet another retailer to carve up a limited pie? What is the competition? Are others trying to do the same thing in the same market area? Have they succeeded? Is there room for more of the same? Inventory what will make you different and dispassionately decide if the benefits will outweigh the risks. Then act from a position of confidence and strength.
2. How can you better serve the needs and demands of the public?
3. Do you know the whole story on demographics in your area (average family or individual income of your likely customers; real estate values; marital status of potential clientele; overall strength of area businesses or industries likely to be your customer base for takeout or catering; stability or transience of local population base)? Do your research using Exhibit 2-1, the feasibility study worksheet.

EXHIBIT 2-1

FEASIBILITY STUDY WORKSHEET

The following worksheet can be adapted and used by the entrepreneur in the start-up phase to help determine the overall feasibility of the business idea. This feasibility worksheet will aid the entrepreneur in assessing the real estate, demographic market, concept, and pricing structure of his/her idea in various locations and under various situations.

Onto this worksheet will go "hard" information such as building prices and lease terms of the areas under consideration as well as "soft" information, such as your impression of particular neighborhoods and design and flow of the stores visited in desirable locations.

There is no score per se to achieve with the feasibility study, which makes its evaluation difficult for some and uncomfortable for many. It is still an important commitment to make. Much of the information derived from the work of completing this study will direct the entrepreneur to rule out certain locations or concepts and very often steer him/her to a concrete direction. It is important for the entrepreneur to evaluate the findings of the feasibility study with his/her partners, potential investors, colleagues, and family in order to remain as objective as possible.

Proceeding to writing a full blown business plan is easier and quicker if a feasibility study is done. Some start-up entrepreneurs are even able to get preliminary financial commitments from investors from a completed feasibility study.

Feasibility Study Worksheet for a Specialty Food Store

I.   **The Competitive Environment**

1.   How busy is this store compared with competing stores in the area?
- ☐ Very busy (people waiting on line)
- ☑ Somewhat busy (store active, no long waits)
- ☐ Has business but not busy
- ☐ Very slow

2.   What does this store that is doing well have in common with other stores doing well in the area?
- ☑ Attractive store design
- ☐ Functional store design
- ☑ Wide array of prepared items offered
- ☑ Wide array of packaged items offered
- ☑ High level of customer service
- ☑ Good signage
- ☑ No/little lines
- ☑ Good prices
- ☑ Delivery service
- ☑ Catering service
- ☑ Other services
- ☑ Accepts credit cards and/or checks

3. Which factors seem to be most important to the success of this store with a high level of business?

- ☑ Attractive store design
- ☐ Functional store design
- ☑ Wide array of prepared items offered
- ☐ Wide array of packaged items offered
- ☑ High level of customer service
- ☑ Good signage
- ☐ No/little lines
- ☑ Good prices
- ☑ Delivery service
- ☐ Catering service
- ☐ Other services
- ☑ Accepts credit cards and/or checks

4. What is wrong with the store if it is not doing well?

- ☐ Unattractive store design
- ☑ Nonfunctional store design
- ☐ Minimal array of prepared items offered
- ☐ Minimal array of packaged items offered
- ☑ Lack of customer service
- ☑ Little/no signage
- ☐ Long lines
- ☑ High prices
- ☑ No delivery service
- ☐ No catering service
- ☐ Other?
- ☐ Doesn't accept credit cards and/or checks

5. In this neighborhood, what would I do better?

- ☐ Store design
- ☐ Store layout /location
- ☐ Increase/decrease prepared items
- ☐ Increase/decrease packaged items offered
- ☐ Customer service
- ☑ Signage /poor
- ☑ Checkout
- ☐ Prices
- ☐ Delivery service
- ☐ Catering service
- ☐ Other services
- ☐ Accept/not accept credit cards and/or checks

6. What attributes of and developments to the area may affect our doing business here?

- ☐ New roads/transportation systems being built
- ☑ Construction that will enhance/deter business in next five years

☒ New businesses coming into
area/businesses leaving
☒ New housing being built
☐ Hospitals/schools/government
centers active and busy in area
☒ High/low shopping district
☐ Easy/difficult access from main roads
☒ Easy/difficult parking
☒ Large supermarket nearby
☐ Other specialty food stores in
immediate range

II. **Customer Profile—Characteristics and Sources of Customers**

1. What is the residential population
of the market area?
    ☐ 5,000–10,000
    ☐ 11,000–20,000
    ☐ 21,000–30,000
    ☐ 31,000–50,000
    ☐ More than 50,000

2. What is the nonresidential population
in the market area?
    ☐ 5,000–10,000
    ☐ 11,000–20,000
    ☐ 21,000–30,000
    ☐ 31,000–50,000
    ☐ More than 50,000

3. What is the source of the nonresidential
population?
    ☒ Local businesses, retail
    ☒ Local businesses, commercial/
    industrial
    ☒ Hospitals
    ☐ Schools
    ☒ Other MAJOR CORPS *P&G LENS GE DUKE*

4. What is our estimate (based on
observation) of hourly pedestrian and
auto traffic that is in addition to the
numbers above?
    ☐ Under 100
    ☐ 100–200
    ☐ 200–400
    ☐ 400–600
    ☐ More than 600

5. Based on observed traffic, will we attract customers at off time
as well as for regular meals?
    ☐ Yes ?
    ☐ No .

6. Based on observation of customer base, is the demand for
services greater than the supply to this area?
    ☒ Yes
    ☐ No

7. Do we have the capability to attract customers away from the
competition? Why? *Quality products*
    ☒ Yes
    ☐ No

8. Can we attract more than one population group in the market
area? Why? – *several mkts*
    ☒ Yes
    ☐ No

? 9. Will customers go out of their way to travel to our store? Why?
    ☐ Yes ?
    ☐ No .

III. **Estimate Customer Counts**

Estimate number of households/businesses in area: _____

Estimate frequency of eating out/purchasing from similar businesses: _____

Estimate the average number of specialty food store visits in the area for a typical period (day/week/month): _____

(*To do this, multiply the total households/businesses by the frequency of eating out.*)

(*Divide the number obtained from above calculation by the total number of competitive businesses, including our store and others known to be planned for the area*)

This will give us an estimate of the average number of customers per period:

_____

IV. **Estimate Overhead (rent) as an Appropriate Percentage of Sales**

1. Say you want your occupation costs to be 10% of gross. Follow this formula:

   $.10 \times$ sales = yearly rent/occupation costs (Let's use $120,000/year)

   Sales = $120,000/.1

   Sales = $1,200,000

   Sales = 100,000/month or $23,500/week

   $23,500 per week/average sale (say $8.00) =

   2,906 sales per week/415 per day (7 days)

V. **Conclusion**

1. Is the competitive environment favorable for a new store with the above specs?   ☐ Yes   ☐ No

2. Is the total customer base favorable for a new store?   ☐ Yes   ☐ No

3. Will our store be able to attract sufficient customers from the total customer base to operate successfully?   ☐ Yes   ☐ No

4. Will our store be able to produce the dollar sales necessary to meet the estimated sales level?   ☐ Yes   ☐ No

5. Which specific population groups in the market area can we identify?

   _____

6. What kinds of stores/services do these groups need and prefer?

   _____

7. Which population groups, or market segments, are being served adequately by existing stores/services in the market area? _____

8. What population groups need or want services that are either not available or performed poorly by the competition? _____

9. What type of store could best fill the needs of the identified market segment(s)?

   _____

Where *Where* should you open your business? In general, when pressed for an answer about their key to success in a specialty food business, owners will repeat the oft-cited three-word answer: "Location! Location! Location!" and there's more than a kernel of truth to that answer. Do you intend to be located where your store will be a destination or just one more stop on the way during routine shopping (freestanding, rural, or downtown, strip mall or large shopping center?) Will you be the anchor for future development of a neighborhood undergoing revitalization or ride the coattails of other successful businesses in the area? What kind of community support (and/or recognition) will you get for your efforts? Are there other complementary businesses (i.e., movie house, other theater/seasonal concert venue or entertainment complex) nearby that will drive your business at particular times of day?

> On the importance of location, Russ Vernon, owner of West Point Market, Akron, OH, says: "Visibility is important but after 59 years, people are still discovering us. . . . Having said that, a lot of your success has to do with the personality of the store and its culture. We have developed a destination store unique in our market so location is not paramount in our case."

What *What* should you sell once you've opened? What products and what services will form the core of your business? Should your store include eat-in facilities as well as takeout, considering the growing demand for affordable, accessible, casual eating environments that serve a public needing to eat on the run? There's always a time for dining experiences that are no-frills, fast, and affordable. Good quality and good value are the buzzwords. If late hours or eat-in capability will be the lure, should you and can you plan for it (after checking on zoning codes related to amount of parking, number of restrooms, handicapped access)?

Based on other stores in your market area, should you try to compete by offering similar lines in your store? Or should you move in another direction entirely, offer a line of foods with a different, perhaps ethnic, slant? How different can your store be (either in content or form) and still draw in the population who is apt to be your clientele?

Would you do best to specialize and make a strong statement with a deep and broad assortment of core items in a single category (coffee, tea, cheese, smoked fish, confections, baked goods including bread) and then offer complementary lines to supplement this main attraction?

When Because timing is everything, you need to take one more thing into account: *when* you intend to open your business. (See the list of questions on personal criteria and business strategies later in this chapter to appreciate the crucial nature of timing when opening a business.) Does opening this kind of business, given the current economic climate, make sense? Just as important, is it the right time in your life to be making such a far-reaching commitment of time and money and incurring debt in the process? Look yourself in the eye and be honest with yourself and with others who depend on you when answering these fundamental questions.

How   Undercapitalization spells an early death for food (and all other kinds of) businesses. So *how* you are going to fund your operation is as important as *why, where,* and *when* you are opening and *what* you will sell. Therefore, before you even begin, have you budgeted capital and space for growth (production as well as retail areas), flexibility, and change (inevitable in a trend-driven, dynamic industry)?

How Do You Conduct a Feasibility Study?

Once the feasibility study is complete and the results yield a green light, you will then proceed to writing the actual business plan, a more detailed road map including directions through all the "back roads" of corporate structure, financing, real-estate, staffing, marketing, and promotion, among other pieces of the total business picture. First things first, however; begin with feasibility.

For new businesses, the feasibility study maps out the exact course you will take to open and grow your venture. It is the predevelopment work in critical areas such as market analysis, demographic study, understanding pricing strategies, and customer flow. When all of this work has been done, you will have a good idea of what you can expect in initial sales and expense projections for your new venture. Think of it this way: if you were driving across country to a well-known destination without a detailed map, you would probably get there all right; but if your plan was to get there directly and without long delays, you'd need a good map listing all of the alternate routes. In a car journey surprise and serendipity may be welcome, helping to make the trip more interesting. When planning a business, however, the goal is to reduce unknowns in an effort to rule out areas of risk that may permanently derail your project. This is where good detective work and a commitment of time and energy, necessary for completing the feasibility study, come in.

How much time will it take to gather the information necessary to fill in *all* the blanks for a truly objective and therefore useful feasibility study? You may say, "Too much time" and feel you would rather spend your precious free minutes making deals and doing the fun stuff, such as securing commitments from your favorite artisanal food producers for exclusive representation of their products. This kind of deal making will have to wait. Be confident that time spent up front in the research phase of your business development will save you untold heartache, not to mention money. With a structure in hand to guide you, you will be able to think more clearly and dispassionately about your next move. From the mere act of researching your idea and writing the outcome of the study, you stand to amass necessary information and learn valuable lessons for the rest of your journey to business ownership.

Often a feasibility study determines whether or not your idea should be pursued at all. You may complete your first feasibility study and discover that the venture as proposed is inappropriate at the present time, or wrong for the location initially desired. Or you may discover that the population you have targeted as your market may not, in fact, be right for your products and services at the price you need to charge for them, or may not be large enough in a particular part of town to support your concept.

Face it: with few exceptions, all retail businesses depend for their viability on having a critical mass of people closely surrounding them who will be their regular customer base (those few exceptions include mail order businesses and the occasional establishment whose customers travel inordinate distances or otherwise tolerate difficult access to obtain the products that they crave and that are unavailable elsewhere). By and large, location counts. Therefore it is important to look at the feasibility of placing your concept and your product in various sites before settling on one. Compare the numbers for each location studied to see which seems the most convincing. In addition to the neighborhood location, many aspects of the physical space itself such as equipment already installed, renovations needed, and prior uses of the space (is it already zoned for food?) will determine whether the investment is appropriate. It's best to arrange close inspection of several locations to help determine your concept, market, product line, and, potential revenue and income. When you are researching each potential site, gather as much information as possible about other businesses in the immediate area, including their longevity, pattern of ownership, and customer base.

Don't simply go through the motions of gathering data to support your unshakable belief that you have a great idea that cannot fail. Don't rely on those pie-in-the-sky projections of revenues generated from your mythical business without regard for the costs, both human and financial, incurred in generating those sales figures. No amount of wishful thinking that you can duplicate that "overnight" success story on the other side of town will make your dream a reality. In fact, a feasibility study misses the point if it is written just to prove that a venture can succeed. Instead, be thorough in your fact gathering and do a realistic data analysis to help you determine if your idea is going to be doable, from capital, energy, and profit perspectives. If it passes this first stage of rational scrutiny, you can then feel comfortable that the business should be explored further.

Where to Begin?

The first place to start with the feasibility study process is more self-questioning. After having seen how well you stack up next to the personality profile of a successful entrepreneur, you should have most of the answers to these questions. They show up again here to help you focus even more. Include your business partner if you have one, and do the following exercise by writing down one-sentence answers to the following questions. Put your answers aside and, without looking at them, revisit the questions perhaps a week later and answer them again. A side-by-side comparison of your answers may be revealing:

Personal Criteria and Business Strategies

1. What is your definition of job security?
2. How important is money (and how much) in your life?
3. What would you like to improve about your lifestyle?
4. What is your definition of power?
5. How will your age affect the potential of your business?
6. Are there any known health issues that may interfere with your commitment to the business in the long term? Short term?
7. What are your primary family considerations and commitments?
8. How does the business' location jibe with where you live?
9. What is the total investment you are willing to raise, make yourself, or risk for this venture?
10. How would you define your attitude in general toward this venture?

> Paul Griffith, owner of Gourmet Foods Warehouse Outlet, Englewood, CO, has this to say: "Individuals who are emotionally caught up in the industry are likely to fail without a strong business partner."

Strategy (*n.*) A skill in managing or planning and a scheme for achieving some purpose

———From *Random House Dictionary of the English Language,* 1967

A feasibility study helps you define your strategy before you get on the road, and a strategy is both a science and an art in its own right. To create art, however, the artist (or business-owner-to-be) must:

1. Have a vision of what is to be created.
2. Have adequate knowledge of the craft.
3. Successfully communicate or present a completed, coherent piece to an audience. (For the entrepreneur, the feasibility study, and later the business plan, will be communicated to prospective investors or other funding sources. Eventually, the business itself will be presented to the community at large.)

Hence as an entrepreneur, you can employ a strategy similar to an artist's. You need to educate yourself about current developments in the market you plan to enter. You also need to have a distinct vision or idea, to work toward refining your concept with specific products and/or market strategies in mind. The knowledge of the craft might come from experience in the field, seeking and getting the necessary training, or hiring professionals to assemble the project with you. Here you are working to turn your business idea into a viable business venture just as a sculptor turns an idea and a piece of store into a statue. Researching the location, market, capital needs, and potential sales, as well as identifying the competition, belong to the feasibility study phase. Exploring what's involved in securing financing, creating full-blown financial projections, and creating your store design will be essential components of the more formal business plan phase, which comes later. You'll need to communicate the results of your feasibility study to possible investors (or other funding sources). This, followed by the presentation of the more complete business plan, is often the one-two punch that will launch your venture. This methodical step-by-step approach, resulting in a guidebook through further development stages, sends a loud, clear message to prospective backers: "This is a potential business owner who has done his (or her) homework thoroughly and well." With really minimal up-front work and investment of time, energy, and money, you will have conquered hurdles it can otherwise take months or years to jump.

Here are some pointers about how to write your feasibility plan that hold true also for your other business writing, including the business plan.

Content Issues

1. Avoid emotionally expressed qualifiers and the use of insupportable superlatives, such as "the most . . . ," "the best ever . . . ," or hackneyed descriptors such as "cutting edge."

2. If you insist on using these terms because they are truly the most appropriate, explain exactly *how* the product or service is "the best ever, " "the highest quality," and so on. Qualify your claims with background, history, or well regarded definitions. Be specific to support your effusiveness; state that you make your chocolate chip cookies truly *by hand* and only from the highest quality ingredients including specifically *French* chocolate or *unsalted, raw organic* butter or. . . . Take credit for what makes you unique.

3. If you use technical terminology specific to the food business, provide definitions to readers from different backgrounds the first time any of these terms appear. Generally, the people who will read your feasibility study, and later your business plan, are not experts in the specialty food industry. Therefore, except where describing techniques that enhance or differentiate your product or service from others available, translate any industry-specific terminology into everyday language.

Mechanical Details

4. Use type that is pleasant to look at and easy to read. Also make sure that the report looks professional and that it is free from typos, misspelled words, or awkward phrasing. Avoid text so tiny that it is tiring to read your document. Conversely avoid text that is so large that you appear to be shouting your message to make up in volume what you lack in quality.

5. Create a cover sheet for the study, use a soft-colored paper for all of the text pages; and have the product professionally bound so that the reader can fold the pages back flat (this service is available at most copy shops).

6. Include photos or other printed materials about you, your product or service, and any diagrams or layouts you may have; they often help to convey your message more compellingly than words can.

Now, before you set out to evaluate the potential of different sites and specific markets, clarify the product and/or service you intend to sell. The first step here is to understand the difference between "product" and "service"—a distinction that is often challenging for food professionals because the two concepts are inherently intertwined in the merchandising, selling, and consumption end of the food business. This fact makes it even more imperative that you first understand the distinctions and interconnections, and then be able to clarify the nature of *your* business to *your* potential investors, many of whom may know nothing about your particular business.

You're now ready to formulate the first part, your "mission statement": "What is the purpose of my business?" Here is where you first clarify the "nature" of your business, whether it is a product or service business, or some combination of the two, and why the need for your business exists.

To use the familiar and illuminating example of Domino's Pizza: At first glance, the units of this chain appear to be simply pizza franchises. But above and beyond product, Domino's is selling *convenience* in the form of pizza guaranteed to be delivered to your door in 20 minutes or less. Additionally, the service is widely available in most US communities. So is Domino's chief business product or service?

Take a look at your proposed products and/or services. Determine which of these is most important to you and most relevant to the total business concept as it is developed so far. Look further to analyze which, at this point, have the potential to generate the most revenue and most profit. Write them down! Again, when tempted to describe your product or service as "the best" or any other superlative, define exactly why it deserves such a description in clear, concise words, using the previous analyses to back up your contentions.

Armed with Exhibit 2-1, the feasibility study worksheet, you're ready at this point to go "out in the field" to begin your feasibility study. Remember that your goal is to obtain information about the observable, empirical characteristics of a market, its population, and the overall business climate. Some of this data (competitive environment) will be relatively easy to find by visiting and observing closely the operations of businesses analogous to what you hope to open. (There's nothing unethical about sending friends and family members to "spy" for you, if it seems more appropriate; you've got to know the competition well before you can hope to compete.) Other bits of information, such as residential and working population of your target area and median income levels (prospective customer profile), will be obtainable from previously compiled databases (see Sources and Resources at the end of this book). Combining the information you glean in the field with supporting general statistics about the specific market area in which you intend to open, you will then be able to narrow the focus of your business concept, zero in on an appropriate site for your business, and move ahead with the next step: Writing your business plan.

THE MARKET FOR YOUR BUSINESS

How do you validate your gut feelings about the essential "rightness" of your business concept? Do you simply bank on the fact that you have found a location that you feel suits you and blindly open your business there in the hopes that you will succeed? Or, before you commit the first dollar to your venture, do you take the much more rational, well-considered path that involves an intensive market study of your area? The occasional fluke success story might support the former approach, but more commonly, entrepreneurs wishing to attract funding for a business project must take the traditional, methodical route and undertake and evaluate a comprehensive market survey before embarking on plans to open their doors. Remember, however, that any marketing study is only as good as the data it contains. If the data is reliable and up-to-date and you know that the area under study has remained relatively stable within the last few years, then the report will have validity. If a major corporation has just downsized or left your area, then all of the data you find may be obsolete.

Remember that marketing studies are tools used to convince the potential entrepreneur and the potential investors in the project of the validity of a business concept for a particular geographical context at a particular point in time. They are predictors of the behavior of a given population with given characteristics. They are not guarantees that a particular business will succeed. In fact, it has been shown time and again that having the right target audience with the "right demographics" will not mean success for a business which is undercapitalized, poorly marketed, underpromoted, and badly operated. The converse is also true: the best run business in the wrong market is not likely to meet success. It's the old "coals to Newcastle" story writ large. (Of course, there are exceptions—but try to convince your funding sources of that!)

Where to begin? And what can you expect to learn from such a study?

When developing your market study, you need to take the following steps:

- Define the geographic market area (what size sample) and the group you wish to study and limit your research to those.
- Define what kind of information you are seeking to gain from doing a survey and market study (how many questions you wish to include in the survey).
- Develop the outline for the study, listing all the measures you wish to include in the study.
- Identify sources for the information you are seeking.
- Look at other businesses in your market area that are analogous to yours or closely approximate yours as clues to the market study you will conduct.

From your marketing study you should be able to isolate the answers to the following questions:

- What is my competition?
- Who would the client base be, including ethnic and racial makeup? (Base this on your location and on the accessibility of your location to the workforce in your area as well as the residential population.)
- How are their needs being met presently?

- In fact, does this targeted population need the services that I propose to offer in my business?
- What needs aren't being met? Can I program those into my plan?
- What am I looking for to show me the answers to these questions?
- What kind of information will be helpful in making the decision about locations for my proposed business?

To find such information contact Economic Development Councils in your area and read their annual reports. Speak with the Chamber of Commerce to learn about start-ups—and hence the level of investment—in your area. Examine local city or county records to learn about the tax base of your area, which indicates how much revenue comes from local businesses, large and small; this will be an indicator of potential sources of customers for *your* business. From real estate sources you can determine the number of houses sold within a given period, which will let you ascertain transience of population in your area.

Go to the largest local library in your area and ask for reference material, including the following:

- *Donnelly Demographics*
- *Sourcebook of Zip Code Demographics*
- *Zip Code Lifestyle Analyst*
- *Lifestyle Market Analyst*

Although these books are apt to be a year or so out of date, they enable you to pinpoint information on a narrowly defined area. From these you will be able to obtain the following information:

- Average annual income
- Home owners versus renters
- Marital status
- Number of kids in household
- Highest educational level attained

ZEROING IN ON THE NUMBERS

After analyzing the market, you must consider the finances involved. Here is a basic list of entries that will comprise the record of your business—useful for projections and for recording actual numbers as you develop your business plan.

Seeing in black and white just what it takes to produce a profit can be an eye-opening experience. To estimate annual projected revenues, you must consider, for example, space requirements (kitchen, seating, bathrooms). Use industry standards (number of square feet) to calculate that amount of space. How large a staff can turn out what amount of your product, times what price? The following list of expenses will help you plan.

Sales:

Taxable

Nontaxable

On-premise

Take-out

Catering

Direct expenses:

Food costs

Nonfood supplies—paper goods, plastics, disposables, stationery

Delivery

Labor costs:

Hourly

Exempt

Workmen's compensation insurance (based on annual payroll)

Benefits, such as health plans, if offered (all or part of the premiums)

Profit sharing

Retirement plans

Indirect expenses (not necessarily proportionate to product):

Rent

Automobiles—nondelivery vehicles

Insurances (product liability, renter's insurance)

Utilities (gas, electric)

Telephone

Maintenance costs

Publicity:

  Promotion
  Advertising (print and other media)
  Printed brochures, newsletters, graphics

Professional fees:

  Lawyer
  Accountant
  Public relations
  Other consultants
  Memberships, dues

Gross profit

Taxes

Net profit

Your calculations will end up something like this: If I can get my space at this figure, and if I can get labor at this figure, and if I can turn out this much product, then I will have a viable business. This plus the business plan, plus the balance sheet, are indicators that the business you wish to open has a chance of making it.

EVALUATING THE FEASIBILITY STUDY

We recommend that the feasibility study be performed on at least five sites that are under consideration for the building of your business. By answering each of the questions thoroughly and honestly about the sites, you will be able to evaluate which site, or type of site, may best suit your concept. To do this, create a summary sheet charting out the answers to all of the questions for each location, so they can be listed next to one another. In comparing the data from one site to that from another, think about what the answers tell you about the number of people who shop in the area, where the potential customers come from (i.e., residential or business), how much it seems that people in each area eat out and spend for meals while eating out, and so on. Then take another look at your concept. Review the summary data of your feasibility study with your concept in mind. Ask yourself questions like, "If I build a specialty food business that specializes in low-fat salads and entrees, are the people I observed in this neighborhood the type of customers for that product? Do these people pay for meals what I want to (and need to) charge? Do I offer enough selections that they will want to return several times a week and become regular customers? Where else are they buying the type of product I intend to sell?" Take a look at what you listed as the aspects of the stores observed that seem to make them most successful. Are you prepared to do at least that, and possibly more, to edge in on the competition and create a novel and important store? Lastly, if these responses all point toward a "go ahead" for your business, try the acid test of overhead: "Will I be able to generate enough business at the price points I want to charge so that my rent equals no more than 10% of my gross sales?" If the answers to all of the questions yield positive and encouraging results for at least one of the locations surveyed, you are probably ready to move on to the more comprehensive preparatory phase of writing a full-blown business plan. Now armed with enough information to confirm that you, your idea, and your intended location are all perfectly suited for opening a new specialty food store, we have four more things for you to think about as you prepare to write your business plan.

FOUR FINAL QUESTIONS

1. What do I/we want out of the business? The first part of the answer to this questions is the most obvious—what do you and your partners want to gain financially from operating this business? About half the people starting the business planning process have some idea of what they want to earn from their efforts owning and operating a business. Common responses are something like "A lot," or "More than I can possibly make at my current job," or "As much as my boss." If you recognize yourself in any of the above answers, then you also need to think about how the business in its early stages will generate enough to pay you and your partners the desired sum. Then, you need to go the next logical step and find out if your investment team agrees with these salary figures.

At this stage, it is important to look at your current finances and make some decisions about what you will be willing to risk to get the business off the ground. Think about your family and other financial obligations. How will they be affected in a period of unpredictable income and potential use of savings? And how will using your savings impact on those who depend on you? Are your assets liquid and available if and when you need them to tide you over until the business is firmly enough established to begin to pay you? Have you engaged your spouse and partner in this decision? Are you and your partners equally prepared to take very little or nothing out of the business until it can afford to pay you? What is the agreed-to time frame for this?

A second and equally important aspect of the question to consider is about what you want this business to give you (and your partners) over and beyond financial reward. Although intimately bound up with money, answers to this revolve more around intangible factors such as quality of life, lifestyle, and to some degree, status. The answers also relate to your personal ideas about mission, purpose, intent, or contribution. Is this business going to provide you with what you require in terms of community, relationships, sense of purpose, and self-fulfillment? Think hard about this. What is important to you besides financial reward? Do you have social, community or family goals in mind, that may perhaps be aided or derailed by opening and running a business?

Why do you want to start your own business? What can you accomplish by having your own company that can't be achieved by staying at your current job or otherwise advancing within the industry? How important are *your* goals in relation to the larger picture? (These vary widely from individual to individual and from partnership to partnership). Think about your life as it is now and what provides you with happiness or pleasure or fulfillment. Will your own business offer you as much or more of this? You are about to make a long-term commitment fraught with a tremendous amount of risk, both financial and personal. Can you commit to it fully and be content with the commitment even if it results in a reduced standard of living for a while?

2. What do I/we want for the company? Many people believe that businesses have their own lives. (Some may go so far as to ascribe a distinctive spirit, personality, or even karma to a business.). As with any other living, evolving thing, what you put into it has an impact on the outcome. Think about your potential business as a child that will mature and have a life of its own. Where do you want the company to be in five, ten, or fifteen years, and what will you put into it to nurture it through those stages?

Perhaps you are thinking of this business as the prototype for other locations and franchises. Are you looking to operate a company that will allow you free time when you want it? Can the store be minded by someone other than yourself when you just need to get away? The answers to these kinds of questions will help formulate the business' mission, and also help determine its location, your market, and who your staff will be and the scope of their roles. They help to define your position in the market, and thus clarify the concept. All of this, in turn, will aid in clarifying the financial potential of the business.

Some important questions to ask to get these answers are:

1. Philosophically speaking, are you (and your partners) in agreement about what products you will be selling and what markets you will be targeting?

2. Can you agree on a location?

3. Do you have a common vision of your commitment to staff training?

4. What resources besides money are you prepared to offer to the business? (You may draw upon special areas of expertise to contribute artistic input on store graphics and signage; with strong writing skills, you may be the one primarily responsible for producing store newsletters, advertisements, promotional pieces; you may also become the company's spokesperson, exploiting any special ties you may have to community organizations, institutions, philanthropies, and movers and shakers in the community. All of these responsibilities imply a willingness to commit more time or effort than that of your partners at times, secure in the knowledge that things have a way of equalizing over time.)

5. What kind of life do you want the business to lead?

6. What businesses in related fields are your models and why?

Here is where some groundwork will be very helpful. Have you researched enough companies and their "lives"? This can be done by examining available publicity and promotional materials of businesses you admire. Take a look at these businesses' positions in the industry and their contribution to local economies and communities. What are their missions? You can glean a lot of information by reading annual reports, available from all public companies. This research will not only help you to understand the financial position of similar companies, but will also let you examine their product lines, markets, and operations. Perhaps most important of all, you will be able to get an understanding of their image and position in the market. You can draw conclusions about how all of the above contribute to the financial health of the companies under review, and from this information fill in some of the blanks about what exactly your business is. This information goes right into the business plan.

3. How well do I/we and the company's objectives measure up to the experience of other owners and other businesses in the same industry? Here is where more research comes in. If you are already in the industry, you may have a head start on this. You may already read the trade journals religiously and be fully conversant about the competition and market trends. You may be aware of industry averages and new start-ups. In preparation for your own business, perhaps you have been comparing your goals with others who are already successful in the industry.

If you have not been doing this, this fact-gathering phase is the time to start. You will have already answered the questions in number 2 above, so you do know what you are searching for. Reading trade journals, joining national and local culinary and trade associations, attending food events, and doing a lot of comparison shopping will all help to point you toward answers to this question.

Allow plenty of time to discuss your impressions thoroughly and frequently with your partners or other business associates. Although you may be researching independently, be sure to dedicate some time to sharing what you have found and discuss how this information will impact on your future business and how each partner will impact the business, separately and together.

Lastly, in the preplan phase, it is important to include this question:

4. What are the investors' or lenders' objectives? By raising money from outside entities you are entering into very specific kinds of partnerships. The degree of these partners' involvement is determined by many factors, only some of which are related to the amount of money they invest in your company.

Let's start with money. Your need for capital may be the only reason you seek partnerships with other people. Let's assume that your business plan, along with other connections, enables you to attract financial investors. Your needs are met by their writing a check. Now what? What are their needs, and how will these be satisfied? Does a mere return on their investment satisfy their need? Maybe, maybe not. Other questions need to be considered here: How much is a fair return on their investment? At what rate will they be paid, and over what period of time?

Once you have arrived at mutually acceptable answers to these questions, there are still many other questions left to answer. Meeting your investors' and lenders' financial needs is only part of the answer. What about their need for decision-making authority? Can you expect these lenders and investors to require an active voice in the day-to-day operations of the business? When negotiating with financial partners, ask yourself if you have built into your business relationship enough leeway to change course when necessary to turn the tide. On a day-to-day basis, how much autonomy you have in running the show depends on many things in an often fluid relationship: the personality of the prime players, the stakes, and the overall economic climate. Before you consider *their* traits and personalities, however, think through *your* intentions, *your* purpose, and what *you* are willing to share or give away. Essential to any partnership are two things: your long-term commitment to making the business work for you, but also your commitment to making the investors' money work for them. The more you prove you can do this, or at least show good probability of it, in the business plan, the stronger footing you will have with your financial partner(s). And this translates to the dollars that will fund the business over the (hopefully) long course of its life. To create a strategy for this takes careful thinking about your objectives, strengths, weaknesses, ability to share control, and that big concept, compromise.

CHAPTER THREE

THE BUSINESS PLAN

A dozen or more times each year we hear from would-be specialty food entrepreneurs: "I just have to put the business plan together and then I'll get the money. They [the potential investors, people of promise] just want to see 'something' on paper." Even more frequently we hear: "I have the business plan in my head. I just have to sit down to write it—it's no big deal." Sometimes it goes: "I'm going to do the business plan using that computer program prototype (for boilerplate text); maybe I'll need a little help, but I'm really going to do it myself. . . ." When asked what, actually, they have down on paper, these entrepreneurs usually hesitate, then admit that nothing is written. When asked what their proposed business structure will be (partnership, corporation, etc.), they usually admit sheepishly that they don't know the difference. When asked what their "investors" want to see and by when, they almost always answer that there is no definite time frame, although they are always in a rush to get "it" done.

The scenario usually goes like this: The would-be entrepreneur starts with a germ of an idea and then bats it around to some people who may or may not have money to invest in a venture such as the one described. (Be prepared for the fact that these would-be "investors" will know even less than you about how much it will take to get this hypothetical retail food venture off the ground.) Like the high school freshman who waits until 10:30 P.M. to start the book report due the next day, the writer of a business plan may be thinking wishfully that the plan will write itself or that the need for it will just go away.

Tenaciously holding onto the dream, this same person may not be ready to put the idea to the first viability tests. That's where a good business plan comes in.

WHAT IS A BUSINESS PLAN?

When you ask potential investors for money to capitalize your business, the first question you will be asked is often, "Do you have a business plan?" Your automatic response, as illustrated by the scenarios above, will most likely be, "Yes," on the assumption that, if someone is indicating interest in your business by asking for a business plan, it is a thing you need to have. At that point, perhaps for the first time, you realize you need such a plan even if you don't know exactly what one is. Perhaps you believe you can throw one together for this potential investor and others. So, perhaps for the first time, you set about thinking, "What is a business plan, exactly?"

A business plan is a document that states the concept of your business in a nutshell, describes your potential market, and gives reasons why there is a need for your proposed products and/or services. It includes financial projections, both for start-up and for the way the business will run once you open. It clarifies the corporate status and nature of the partnerships, proves the credibility of the management team, and includes many supporting documents, such as renderings of your store's interior, a map that indicates where your business will be located in relation to other businesses, a menu of offerings, and perhaps even press reviews from past ventures. The business plan can be large (75 pages or more) or small (20 pages)—there are different schools of thought on this—but it must be thorough, convincing, and, to the best of your ability, realistic.

A business plan is your best ally in raising money and interest for a new venture. Formulating a business plan is the single most important thing you can do before you consider going into business. It is a tool you should use to evaluate your business idea, and a touchstone you need to return to again and again to confirm the viability of your idea. As the blueprint or roadmap for your business, a well-researched business plan can clarify your goals, focus your energy, give direction to your work and help you gauge your progress before *and after* you are in operation.

A business plan is not to be taken lightly. Any business proposed will probably dominate the entrepreneur's life for many years to come. In the food business in particular, the break-even point is not usually seen before the third or fifth year, with high growth years and profits often further off on the horizon. When it comes, success usually comes slowly and steadily. A meteoric rise often precedes an equally dramatic roller coaster trajectory to failure. If you look at "overnight successes" in business, you will most likely find that a slow and steady progress toward profitability was the real story behind an enduring business.

Everything takes time. The process from the inception of a business idea to its incubation and eventual implementation takes time and patience. In fact, a typical five-year time line of the process might show development of the concept and writing the initial draft of the business plan within the first six months. The next year or two will then be devoted to raising the money, securing the location, building and fixturizing the store (on average, retail food businesses take anywhere from 1½ to 3½ years to opening day from the time the initial idea was hatched). See Exhibit 3-1 for a typical timeline for opening a business. Although the business plan is the first step in that long process and provides the least expensive testing ground a potential business owner can use, people are often reluctant to make a commitment to writing one or to engaging the services of a professional to help them write one. (To write a comprehensive business plan, a good business consultant can charge upwards of $10,000, depending on your market. Bite the bullet and consider these services as part of start-up costs and money well spent.)

Whether you write the plan yourself or choose to hire a consultant for all or part of the process, you need a plan before you can proceed any farther. We have found that, anxious as they may be to implement their ideas, many would-be business owners have a hard time confronting head-on the need for a business plan. Psychological or emotional obstacles often stand in the way. Here's why:

When the proposed business owner is inexperienced in any of the primary areas of research and development crucial to his/her idea, simple procrastination sets in and the plan is never properly written, if at all. This same lack of experience will have a negative impact on the analysis of the data retrieved once the research for the plan actually begins. The sheer act of sitting down and putting thoughts and ideas on paper, however unrefined, can serve to crystallize the potential entrepreneur's feelings about the intended business. This initial scribbling is often the truest, most basic expression of why someone wants to start a new business. Once you, as a hopeful business leader, begin the process, you may discover that, rough though it is, the resulting digest of information about the business-to-be can be an anchor to which you return again and again when the formal writing of the business plan is actually being done. It can also be highly revealing about a whole host of other underlying agenda, and it pays to examine it frequently as you proceed with the business plan itself.

The final business plan is *not* just a haphazard, casual array of ideas on paper, however, even if that's where you start. Appropriately named, it is indeed a plan for transforming those ideas from your head into a way to operate your future business. The act of writing a business plan is a process of discovery about your business—what it is, what it will (and will *not*) be, and what your relationship is to it. Preparing to write the plan will set you on the first of many paths toward getting those important questions answered. Turning your basic, and often diffuse, ideas into reality, into a coherent business plan, is the single most important thing you can do before going into business.

EXHIBIT 3-1

GOURMET-TO-GO BUSINESS PLANNING CHECKLIST AND TIME LINE

Although your own time frame may differ somewhat from the one shown here, the following is provided as a basic guideline and a preview of the steps any entrepreneur-to-be needs to take on the road to opening a business.

I. **Research and Development Phase, 2–6 months**
    A. Identify concept and establish preliminary parameters, including:
       • Menu
       • Location
       • Market
       • Pricing
       (Explore two–three possibilities for each)
    B. Get some clear ideas about cost:
       • Leasehold improvements and cost of lease
       • Cost of goods and other fixed expenses (industry standards)
       • Professional fees
       • Projected sales volume and bottom line

II. **The Business Plan, 2–8 months**
    A. Conduct feasibility and market studies for proposed site(s)
    B. Solidify partnership agreements
    C. Incorporate
    D. Interview architects, contractors, accountants, lawyers, and other consultants and assemble team to write plan
    E. Write the plan with scheduled goals/time line (including all pertinent financial information such as start-up and operating budgets, return of investment to financial partners)
    F. Line up investors

III. **Raising Capital, from 6 months to an indeterminate amount of time**
    A. Identify the capitalization structure for your business (can be combination of own money, loans, private investors—including family and friends—venture capital, and economic development or other grants)
    B. Create strategy for making contacts and pitching business
    C. Create goals and deadlines for raising capital

Phase III coincides with other development, within same time frame, and Phase IV:

IV. **Location Planning, 3–8 months**
    A. Select top three location sites
    B. Negotiate lease
    C. Have architect and contractor do preliminary planning
    D. Have lease prepared, reviewed, and summarized.

V. **Build-Out of Leased or Purchased Space, 3 months–1 year, depending on size of space and scope of renovations or new construction**
   A. Have architect draw up plans
   B. Hire the contractor
   C. Schedule/prepare a time line
   D. Obtain permits
   E. Confirm budget (and readjust business plan throughout process)
   F. Arrange for multi-phases of construction, including equipment installation
   G. Revise budget (every 2–4 weeks)
   H. Arrange for inspections

Phase V also coincides with other aspects of project development, especially Phase VI.

VI. **Preopening, 3 months–1 year**
   A. Write menu/establish product mix and pricing
   B. For packaged goods: establish manufacturer and distributor sources and relationships
   C. Assemble management team
   D. Select interior fixtures (shelving, display, tableware, cookware, etc.)
   E. Select insurance company, credit card company, telephone system and company, bank, and other services (e.g., linen, garbage, maintenance services, security)
   F. Establish accounting system and other software/management systems [select point of sale system (POS), recipe costing, inventory, payroll]
   G. Solidify marketing plan and execute preopening activities according to construction and opening schedule
   H. Test and cost out recipes of prepared foods
   I. Install POS and train staff
   J. Write operations manual, including job descriptions for all positions
   K. Develop system and strategy for hiring (begin two–three months prior to opening) and training (two weeks to a month prior to opening)
   L. Revise operating budget (every two months)
   M. Reassess partners, goals and job descriptions
   N. Create daily operating checklist
   O. Create manager's "punch list" for construction items

VII. **Opening, 1 month**
   A. Solidify daily operating checklist
   B. Clarify daily bookkeeping procedures
   C. Create weekly P+L statements and compare to operating budget
   D. Create checklist for contractor
   E. Verify total opening costs to budget, adjust operating budget or raise more capital to compensate for overages
   F. Continue preopening marketing plan and prepare for ongoing marketing efforts

HOW DO YOU START?

The first steps in writing a business plan are like testing the waters. For most first-time business owners-to-be, it is a process riddled with fear, passion, desire, and more fear (what will happen once I get started?). No matter what, preparing to write a plan and then doing it are difficult steps, often laden with conflicting emotions. Your interior voice may be whispering, "Should I take this risk? Can I afford to lose my shirt, my pride, or my dignity and self-respect if I fail?" At the same time, your ego may be propelling you onward, fueled by a blind and often unreasonable attachment to the idea.

The process of writing a business plan is somewhat akin to setting your first boot-clad foot out the door on a numbingly cold, snowy day. You place one toe on the pavement but the rest of you wishes to hang back, to stay inside, safe and warm, hidden behind the thick protective door. Then, because you have gone a bit public with the concept already, you feel the need to go all the way. You do it—you step out into the cold completely. With a business idea, that same kind of reluctance in confronting reality often prevents you from making a commitment to do a formal business plan for your proposed business. Some of this reluctance may stem from believing that you are sure of what you are going to do, how much money it will cost, and that it's "not necessary" to create this formal document. If you went through the feasibility study process, you now know that can't be true, and you probably have come up with a variation on your initial concept. This is good!

The business plan takes the results of your feasibility study and explores the business potential within those findings. In the business plan you will dig out every possible aspect of your new business in a particular location and under particular circumstances. You will have a document that outlines all of the important aspects of your business, from concept to financing to design to staffing to daily operations, and even a plan for the future. The business plan will become a point of reference when in the middle of a million tasks, either pre- or post-opening. It will be there to remind you what you planned to do, why you planned it, and how you projected the business to work both operationally and financially for your start-up years.

THE FIRST STEP—THE MISSION STATEMENT

After passing the self-assessment stage, proceed with writing your plan on the assumption that you will raise the money you need, you will find that great location, and you will get your business up and running within two years. Plan on spending between three and six months to complete the business plan. This is not a lot of time to plan for something that you expect to spend a good part of your career operating! If you give yourself this time, you can make a realistic outline of how to get it done and who will help you. The worst mistake you can make now, and throughout your life as a business owner, is to overpromise. If you don't overpromise now, you will have a better chance of maintaining that posture throughout.

Here's the first step: *Write a mission statement.* This will be easy if you spent some time in the self-assessment phase. A mission statement is the springboard to your business plan, and will serve as your grounding throughout. The mission statement is a paragraph of a few sentences that states *what* your business is, *where* your proposed business will be, *who* is operating the business, *who* or *what market* you are catering to, *what products* you will be carrying, what *services* you will be rendering, *what* will distinguish your business from the rest, and *what* you want to get out of operating the business. The mission statement may be the toughest part of writing your business plan. After writing it, read it to yourself and your friends and family. How does it sound to you? Does it sound like the kind of business that you want to own and live with for years to come? All of the information in your business plan will come out of words or sentences of your mission statement.

Sutton Place Gourmet is a leading chain of large specialty food emporia in Washington, DC, and Virginia, as well as owner of Hay Day Markets with stores in Connecticut and New York; it sets a lofty goal in its mission statement:

> To be the leading specialty food retailer in the U.S., by providing the finest quality foods available worldwide, delivering exceptional service from friendly and knowledgeable food specialists, and presenting a unique and inviting shopping environment.

Another well-known retailer, Zingerman's (in Ann Arbor, MI.), expresses its mission statement in terms of its employees' overall role in making the business successful:

> We share the Zingerman's Experience
> Selling food that makes you* happy
> Giving service that makes you* smile
> In passionate pursuit of our mission
> Showing love and caring in all our actions
> To enrich as many lives as we possibly can.
>
> *"you" = "customers and staff"

In more than five pages, it then goes on to elaborate the following four major areas, or guiding principles, which underlie the store's philosophy: Great Food!, Great Service!, A Great Place to Shop and Eat!, and Solid Profits!, with descriptions below each to elaborate. This retailer makes an unconditional commitment to "selling high-quality food" and states that "first and foremost we are in business to sell food. Our other work—including accounting, design and management—is done to support and advance the sales of our food." Rather than catering to an elite of foodies ("Good food is for everyone, not just a select, 'gourmet' few"), Zingerman's makes the egalitarian claim that "No advanced degrees are needed to appreciate it [good food]—just a willingness to taste and experience the pleasure it provides." About service, Zingerman's mission statement promises that "Our guests leave happy or they don't leave. Each of us takes full responsibility for making our guest's experience an enjoyable one, before, during and after the sale." These are lofty but not unreachable goals, and all of the best operators in the specialty food industry embody them and are successful because they recognize the importance of doing so.

Profits Are Also Part of the Picture

Amidst all the talk about great food and great service, Zingerman's philosophy acknowledges that:

> Profits are the lifeblood of our business. Profits provide us with security and growth potential—both for the business as a whole and for each of us as components of that business—in order to fulfill our mission. Attaining healthy profits requires a concerted and consistent contribution from everyone at Zingerman's. Toward that end we educate our entire staff about the financial workings of the business.

Tied to that commitment, the Zingerman's manifesto goes on to describe its corporate culture by stating that "We are empowered by the creativity, hard work and commitment of our staff." It asserts further that its success is based on strong relationships with customers, staff, suppliers, and other businesses. In addition to this, providing a safe workplace and using safe food-handling procedures underlies all else that they do. And since staying current is essential to the continuing success of the business, Zingerman's works to "Actively educate our guests, our staff and ourselves about the food we sell." Echoing its food-driven raison d'être, the statement continues: "We believe that the more we learn about food (where it comes from, how it's made, how to use it) the more effectively and profitably the business will operate." What's more, Zingerman's strives to "give back to the community of which it is a part" by "contributing time, food, money, energy and information."

All of this would ring hollow if the store did not live up to its stated objectives and philosophies. Going through the motions of writing a mission statement without a deeper commitment to carry out the stated goals and abide by the stated philosophies and guiding principles is an exercise in futility. Whether stated in simple terms, in a few lines, or set forth in great detail, the statement should act as a goal to which both owner and staff aspire. The mere act of sitting down to write a well-thought-out mission statement allows the store owner to examine and then express his or her core beliefs. What you stand for is at the heart of any mission statement. What you express in it should give a clear indication of how you will operate your business as well. Let all of your employees know where you stand. Share your goals with them (give each a copy of your mission statement and then follow up with a face-to-face meeting to go over its contents with them). The statement should make clear to all of your staff that your success is their success and vice versa. But the statement is valuable only insofar as it keeps you on track, even while acknowledging your shortcomings and taking credit for your strengths. Bear in mind that there is no one right way to cast your mission statement. The only requirement is that you give it a lot of thought, be honest with yourself, be sure that it represents the "real" you and your "real" goals. Then do all that it takes to "live it" once you have committed it to paper.

THE SECOND STEP

Once your mission statement is completed, create an outline of your business plan (see the following section, "The Nitty-Gritty," for a sample business plan outline). Sit down with that outline and figure out who on your team has the most expertise in the different areas and "assign" appropriate team members the task of completing what will turn into sections.

If you are going it alone, sit down with the outline and honestly assess which sections you will have trouble completing and then think about the resources available to you to get them written. If you will be utilizing friends and family to assist you, be clear about your needs and get commitments from them. Most importantly, if you need help from professionals, seek it. An accountant can assist with the financials. A lawyer can draft sample partnership agreements. A marketing specialist can help you assess the local markets. A consultant specializing in food service operations can help with any of the above areas, and also help to round out the plan, filling in any necessary gaps before you present it to potential funding sources. Consider the cost of outside help to be money well spent. Don't be tempted to use cookie-cutter prototypes such as those in an off-the-shelf software package; these simply do not offer the kind of detail or subtlety you may need to really sell your idea.

Business consultants concur that each business plan is unique. While there are elements that are essential and common to every business plan, a business plan for a specialty food business must take into account the uniqueness of products and services in such a business and the specialized market you are trying to reach. How you plan to operate should certainly incorporate the best of what the stars in your field are doing, but build your own plan from scratch. Otherwise you are robbed of the opportunity to express the uniqueness of your business.

To begin formulating the business plan, start with the core of your operations, your principal products and services, in order to arrive at the kinds of revenues you may expect from your business. Follow up with extensive research, comparison studies, interviews, attending events, and a lot of calculations based on differing scenarios. Construct a summarized description of how the operation will function and a statement of current performance (if you're already in business and writing the business plan as a tool to gain funding for expansion). If, in your self-assessment, you realized that you need some help, either with the marketing, financials, writing, or coordinating everything from your head to paper, there are several ways to get it. You need a seasoned, dispassionate, rational ally to help sort out fact from fiction, reality from dreams.

Since the decision to open and operate any business comes down to money— you need to know how much you have and how much you need. Will you be drawing from funds on hand, or needing to borrow (or both)? A detailed business plan will help clarify this and many other questions besides. Before any business plan can be formulated, however, you need to assess accurately and realistically what your financial resources are.

Each plan differs enough that there is no one "right" way to formulate its language and claims. In fact, very often, the individualistic style of the business plan itself will interest potential investors. The examples in Exhibits 3-2 and 3-3 will doubtless give you some ideas.

EXHIBIT 3-2

KITCHEN/MARKET BUSINESS PLAN EXCERPT

Executive Summary

In this plan we propose Manhattan's most comprehensive Pan-American food emporium and prepared meals shop. The new *Kitchen/Market* will evolve from the current businesses of *Kitchen* and *Bright Food Shop*, owned by Stuart Tarabour. The current locations will be expanded by incorporating two adjoining stores, increasing the retail space to 2,500 square feet. The total area will be renovated and redesigned to aggressively market the expanded concept.

Established in 1985, *Kitchen* is a takeout/delivery and Pan-American market. Prepared foods are primarily California-Mexican style, quality fast food. The market area of the store sells food products from many Pan-American sources along with some Asian ingredients. The most important prepared food product is a Mission District San Francisco-style burrito. This is a 1 lb. combination of rice and beans, with either meat, vegetable, or dairy, served with salsa and wrapped in an oversized flour tortilla.

The burrito has an overwhelming sellable quality as has been evidenced by the explosion of burrito shops in New York and other cities in the U.S. It is full-flavored, filling, nutritionally balanced, portable and affordable. The burrito has also been the catalyst to widespread interest in Pan-American food products in the U.S. Part of the marketing plan includes the production of frozen *Kitchen/Market* burittos for supermarket distribution.

Bright Food Shop opened in 1990 and offers an extension of the menu at *Kitchen* in a restaurant setting. *Bright Food Shop* is housed in a former luncheonette, dating back to 1905. The menu is a whimsical blend of Southwestern (U.S.) and Pacific Rim flavors.

A coordinated plan to create a corporate image as *the* source for Pan-American products and the finest in prepared foods will begin at the time of funding. Plans include the expansion of private labeling, mail order (some of the greatest growth potential), expanded wholesale division, multi-unit markets, a prepared foods line, and promotional products campaigns.

Every effort will be made to recruit the best possible employees, continue to use our successful management techniques, and nurture and support our staff to educate the public.

In all, the extensive selection of both packaged and prepared Pan-American food products will position *Kitchen/Market* strongly in the New York market. The continued promotion of the company will come easily from the excellent relationships with the press that have been culled over the last ten years.

Reprinted courtesy Stuart Tarabour, Kitchen/Market.

EXHIBIT 3-3

LIBRE TABACALERA BUSINESS PLAN EXCERPT

The following is an excerpt from the business plan for Libre Tabacalera, an upscale specialty cigar store. Although not a specialty food, cigars are similar in that they're a consumable commodity. Therefore, the language and intent of the following can serve as an example when you describe your store concept to potential investors and lenders. The point here is to give your prospective investors a feel for what your operation will be and how it will fit into the local retailing landscape and business climate of your area.

Introduction

A well-known Soho maître d' often complains: "My patrons constantly ask me where they can buy a good cigar in Soho, and I have nowhere to send them. The only thing they can buy here is a cheap drugstore smoke."

To think about trends of affluence and sociability in the 90s is to think about cigars. *The New York Times* wrote last year, "With the eschewing of alcohol and drugs, they [cigars] have become the 'acceptable' vice."

To know Soho in the 90s is to think of a neighborhood that has blossomed in the last two decades from a dark industrial district pioneered first by artists.

In the 70s a few brave restaurateurs first ventured into the neighborhood. Then, a few art galleries moved down from uptown. About ten years ago more buildings were opened to residential tenants and it was like a floodgate: The area has become one of the most upscale retail specialty districts in the United States, and, perhaps, the world. Shoppers from all over scour the streets for the most unusual clothing, jewelry, shoes, housewares, toys, and furniture available. Often, these are the most expensive as well. Controversial but noteworthy is the recent "malling" of Soho's main corridor, Broadway, bringing in such national chains as *Banana Republic, A/X (Armani Exchange), Williams-Sonoma, Eddie Bauer, Nine West*, and *Pottery Barn*. Now a middle class of shoppers has been added to the international and upper class mix. The streets are crowded (*The New York Times* reports visitors to the area total 100,000 on the weekends). People are there for leisure, they have money, and they are spending it.

There's very little missing from the retail mix in Soho, except, strangely, a store that specializes in cigars. This is LIBRE TABACALERA, the first downtown specialty cigar store, and the first such establishment that will cater to the *new* cigar smoker.

A novel retail concept, LIBRE TABACALERA will be a special environment to shop for cigars and smoking accessories. It will also be a place that offers respite for the weary cigar-loving shopper, with its comfortable smoking room. LIBRE TABACALERA will also offer private humidor lockers for rent to downtown connoisseurs who wish to store their prize smokes (and show them off to their friends in public).

Understated yet sophisticated and elegant, the design of the tabacalera will be a stylish combination of classic and fun forms. LIBRE TABACALERA will cater to cigar connoisseurs as well as a discriminating clientele from the worlds of fashion, food, music, art, design, politics, theater, sports, finance, and film.

Designed to also offer local restaurants, other businesses, and residents a delivery service of cigars into the late night hours, LIBRE TABACALERA is where you will find the most extensive and well-priced selection of premium cigars in any store this side of the Caribbean. At the store, the cigars will be paired with the most stylish accessories and cigar- and smoking-related artifacts and antiques. The well-heeled clientele of Soho will be well served by LIBRE TABACALERA.

Reprinted courtesy Diane Ghioto.

THE NITTY-GRITTY

Following is a list of the chapters of a business plan:

1. Introduction
2. Executive Summary
3. Statement of Purpose
4. Concept
5. History of Concept
6. Proposed Location
7. Market Study and Analysis
8. Competition—Description and Analysis
9. Preliminary Marketing Plan
10. Description of the Management Team
11. Design and Decor
12. Menu or Product Line
13. Financials
14. Appendix

We next outline what information should be included in each section of the business plan and how you should proceed in getting that information. Please note that the process of arriving at your business plan will involve some backing and filling. Think of it as putting together a jigsaw puzzle. As with any jigsaw puzzle, it's easiest to start fitting together all the pieces with flat edges first. Begin at the borders and then fill in the middle pieces. So it is with the business plan—start with the pieces of the picture that you know or feel confident about and then start to fill in the rest of the blanks after you have done your research, as you (and your partners or team members) gather more information.

Introduction

The introduction is the first selling tool of the business and its function is to bring the readers in, grab their attention, set the tone, and get investors excited. The structure of your plan's introduction can take many forms. In some plans it is simply a carefully crafted cover sheet, complete with graphics and some catchy, attention-getting text that introduces the idea. For others, it is a page or so of text introducing the concept through a more literary or artistic means than the rest of the plan, a page to put forth the flavor and craft of what you are about to propose in more technical words and numbers.

It is not necessary (nor is it recommended) to get too detailed in the introduction. That is, after all, the purpose of the rest of the plan. The introduction is your first stab at advertising your idea, and in this advertisement you get to communicate your mission, product(s), and market position with a quick brushstroke. As with all the other sections of your plan, creating a catchy introduction page is one of your first marketing lessons.

Executive Summary

Although the first full section of your plan, the executive summary is often the last section written. The executive summary is between one and two pages long and the first paragraph is your mission statement. Following this is a compilation of the two to three most important ideas from each of the subsequent sections of your plan, organized in a way that communicates every important thing about your business briefly but to the point.

Sad to say, after your hard work in putting together a complete business plan, not everyone is going to read it cover to cover. Many people, particularly financial people, will read over the executive summary first and then go right to the financial documents. The purpose of the executive summary is to give each potential reader an overview of what your concept is, what you are raising money for, how much money you need, and how you propose to operate.

The executive summary needs to be clear, concise, and still be a convincing selling tool on its own. You will want to write and rewrite this throughout the business plan writing process. You will probably have to (or want to) show this section to people (bankers, advisors, potential investors, real estate brokers, etc.) along the way and in combination, perhaps, with one or two other sections of the plan (the most common is to submit the executive summary with the financial documents), so it really needs to be a complete overview. As with every section of your business plan, successfully creating an executive summary that is brief but complete is a useful exercise in effective salesmanship. The sample in Exhibit 3-4 will give you a clearer idea of what's involved.

EXHIBIT 3-4

Here is an example of the executive summary from a business plan that sets the stage for a proposed expansion for a frozen soup manufacturer. Although this company seeks to enter the wholesale food arena, a retailer-to-be would include much of the same kinds of information in the executive summary of his/her business plan. *Reprinted courtesy Beth Feehan, Live to Eat.*

Executive Summary

Live to Eat, Inc. (LTE), a manufacturer of frozen organic vegetable stock, desires to expand its distribution and increase its market share according to the plan outlined in this document. This plan specifies not only the capital required for expansion, but a schedule of work to be carried out over the next 12 months, through February 1997.

Owner-entrepreneur Beth Feehan has taken the preliminary and necessary steps to prepare the company for expansion: In 1995 a market survey was conducted and the results were compiled and analyzed. Originally a home-based business, production of the stock was moved to a nearby co-packing facility, and a distributor was contracted to both market and deliver the product to metropolitan area specialty food stores in fall 1995. Finally, a commitment was made to research the natural, and, specifically, the organic food industry to clearly and methodically understand the areas for immediate growth as well as overall market potential for this organic frozen stock.

The history of the company, in both text and financials, documents the increasing market and distribution range as well as the increase in sales over the past 18 months. The reader is here introduced to the fast-growing market of organic foods, and, specifically, *organic convenience foods*. While national studies and statistics verify the increasing trend, it should not go unnoticed that the increasing interest of LTE organic soup stock is also attributed to the diligent efforts of Ms. Feehan and her development team. Ms. Feehan was trained at the French Culinary Institute and has lived and worked as a chef in New York City for more than 12 years. Ms. Feehan has developed this project from a commitment to healthful eating and a vision, verified by market research, that healthful convenience foods are a huge growth area in the natural foods sector.

National statistics show that retail sales of health and natural food rose an overwhelming 14 percent in 1994, a $2 billion increase since 1991. Additionally, the organic market has been growing about 23 percent a year at retail level, according to Katherine DiMatteo, executive director of the Organic Trade Association in Greenfield, MA. Health food stores are responding with similar growth. Fresh Fields, the natural supermarket chain that began just three and a half years ago, now has 16 stores and 22 more planned by the end of 1997. To make it in this new environment health foods have had to live up to the same standards as more traditional, mass-marketed foods: they must look good on the shelf and be easy to use. Now, the natural food consumer "wants to be able to open up a container and pop it in the microwave and have it in four minutes," according to Danny Wells, consultant to the natural foods industry both here and abroad. Buying something ready-made also helps mainstream people cross the "arrgghh barrier" says Melanie Melin of Glencove, NY's Rising Tide.

Local distribution of the LTE product has expanded to all of Manhattan and the product can be found on the shelves of Dean and DeLuca, Grass Roots, and Down to Earth. By the end of 1996 LTE anticipates seeing a 100% increase in sales over 1995. With production facilities secured and distribution system now in place, profits are anticipated at 8% of sales.

Competition in the organic, frozen organic vegetarian soup stock market will not inhibit the projected expansion of the LTE product. In both local and regional stores there is only one product that nearly competes with LTE. *Perfect Addition*, a frozen stock product available in markets and specialty food stores, offers a vegetable stock along with concentrated chicken and fish stocks. Although they are specialty products, they are neither organic nor vegetarian. Some of the newer health/whole foods Supermarkets such as Healthy Pleasures and Life Thyme in New York City are producing their own soup products, some of which may be organic or vegetarian. These are not sold frozen and they have a limited shelf life, offering in-store distribution only.

The LTE product is more appealing to a wider audience of consumers for a variety of reasons: It is sold frozen, and thus has a long (up to eight months) shelf life; the stock is both vegetarian and organic, which meets the increasing needs of health-conscious consumers. It is conveniently packaged in pint-sized containers; the product can be used as a base for soups, pasta and risotto dishes, and in recipes for gratins and casseroles. In any application the product meets the needs of a growing number of people, families in particular, who want to cook but do not have the time to prepare everything from scratch. LTE organic stock offers the consumer a value-added product as the basis for a complete, home-prepared meal.

Simultaneous to expanding distribution of the product, recipe development has begun that will expand the line of LTE products. A mushroom stock, followed by either a fish or seafood stock, is planned. Development of these products and complementary marketing efforts are fully outlined and explained in this document along with a budget (see Appendix A). A fully expanded line will be financed primarily with profits from sales predicted over the next five years, with returns equal to or superseding profits predicted for the original LTE frozen organic vegetable stock.

Statement of Purpose

Different from both the introduction and the executive summary, the statement of purpose is solely about the business' structure and money. This is perhaps the section that is best-served by a cookie-cutter approach or structure; in other words, it is about facts and not about creativity. It should include certain information, stated plainly and simply, with the craft and salesmanship left to the other sections.

In the statement of purpose you first state who you are (your names and name of the proposed business), what sort of company you are or will be (corporate structure, date of incorporation, state of incorporation, et al.), and how much money you are seeking to raise.

The second paragraph explains what the start-up money (capital) will be used for. You can describe this a bit here, particularly by providing a general outline of what percent of the total sum is going to be used for the major expenses (lease down payments or building purchase, construction, equipment, inventory, professional fees, and preopening operating expenses). Be general about this and don't get too detailed. For the detail you will include a capital expense schedule, and this should be referenced in this section as your first appendix document.

In the third paragraph we suggest you provide a brief summary of your financial projections. Most simply, state what your projected sales are for the first three years, and your projected profits for the same period. If your business will generate revenue from multiple divisions, you may want to state what percentage of the revenue and profits are coming from the three major divisions. You will cite your next few appendix documents here, the projected income statements. These statements, usually comprising three projections—one with three scenarios (low, medium and high projections) for your first year; one that details the first year by month, based on the medium year one scenario; and one that projects your operations out for five years—are the meat of your business plan. They will be reviewed with scrupulous detail by nearly everyone who reads your plan. We will go into detail about how to construct these documents later. For now, simply note how they are tied into the text of your business plan.

The fourth paragraph should explain something about how you propose to structure the partnerships—general partners, limited partners, shareholders, with loans, and so on. You should also detail what the investment units are, the desired time frame for raising capital and structuring the partnerships, and a preliminary plan for how the investment will be returned. Usually a plan for how the investment will be returned is provided in the projected income statements. There should be line items at the bottom (i.e., after your operating profit or loss) of these documents that provide some indication of capital payback over time. Your investors will be looking for this, first in words, provided in the statement of purpose, and then in numbers, in the projected income statements.

In the early stages of writing your business plan, you may not know or be prepared to construct these financial structures nor be able commit to a payment schedule. That's okay. You can state something about preliminary structures being explored and that a complete offering will be made by prospectus later on. This gives you some time to work a lot of logistics out and to get professional help to structure the deals. You can create a smaller, separate document later that provides this crucial information.

The statement of purpose is a one-page section, and since it includes numbers, you will need to revise it several times over the course of writing your plan. Don't let this steer you away from starting to write this section in the beginning. It is important to begin to understand the financial needs and structure of your proposed business from the start. It will feed into and out of the concept, market, and pricing structure of your business, and provide some good guidelines for the rest of your business. Exhibit 3-5 shows how one retailer attempted to sell his concept to investors.

EXHIBIT 3-5

DINO'S PASTA MARKET PROSPECTUS

"You've got to spend money to make money," says Richard Heyman, the owner of Dino's Pasta Market in Brentwood, CA. Before opening, when attempting to raise interest in and capital for his venture, Heyman designed and produced a full-color prospectus detailing his retailing philosophy. It included photographs of mock-ups of the store and product offerings to be carried, as well as marketing and promotional strategies. Note how the graphics, typeface, and layout of this piece all contribute to conveying the company's upscale, trend-conscious image. Strong graphic image combined with a well-defined concept helped Heyman to sell his idea to investors.

Reprinted courtesy Richard Heyman, Dino's Pasta Market.

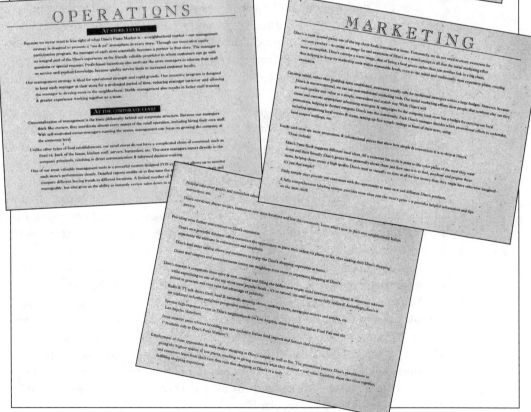

Concept

Finally, in the section on concept, you get to talk about your great business idea! It is here that you first reidentify your business by name, and the products and services offered. Then, still in the first paragraph, give a simple but complete description of your product or service. If it is a store, give the reader a snapshot of the place. If you are promoting a service, such as catering, delivery, or mail order, describe in a sentence or two how the business will work and to whom the concept is targeted.

In the subsequent paragraphs of this section (totaling between two to three pages) go into a complete description about the place, products and services you will be offering your potential customers. Briefly describe how you came up with the idea. If your concept is original or unique to the area, say why you believe that it will work now and in your proposed location. If you are opening a business that will exist in direct competition with other businesses in the area, state what it is about your idea that will be different, and, therefore, successful.

Describe the location and how it will work to support your concept financially. Are you buying or leasing and significantly renovating a space to be a showcase for a particular line of products? How will the location enhance your business idea? Get information from real estate brokers and architects about your location and how to build it out to suit your concept (more details on this will go in the section on location).

Describe your products in detail. Here is where you will either include a product and price list, or refer to such a list in an appendix document. Talk about pricing, packaging, marketing, in-store merchandising and contribution to the community. Each of these aspects must complement your basic concept and support your projected profitability. Beware of clashes between concept and packaging, location, product and pricing, hours of operation, or the nature of the location. In the section on concept you are pulling all of the aspects of your business idea *and proposed operations* into a cohesive argument for the greatness of your business idea.

Basically, in the concept section, you identify your business and then present a case for why it is a good idea, conceptually as well as financially, at this time.

You may want to include, as a subsection to the concept section of the business plan, a brief description of your operations. This can include days and hours of operation, how many staff people will be working, and in what capacity, per day and per week. You can describe your product mix here, and how the staff and customer flow will support your projected sales of this mix, who will be managing and what their style will be, and any related activities you will be involved in on a daily, weekly, or other regular basis.

History of Concept

This is a optional section to your business plan and we mention it for one main purpose: If you are opening a specialty food store in an area where there are many, for example, you will need to present a case for why there should be another one. Or, conversely, if there are no specialty food stores in your area you will need additional backup as to why opening one is a good idea. By researching the history (long- and short-term) of your concept, you will not only learn how the specialty market evolved as a significant force in food retailing, but also, most likely, gain some insight into how your concept can be unique and profitable within the scope of these businesses over time.

By researching your concept you will provide the reader, and the funders of your new business, additional support for its place in the economy. You may also be recreating a prototype or an institution of some sort. This section will help place that in context with the rest of the plan for your business' start-up and profitability.

Proposed Location

You may have heard that location is everything. We agree with that line of thinking, and you will understand why once you set upon your search for a place to open your business as well as researching other similar businesses.

It is often the case that you will not know the exact location of your proposed business while you're writing your business plan. How, then, to go about describing it? If you have not selected a particular location, use this section to discuss what decisions about location you have made and the process by which you will be making these decisions. If you are still evaluating different neighborhoods, discuss each of these in relation to your concept, why each of these would support a healthy business. Discuss the opportunities and risks of each neighborhood or potential location and be honest about what will make it easier or tougher to make a go of things in each possible spot. As we have previously stated, writing the business plan is a process and there will be many changes and additions to your first draft over time. This is okay!

If you have selected the neighborhood, but not the site, where you will be building or starting your new business, begin with a demographic description of the area. Demographic information can be collected from community boards, town halls, local chambers of commerce, local business associations, or the census bureau. Call these sources and ask to get a copy of their area statistics. Extract information about the area's total population, both residential and business. In the text of the plan describe the ethnic and racial breakdown, the breakdown by education and economic bracket. Once these statistics are pulled out, prepare a case for why your concept will succeed in this location. Describe whether you will be catering to a day or evening crowd and why that is supported by the demographic information; explain why your product line is suitable to this area and this market. State what other similar businesses are already in the neighborhood, and who they target. Give a brief history of their operation. Next, describe the potential sites within this area that are under consideration. How are they different and how are they similar? What are the virtues and drawbacks or risks of each proposed site? How do they differ in size, exact location, and price, and how will these factors contribute to your bottom line?

If you already have one, describe your particular site. Say how large it is, how many floors, and what floors, of the building you will be occupying. Talk briefly about how your store will be designed—how many square feet or what major divisions. Mention the lease (or lease in negotiation) terms and how that will affect your overall profitability. Talk about the basic structure and architectural details of the space and how these enhance your idea or will have to be overcome by good design to make your idea work. This is important, as these kinds of details about the location will assist you with your capital budget as well as helping you evaluate the potential site.

Always remember to use the theme of the business plan section to support your business idea overall, that is, explain why this location will enhance the marketability and profitability of your business. Remember that your business plan is meant to prove a case to your potential funders.

Get as much information as possible from possible suppliers of kitchen equipment, but know that you need not feel tied to that particular supplier; the actual costing out of equipping your kitchen only happens after your designer or architect creates a firm blueprint into which kitchen equipment is fit. Then a budget is proposed with the plan going out to bid to several equipment suppliers. Only then are commitments made from you to the supplier and the supplier to you in a contract, with all specifications, delivery dates and costs clearly spelled out and agreed upon by all parties.

To get a feel for product-to-sales space ratios, always look with a critical eye at operations similar in concept to what you hope to open. Gauge their production facilities in relation to the scope of the in-house prepared product lines they carry. Touring other analogous businesses with your eyes wide open, you can gain valuable insights about the industry in general and then apply what you have seen to your business, in particular.

Since the location will drive the capital budget, and, inevitably, the operating projections, make note of this in the text and provide a few budget prototypes in the plan's appendix. If your actual site is not yet decided, provide data to support each of three potential sites.

Market Study and Analysis

The market study and analysis is a thorough examination of how the market will support your concept. This section will partially be comprised of information you have stated in previous sections on concept and location. After a brief reiteration of your concept and proposed location or locations, this section offers the structure to communicate the market viability of your concept.

One Retailer's View:

"It helps to grow up in the business," says Pud Kearns, Vice President and CEO of Mary of Puddin' Hill, a long-established Texas specialty food company and mail-order candy and cake business, on the interstate 50 miles from Dallas. Since 1982, Kearns has been actively involved in the business her parents founded almost fifty years ago but she's the first to admit that in order to grow, you need to make yourself a leader in your niche or category and stick to that plan. She asserts that, as a specialty food retailer, one must never lose sight of who you are in your customers' eyes. Kearns's only failures have resulted from trying to be too advanced and city-style for her client base. She says that "her customers just aren't willing to pay the high prices for the newest things, but the kind of home-style food drawn from community cookbooks keeps the customers coming back again and again."

With a fashion design and merchandising background and a mother and grandmother with excellent food backgrounds, Kearns has been able to parlay her years of being around the business into a multimillion dollar enterprise with the bulk of revenues derived from mail-order sales of in-house made candies and fruitcakes, private-label condiments, and gift baskets. And candy, particularly their chocolates, in her words, "the ultimate comfort food," supports a 45,000-square-foot production area and continues to be a growth area for the business.

Keeping the customers satisfied is an ongoing challenge but Kearns leads her staff by example and expects her managers to do the same. During the holiday crunch, Kearns brings in a local staff trainer who has developed a program tailored to her store. Being a "typical friendly Texan" seems to stand Kearns in good stead with locals and tourists alike.

All in all, a simple, homespun, commonsensical approach, coupled with a strong "guerilla marketing" strategy, has kept this long-established family business vital and responsive.

Questions to answer in this section include: Who is your target market? What other like products and services are they buying now? How often are they buying them? Where are they buying them and how much are they paying for them? This information can be tedious or difficult to get, but here are some hints: Contact both general and product-specific trade associations. Go to university libraries of schools that have food service, restaurant, or hotel departments and read trade journals. Bone up on the trends, and come up with an argument of where your business fits in. Contact marketing firms and trade groups. These organizations have most likely conducted surveys and collected data on businesses related to yours. See what they will give you for free. If you are starting a business that will be unique to the area, or are introducing a product that is innovative, you may want to conduct your own survey. Market research firms can do this for you, usually at a significant cost. Business support centers can also, occasionally, help you structure a survey and give you directions how to conduct one and how to analyze the data.

While conducting a survey may seem like a laborious task (and it is), bear in mind the information you will glean from it and the format in which it will be presented: statistics and quick, numerical facts. Funders and business people love this stuff and will be very impressed that you have gone the length to do it. It demonstrates commitment.

Competition—Description and Analysis

In the section on competition you will present and describe the products and services of pertinent competing businesses in a comprehensive way that makes your business seem poised for success. Before drawing conclusions about your competition, you will need to do some research, and before the research you will have to decide whom to investigate. Look at businesses in the immediate neighborhood of your intended site. If you haven't yet chosen a location, this is an opportunity to really investigate businesses in several areas and understand their differences and strengths. If you know the neighborhood where you want to build your business, carefully research many other businesses in the vicinity, not only those that will be directly competing with you, but even ones that are not related. Look carefully at products and services offered by others, at the prices charged, and at the number of customers that patronize the businesses daily (yes, you will have to stake out and count the number of people going in and out of the place!). This will supply you with vital information about what you will want to sell and how you will want to sell it. Looking at businesses in related industries will tell you more about the total population of people who patronize the businesses. You can even interview these customers about what they would like to see in a new food venture.

A thorough way to compile the information you get is to create a chart that lists businesses like yours, indicating their location, products, services, markets served, and price range for products and services. At the end of the chart you can list your business and fill in the subsequent columns with data for your proposed location, services, prices, and so on. A concluding paragraph should explain why your business will successfully compete with the others you chose to cite. You will undoubtedly leave some conclusions to be drawn by the readers, and that will help them get involved in the business development process.

Preliminary Marketing Plan

The marketing plan you include in your business plan should be an overview of the methods and activities you will pursue to launch your business. The plan should encompass preopening events and other publicity efforts—what you will do to launch the business. It should also provide an outline of what you will do over the first year or so of operations to keep the marketing momentum up. We discuss in a later chapter the various kinds of marketing tools and activities in which you can participate and how effective they can be. For purposes of the business plan it is most important to acknowledge the *need* to do marketing and provide a rough outline of what you plan to do.

Some businesses rely more heavily than others on marketing; some entrepreneurs place a greater emphasis on this aspect of operations. If you're one of those folks, it's probably a good idea to consult a marketing or public relations firm for help in devising a plan for preopening, launch, and the first year of operations. Whether you should use a marketing company is often a factor of the target market of your proposed business. As a general rule, the more you intend to target the upper level of any market, the more you will want to commit (in dollars and effort) to marketing. In all cases it is important to mention, in the business plan text, how much of your capital and first year's operating budget will be committed to marketing. Again, any reference in the body of the plan to your financial documents will help the investors understand the scope of your concept and your operations. For you, the more various elements interrelate to each other, the more complete a business you are putting together, and the more you will understand how to captain the ship you are building.

Description of the Management Team

This section is brief, with an opening paragraph on the basic structure of your management team and then subsequent paragraphs on the principal members of the team and their roles. You can supply appendix documents to support this section of the plan: an organizational chart will demonstrate graphically who is where and what they (and you) will each be doing. Résumés of the key players might also go in the appendix.

In the text of this section you have an opportunity to explain to the investors your commitment to team building, staff training, and where and how you have gleaned this team. It's easier to convince someone to loan you money if you and your team members can show a track record of success and a plan for growth based on your experience in the industry.

You can build your team up by highlighting the most positive and advanced skills and contributions that each member will make and by showing how their experience working for someone else will directly benefit your new business. You can also compare your team to teams in competing businesses and describe why yours will be cutting edge and how they will contribute to your profitability. Remember, everything comes down to the business' profitability.

If you do not yet know who your key management team will be, include in this section who is on your development team. This includes: yourself (describe your role in detail); your partners; your consultant; designer/architect; accountant; lawyer; other professionals such as marketing expert or public relations consultant; your chef; your head salesperson. Next to the numbers, what investors are looking for is the strength of your operating infrastructure.

Design and Decor

Assign a designated chapter to design and decor if you have gotten as far as this in your planning, particularly if you have renderings (include as an appendix document) or other references to what your business will look like. People love pictures and need visual references to fully understand what has already been presented to them in words.

If you have not chosen a site or a designer yet but have clear ideas about the look and layout of your store, fully explain them in this section. Often this will be a reasonable substitute for actual pictures, but more importantly, by putting some of your mental images down on paper you will be able to begin understanding their practicality in operations.

Be as descriptive and fluid in this section as you like; this is the fun part, one of the sexy aspects of building your business.

Menu or Product Line

You will have discussed this briefly in the concept section, but here is where you will dive into detail about the goods and services you will be offering. Talk about your chef or your buyers and how they have come up with the product mix. Discuss pricing and what you anticipate to be an average sale—in dollars and products. Include a menu/product list in the text here or as an appendix document. Again, this is another sexy aspect of your business, and the nuts and bolts of your potential profitability. Present a case as to why your product list and/or menu will be optimum for financial success, due to the talent of your chef and the quality of your merchandise. This section can be handled in one to three pages, depending on the size of your projected inventory.

Financials

Here's your chance to dazzle the investors with the financial viability of your concept in words. One word of advise for this section is: keep it to the point.

You will be again referencing the various financial documents you are including as appendices to the plan here. When creating the documents themselves, be realistic about what you can hope to produce within the confines of the kitchen space you expect to be working within. Estimate probable revenues given staffing, number of shifts for production, refrigerated storage space, projected turnaround of inventory. Combine these revenues with a conservative estimate of sales from other potentially profitable areas of your business (shelf items, gift baskets, wines, books, hardgoods like kitchen equipment, tools, tabletop are all areas you may consider, depending on space and marketability to your projected clientele) and then compute an annual estimate. Account for dramatic seasonal peaks and valleys. Some food-centered enterprises do the bulk of their business in the last quarter of the year. Others report revenues that hover at about the same levels each month. Location and sheer marketing savvy can greatly affect the sales picture.

Use this section of text to do the following but not a lot more: Name the financial documents you are including in the appendix; state what each document shows or proves; describe, minimally, the process by which you created the documents (i.e., who prepared them and what kind of information and criteria were used to generate the numbers); make one to three points about each document that are definitive and support your case for raising money; and state in one or two sentences your conclusions about the financials, conclusions that will demonstrate why funders should invest money in your concept. The financial documents in the appendix themselves should have explanations for sales and expenses (i.e., how many customers per day and the average ticket for sales; how you arrived at projected expenses, such as by utilizing industry standards or other calculations), so you need not repeat those here. Be sure, however, that there is sufficient backup for your numbers and that you are comfortable supporting the figures you drew up both in the text and in future interviews with investors.

Models of the sort of documents investors will expect to see are included as Exhibits 3-6 to 3-8.

EXHIBIT 3-6

CAPITALIZATION BUDGET

The following capital budget was created in 1992 for a home-based caterer who was expanding her business to an existing commercial kitchen with an attached retail space. The budget allows for some kitchen renovation, construction of office and storage space, and complete renovation of the retail space to become a showplace for her prepared foods.

Emphasis was on the aesthetic design and so considerable money was put into purchasing furniture and custom-designed food displays, such as a "market table" (elaborate salad bar) and display refrigeration.

The budget also allows for considerable marketing efforts and systems consultants, as well as general consultants. This specialty food retailer had to pay a lot for consulting assistance since she was running an active and growing catering business during construction and start-up of her store.

Capital Expense Projections

	Purchase	Lease Option, Where Available[1]
Leasehold Improvements		
Floors and walls		
Structure	$5,000	$5,000
Decorative (tile, e.g.)	1,000	1,000
Electrical—wiring	12,000	12,000[2]
Plumbing—gas and water lines	15,000	15,000
HVAC		
Air conditioning	20,000	20,000
Ventilation—hoods and ducts		
Inspection/filing	1,600	1,600
Cleaning	400	400
Security		
Alarm system	650	650
Gates, locks, etc.		
Skylight	2,000	2,000
Storefront and windows	5,000	5,000

	Purchase	*Lease Option, Where Available*[1]
Equipment and Fixtures		
Refrigeration		
Walk-in—new one, installed	6,500	2,200 [3]
Walk-ins—repair/transform	500	500
2 Lowboys (back bar)	2,400	2,400
2 Single door lowboys (dairy/juice bar)	1,700	1,700
2 stand-up reach ins	4,000	4,000
Fish refrigerator	2,000	2,000
Deli cases (12 feet)	10,000	10,000
Display/point of sale (juice/water)	1,200	1,200
Freezers		
Reach-in (2-door)	3,500	3,500
Chest freezer (if no walk-in)	800	800
Display (customer access)	1,050	1,050
Cooking equipment		
6 Burner range	1,100	1,100
Salamander	950	950
Gas grill—2 feet	500	500
Candy stove	450	450
Fryer	595	595
Double convection oven	4,200	4,200
Hot top with oven	1,000	1,000
Vacuum steamer	2,200	770
Small cooking equipment (food processors, etc.)	3,000	3,000
Pots, pans, etc.	2,000	2,000
Miscellaneous	1,000	1,000
Preparation		
Workstation—1, chef's table, casters, cabinets	900	900
Workstation—stainless table 4 feet	300	300
Salad dryer	500	500
1 Slicer	2,500	875
Shelving (kitchen)	1,500	1,500
Pot sink	300	300
2-Three compartment sinks w/drain boards	1,700	1,700
Retail		
Shelving and display	6,000	6,000
Salad bar—pine table, sneeze guard, custom	4,000	4,000
2 Cash registers	2,000	500
Soup terrine	350	350
Heated display—5 feet	1,200	1,200
2 Sinks—one compartment	600	600
1 Sink—three compartment	850	850
Food display (platters, serving utensils, etc.)	1,500	1,500
Misc. small equipment	2,000	2,000
Back of house		
Store room construction	500	500
Shelving	1,500	1,500
Bathroom fixtures	1,000	1,000

	Purchase	Lease Option, Where Available[1]
Design		
Painting	7,500	7,500
Lighting—fixtures	5,000	5,000
Music	1,500	1,500
Awnings and signage	7,500	7,500 [4]
Decorations/artwork	5,000	5,000 [5]
Other (fabric, etc.)	1,000	1,000
Tasting room furniture	3,000	3,000
Coffee/juice bar		
Service counter	8,000	8,000
Espresso machine/grinder	6,000	650
Coffee machine/grinder	n/c	n/c
2 Juicers (extractor)	1,400	1,400
2 Juicers (citrus)	800	800
3 Blenders	750	750
Misc. other small equipment	1,000	1,000
Dishwasher	2,700	945
Glassware (1012 dozen, one size)	300	300
Tabletop	250	250
Tables and chairs (café, sit/down)	3,400	3,400
Office/administrative		
Computers	10,000	2,500
Office furnishings (desks, chairs, etc.)	2,500	2,500
Telephone system	6,500	1,620
Inventory		
Cooking ingredients	6,000	6,000
Packaged foods	10,000	10,000
Paper/packaging products	1,500	1,500
Printed materials	5,000	5,000
Office supplies	1,000	1,000
Uniforms (special order/printed)	500	500
Fees		
Contractor's fees	20,000	20,000
General construction	10,000	10,000
Architect/designer fees	25,000	25,000
Lighting design	2,500	2,500
Graphic designer	5,000	5,000
Legal	5,000	5,000
Accounting	5,000	5,000
Consulting	10,000	10,000
Computer consultant	2,000	2,000
Filing/permits and licenses	3,000	3,000
Preopening Operating Expenses		
Rent security	15,000	15,000
Utility deposit	3,000	3,000

	Purchase	Lease Option, Where Available[1]
Marketing/advertising	15,000	15,000
Preopening salaries		
Chef @ 3 months	10,350	10,350
Manager @ 1 month	3,100	3,100
Administrative—part time @ 5 months	6,000	6,000
Full staff @ 1 week	1,500	1,500
Insurance		
Preopening/construction policy	2,500	2,500
Premium deposit	6,000	6,000
Utilities—preopening		
Electric/gas (3 months @ 750/mo)	2,250	2,250
Telephone (3 months @ 100/month)	300	300
Contingency	39,310	36,475
Working Capital (3–6 months)	100,000	100,000
Total	**$532,405**	**$501,230**
Equipment to be purchased later		
Steam kettle (40 gallon)	4,500	4,500
Hobart mixer (25 quart)	4,700	1,645
1 Slicer	2,500	850

Notes:

[1]Generally, the left column represents the cost for buying equipment outright, the right column represents the down payment or start-up costs for a lease situation.
[2]Electrical wiring does not include new, expanded service to the space, which is to be provided by the landlord as part of lease agreement.
[3]Prices are quoted for a 10×12 foot walk-in refrigerator. The figure on the left is for a new one, the one on the right is for the purchase of used equipment.
[4]This number could be less, depending on landmark restrictions.
[5]This is a soft number; actual amount will depend on final design and budget available.

Appendix

The appendix is a catchall section for any bit of pertinent and convincing information (in the form of charts, press clippings, and other exhibits) that may help to clinch the deal. This can be as extensive or as minimal as you see fit, and any possible appendix document that can be referenced in the main body of the business plan should be here.

EXHIBIT 3-7

SAMPLE BUDGET: FIRST YEAR BY MONTH (7/1/94–6/30/95)

The following budget breaks down the projected business of a catering and carry-out shop for the first year after the business moves to its newly renovated retail space.

Considerations were first given to the overall breakdown of the business's sales between custom catering (growth of her previous business, events such as weddings, receptions and other off-premise affairs); corporate catering, a new segment of the business consisting of breakfast and lunch "drop offs" to business locations throughout Manhattan; and the new retail space.

A second round of considerations was given to the flow of each of these segments over the course of a year. Month one was, conveniently, planned for January, so an entire year's flow was laid out in order. Each of the segments was expected to perform differently according to high seasons for each area: custom in spring and the holiday season; corporate catering during the winter and fall months; and retail during the fall, winter, and spring but light in the summer and winter vacation time.

A third round of considerations was given to how each segment would grow over the course of the year, with seasonal considerations mentioned above in mind: The custom catering business was already a proven entry so its growth over the year was extrapolated from prior years' experience; the other two segments were start-ups and would grow at the rate of first-year businesses.

	7/94	% of sales	8/94	% of sales	9/94	% of sales	10/94	% of sales	11/94	% of sales	12/94	% of sales
SALES												
Store Sales	45,000	.55	45,000	.55	47,300	.51	52,000	.43	55,000	.36	55,000	.29
Corporate Catering	12,000	.15	12,000	.15	14,000	.15	19,000	.16	21,000	.14	35,000	.18
Catering	25,000	.31	25,000	.31	30,000	.33	50,000	.41	75,000	.49	100,000	.52
Wholesale/Other	00	.00	00	.00	1,000	.01	1,000	.01	1,000	.01	1,000	.01
Discounts/Barter	−258	.00	−258	.00	−258	.00	−258	.00	−258	.00	−258	.00
TOTAL SALES	*81,742*		*81,742*		*92,042*		*121,742*		*151,742*		*190,742*	
COST OF SALES												
Variable												
Food	20,926	.26	20,926	.26	23,563	.26	31,166	.26	38,846	.26	48,830	.26
Kitchen Supplies	400	.00	400	.00	400	.00	400	.00	400	.00	400	.00
Store Supplies	400	.00	400	.00	400	.00	400	.00	400	.00	400	.00

	7/94	% of sales	8/94	% of sales	9/94	% of sales	10/94	% of sales	11/94	% of sales	12/94	% of sales
Laundry/Linen	850	.01	850	.01	850	.01	850	.01	850	.01	850	.00
Paper/Packaging—Retail	900	.01	900	.01	946	.01	1,040	.01	1,100	.01	1,100	.01
Paper/Packaging—Corporate	360	.00	360	.00	420	.00	570	.00	630	.00	1,050	.01
Paper/Cleaning Supplies—Kitchen	409	.01	409	.01	460	.01	609	.01	759	.01	954	.01
Repair and Maintenance	225	.00	225	.00	225	.00	225	.00	225	.00	225	.00
Flowers/Decoration	250	.00	250	.00	300	.00	500	.00	750	.00	1,000	.01
Bar Set-ups	500	.01	500	.01	600	.01	1,000	.01	1,500	.01	2,000	.01
Party Rentals	2,000	.02	2,000	.02	2,400	.03	4,000	.03	6,000	.04	8,000	.04
Catering Staff—FOH	4,750	.06	4,750	.06	5,700	.06	9,500	.08	14,250	.09	19,000	.10
Catering Staff—Kitchen	500	.01	500	.01	600	.01	1,000	.01	1,500	.01	2,000	.01
Payroll Taxes	893	.01	893	.01	1,071	.01	1,785	.01	2,678	.02	3,570	.02
Subtotal Variable	**33,362**	**.41**	**33,362**	**.41**	**37,935**	**.41**	**53,045**	**.44**	**69,887**	**.46**	**89,379**	**.47**
Fixed												
Salaries												
Operations Manager (1/2)	1,300	.02	1,300	.02	1,300	.01	1,300	.01	1,300	.01	1,300	.01
Chef—store	1,084	.01	00	.00	00	.00	00	.00	2,167	.01	2,167	.01
Chef—catering	2,917	.04	2,917	.04	2,917	.03	2,917	.02	2,917	.02	2,917	.02
Chef—corporate	1,750	.02	1,750	.02	1,750	.02	1,750	.01	1,750	.01	1,750	.01
Prep staff	5,200	.06	5,200	.06	5,200	.06	5,200	.04	5,200	.03	5,200	.03
Dish/porters	3,500	.04	3,500	.04	3,500	.04	3,500	.03	3,500	.02	3,500	.02
Delivery staff	1,032	.01	1,032	.01	1,032	.01	1,032	.01	1,032	.01	1,032	.01
Taxes/benefits	2,632	.03	2,448	.03	2,448	.03	2,448	.02	2,816	.02	2,816	.01
Subtotal Salaries	**19,415**	**.24**	**18,146**	**.22**	**18,146**	**.20**	**18,146**	**.15**	**20,681**	**.14**	**20,681**	**.11**
Other Fixed Expenses												
Garbage Removal	478	.01	478	.01	478	.01	478	.00	478	.00	478	.00
Pest Control	140	.00	140	.00	140	.00	140	.00	140	.00	140	.00
Equipment Lease	617	.01	617	.01	617	.01	617	.01	617	.00	617	.00
Subtotal Other Fixed	**1,235**	**.02**	**1,235**	**.02**	**1,235**	**.01**	**1,235**	**.01**	**1,235**	**.01**	**1,235**	**.01**
Subtotal Fixed	**20,650**	**.25**	**19,381**	**.24**	**19,381**	**.21**	**19,381**	**.16**	**21,916**	**.14**	**21,916**	**.11**
TOTAL COST OF SALES	*54,012*	*.66*	*52,744*	*.65*	*57,316*	*.62*	*72,426*	*.59*	*91,804*	*.60*	*111,295*	*.58*
GROSS PROFIT	*27,730*	*.34*	*28,998*	*.35*	*34,726*	*.38*	*49,316*	*.41*	*59,938*	*.40*	*79,447*	*.42*

	7/94	% of sales	8/94	% of sales	9/94	% of sales	10/94	% of sales	11/94	% of sales	12/94	% of sales
SELLING EXPENSES												
Salaries												
Retail Manager	3,250	.04	3,250	.04	3,250	.04	3,250	.03	3,250	.02	3,250	.02
Operations Manager (1/2)	1,300	.02	1,300	.02	1,300	.01	1,300	.01	1,300	.01	1,300	.01
Store Clerks	3,660	.04	3,660	.04	3,660	.04	3,660	.03	3,660	.02	3,660	.02
Catering Sales	4,333	.05	4,333	.05	4,333	.05	4,333	.04	4,333	.03	4,333	.02
Commissions	892	.01	892	.01	1,064	.01	1,704	.01	2,436	.02	3,360	.02
Taxes	2,284	.03	2,284	.03	2,313	.03	2,422	.02	2,546	.02	2,704	.01
Subtotal Salaries	**15,719**	**.19**	**15,719**	**.19**	**15,921**	**.17**	**16,669**	**.14**	**17,526**	**.12**	**18,607**	**.10**
Other Selling Expenses												
Public Relations	750	.01	750	.01	750	.01	750	.01	750	.00	750	.00
Advertising	667	.01	667	.01	667	.01	667	.01	667	.00	667	.00
Mailings		.00		.00		.00		.00		.00		.00
Travel	50	.00	50	.00	50	.00	50	.00	50	.00	50	.00
Entertainment	50	.00	50	.00	50	.00	50	.00	50	.00	50	.00
Local Transportation	225	.00	225	.00	225	.00	225	.00	225	.00	225	.00
Subtotal Other Expenses	**1,742**	**.02**	**1,742**	**.02**	**1,742**	**.02**	**1,742**	**.01**	**1,742**	**.01**	**1,742**	**.01**
Subtotal Selling Expenses	**17,461**	**.21**	**17,461**	**.21**	**17,662**	**.19**	**18,411**	**.15**	**19,267**	**.13**	**20,349**	**.11**
G&A												
Occupancy												
Rent	5,100	.06	5,100	.06	5,100	.06	5,100	.04	5,100	.03	5,100	.03
Real Estate Taxes		.00		.00		.00		.00		.00		.00
Rent Tax	332	.00	332	.00	332	.00	332	.00	332	.00	332	.00
Utilities	1,985	.02	1,985	.02	1,985	.02	1,985	.02	1,985	.01	1,985	.01
Subtotal Occupancy	**7,417**	**.09**	**7,417**	**.09**	**7,417**	**.08**	**7,417**	**.06**	**7,417**	**.05**	**7,417**	**.04**
General Operating Expenses												
Insurance (property/liability)	958	.01	958	.01	958	.01	958	.01	958	.01	958	.01
Workman's Compensation	1,500	.02	1,500	.02	1,500	.02	1,500	.01	1,500	.01	1,500	.01
Insurance (health)	355	.00	355	.00	355	.00	355	.00	355	.00	355	.00
Officer's Salaries	2,083	.03	2,083	.03	2,083	.02	2,083	.02	2,083	.01	2,083	.01
Administrative Salaries	5,650	.07	5,650	.07	4,683	.05	4,683	.04	4,683	.03	4,683	.02
Payroll Taxes	1,315	.02	1,315	.02	1,150	.01	1,150	.01	1,150	.01	1,150	.01
Credit Card Expense	121	.00	121	.00	136	.00	180	.00	224	.00	281	.00
Bank Fees	100	.00	100	.00	100	.00	100	.00	100	.00	100	.00
Repairs and Maintenance	150	.00	150	.00	150	.00	150	.00	150	.00	150	.00
Telephone	1,050	.01	1,050	.01	1,050	.01	1,050	.01	1,050	.01	1,050	.01

	7/94	% of sales	8/94	% of sales	9/94	% of sales	10/94	% of sales	11/94	% of sales	12/94	% of sales
Postage	150	.00	150	.00	150	.00	150	.00	150	.00	150	.00
Office Supplies	200	.00	200	.00	200	.00	200	.00	200	.00	200	.00
Payroll Service	160	.00	160	.00	160	.00	160	.00	160	.00	160	.00
Accounting	500	.01	500	.01	500	.01	500	.00	500	.00	500	.00
Computer	2,000	.02	2,000	.02	2,000	.02	2,000	.00	2,000	.00	2,000	.00
Legal	125	.00	125	.00	125	.00	125	.00	125	.00	125	.00
Consulting/R&D	400	.00	400	.00	400	.00	400	.00	400	.00	400	.00
Printing (Incl. Menus)	225	.00	225	.00	225	.00	225	.00	225	.00	225	.00
Cleaning Supplies	350	.00	350	.00	350	.00	350	.00	350	.00	350	.00
Contributions	50	.00	50	.00	50	.00	50	.00	50	.00	50	.00
Interest Expense	15	.00	15	.00	15	.00	15	.00	15	.00	15	.00
Cash Shortages	25	.00	25	.00	25	.00	25	.00	25	.00	25	.00
Licenses and permits	75	.00	75	.00	75	.00	75	.00	75	.00	75	.00
Dues/subscriptions	30	.00	30	.00	30	.00	30	.00	30	.00	30	.00
Subtotal General Operating	17,587	.22	17,587	.22	16,471	.18	14,865	.12	14,909	.10	14,966	.08
GROSS PROFIT	27,730		28,998		34,726		49,316		59,938		79,447	
TOTAL OPERATING EXPENSES	42,464	.52	42,464	.52	41,550	.45	40,692	.33	41,593	.27	42,731	.22
Interest Expense	3,667	.04	3,667	.04	3,667	.04	3,667	.03	3,667	.02	3,667	.02
NET INCOME	-18,401	-.23	-17,133	-.21	-10,491	-.11	4,957	.04	14,679	.10	33,048	.17

	1/95	% of sales	2/95	3/95	% of sales	4/95	% of sales	5/95	% of sales	6/95	% of sales	Total 7/94–6/95	% of sales
SALES													
Store Sales	50,000	.55	50,000	55,000	.56	60,000	.44	60,000	.41	60,000	.37	634,300	.44
Corporate Catering	20,000	.22	20,000	22,000	.23	25,000	.18	26,000	.18	26,000	.16	252,000	.17
Catering	20,000	.22	20,000	20,000	.20	50,000	.37	60,000	.41	75,000	.46	550,000	.38
Wholesale/Other	1,000	.01	1,000	1,000	.01	1,000	.01	1,000	.01	1,000	.01	10,000	.01
Discounts/Barter	-258	.00	-258	-258	.00	-258	.00	-258	.00	-258	.00	-3,096	.00
TOTAL SALES	90,742		90,742	97,742		135,742		146,742		161,742		1,443,204	
COST OF SALES													
Variable													
Food	23,230	.26	23,230	25,022	.26	34,750	.26	37,566	.26	41,406	.26	369,460	.26
Kitchen Supplies	400	.00	400	400	.00	400	.00	400	.00	400	.00	4,800	.00
Store Supplies	400	.00	400	400	.00	400	.00	400	.00	400	.00	4,800	.00
Laundry/Linen	850	.01	850	850	.01	850	.01	850	.01	850	.01	10,200	.01

	1/95	% of sales	2/95	% of sales	3/95	% of sales	4/95	% of sales	5/95	% of sales	6/95	% of sales	Total 7/94–6/95	% of sales
Paper/Packaging—Retail	1,000	.01	1,000	.01	1,100	.01	1,200	.01	1,200	.01	1,200	.01	12,686	.01
Paper/Packaging—Corporate	600	.01	600	.01	660	.01	750	.01	780	.01	80	.00	7,560	.01
Paper/Cleaning Supplies—														
Kitchen	454	.01	454	.01	489	.01	679	.01	734	.01	809	.01	7,216	.01
Repair and Maintenance	225	.00	225	.00	225	.00	225	.00	225	.00	225	.00	2,700	.00
Flowers/Decoration	200	.00	200	.00	200	.00	500	.00	600	.00	750	.00	5,500	.00
Bar Set-ups	400	.00	400	.00	400	.00	1,000	.01	1,200	.01	1,500	.01	11,000	.01
Party Rentals	1,600	.02	1,600	.02	1,600	.02	4,000	.03	4,800	.03	6,000	.04	44,000	.03
Catering Staff—FOH	3,800	.04	3,800	.04	3,800	.04	9,500	.07	11,400	.08	14,250	.09	104,500	.07
Catering Staff—Kitchen	400	.00	400	.00	400	.00	1,000	.01	1,200	.01	1,500	.01	11,000	.01
Payroll Taxes	714	.01	714	.01	714	.01	1,785	.01	2,142	.01	2,678	.02	19,635	.01
Subtotal Variable	**34,273**	**.38**	**34,273**	**.38**	**36,260**	**.37**	**57,039**	**.42**	**63,497**	**.43**	**72,747**	**.45**	**615,057**	**.43**
Fixed														
Salaries														
Operations Manager (1/2)	1,300	.01	1,300	.01	1,300	.01	1,300	.01	1,300	.01	1,300	.01	15,600	.01
Chef—store	2,292	.03	2,292	.03	2,292	.02	2,292	.02	2,292	.02	2,292	.01	19,167	.01
Chef—catering	2,917	.03	2,917	.03	2,917	.03	2,917	.02	2,917	.02	2,917	.02	35,000	.02
Chef—corporate	1,750	.02	1,750	.02	1,750	.02	1,750	.01	1,750	.01	1,750	.01	21,000	.01
Prep staff	5,200	.06	5,200	.06	5,200	.05	5,200	.04	5,200	.04	5,200	.03	62,400	.04
Dish/porters	3,500	.04	3,500	.04	3,500	.04	3,500	.03	3,500	.02	3,500	.02	42,000	.03
Delivery staff	1,032	.01	1,032	.01	1,032	.01	1,032	.01	1,032	.01	1,032	.01	12,384	.01
Taxes/benefits	2,837	.03	2,837	.03	2,837	.03	2,837	.02	2,837	.02	2,837	.02	32,632	.02
Subtotal Salaries	**20,828**	**.23**	**20,828**	**.23**	**20,828**	**.21**	**20,828**	**.15**	**20,828**	**.14**	**20,828**	**.13**	**240,183**	**.17**
Other Fixed Expenses														
Garbage Removal	478	.01	478	.01	478	.00	478	.00	478	.00	478	.00	5,736	.00
Pest Control	140	.00	140	.00	140	.00	140	.00	140	.00	140	.00	1,680	.00
Equipment Lease	200	.00	200	.00	200	.00	200	.00	200	.00	200	.00	4,902	.00
Subtotal Other Fixed	**818**	**.01**	**818**	**.01**	**818**	**.01**	**818**	**.01**	**818**	**.01**	**818**	**.01**	**12,318**	**.01**
Subtotal Fixed	**21,646**	**.24**	**21,646**	**.24**	**21,646**	**.22**	**21,646**	**.16**	**21,646**	**.15**	**21,646**	**.13**	**252,501**	**.17**
TOTAL COST OF SALES	*55,918*	*.62*	*55,918*	*.62*	*57,905*	*.59*	*78,684*	*.58*	*85,142*	*.58*	*94,393*	*.58*	*867,558*	*.60*
GROSS PROFIT	*34,824*	*.38*	*34,824*	*.38*	*39,837*	*.41*	*57,058*	*.42*	*61,600*	*.42*	*67,349*	*.42*	*575,646*	*.40*

	1/95	% of sales	2/95	% of sales	3/95	% of sales	4/95	% of sales	5/95	% of sales	6/95	% of sales	Total 7/94–6/95	% of sales
SELLING EXPENSES														
Salaries														
Retail Manager	3,250	.04	3,250	.04	3,250	.03	3,250	.02	3,250	.02	3,250	.02	39,000	.03
Operations Manager (1/2)	1,300	.01	1,300	.01	1,300	.01	1,300	.01	1,300	.01	1,300	.01	15,600	.01
Store Clerks	3,660	.04	3,660	.04	3,660	.04	3,660	.03	3,660	.02	3,660	.02	43,920	.03
Catering Sales	4,333	.05	4,333	.05	4,333	.04	4,333	.03	4,333	.03	4,333	.03	52,000	.04
Commissions	880	.01	880	.01	912	.01	1,800	.01	2,096	.01	2,516	.02	19,432	.01
Taxes	2,282	.03	2,282	.03	2,287	.02	2,438	.02	2,489	.02	2,560	.02	28,892	.02
Subtotal Salaries	**15,705**	**.17**	**15,705**	**.17**	**15,743**	**.16**	**16,782**	**.12**	**17,128**	**.12**	**17,619**	**.11**	**198,844**	**.14**
Other Selling Expenses														
Public Relations	750	.01	750	.01	750	.01	750	.01	750	.01	750	.00	9,000	.01
Advertising	667	.01	667	.01	667	.01	667	.00	667	.00	667	.00	8,000	.01
Mailings		.00		.00		.00		.00		.00		.00	00	.00
Travel	50	.00	50	.00	50	.00	50	.00	50	.00	50	.00	600	.00
Entertainment	50	.00	50	.00	50	.00	50	.00	50	.00	50	.00	600	.00
Local Transportation	225	.00	225	.00	225	.00	225	.00	225	.00	225	.00	2,700	.00
Subtotal Other Expenses	**1,742**	**.02**	**1,742**	**.02**	**1,742**	**.02**	**1,742**	**.01**	**1,742**	**.01**	**1,742**	**.01**	**20,900**	**.01**
Subtotal Selling Expenses	**17,447**	**.19**	**17,447**	**.19**	**17,484**	**.18**	**18,523**	**.14**	**18,870**	**.13**	**19,361**	**.12**	**219,744**	**.15**
G&A														
Occupancy														
Rent	5,100	.06	5,100	.06	5,100	.06	5,100	.04	5,100	.03	5,100	.03	61,200	.04
Real Estate Taxes		.00		.00		.00		.00		.00		.00	00	.00
Rent Tax	332	.00	332	.00	332	.00	332	.00	332	.00	332	.00	3,978	.00
Utilities	1,985	.02	1,985	.02	1,985	.02	1,985	.01	1,985	.01	1,985	.01	23,820	.02
Subtotal Occupancy	**7,417**	**.08**	**7,417**	**.08**	**7,417**	**.08**	**7,417**	**.05**	**7,417**	**.05**	**7,417**	**.05**	**88,998**	**.06**
General Operating Expenses														
Insurance (property/liability)	958	.01	958	.01	958	.01	958	.01	958	.01	958	.01	11,500	.01
Workman's Compensation	1,500	.02	1,500	.02	1,500	.02	1,500	.01	1,500	.01	1,500	.01	18,000	.01
Insurance (health)	355	.00	355	.00	355	.00	355	.00	355	.00	355	.00	4,256	.00
Officer's Salaries	2,083	.02	2,083	.02	2,083	.02	2,083	.02	2,083	.01	2,083	.01	25,000	.02
Administrative Salaries	4,683	.05	4,683	.05	4,683	.05	4,683	.03	4,683	.03	4,683	.03	58,133	.04
Payroll Taxes	1,150	.01	1,150	.01	1,150	.01	1,150	.01	1,150	.01	1,150	.01	14,133	.01
Credit Card Expense	134	.00	134	.00	144	.00	200	.00	216	.00	239	.00	2,129	.00
Bank Fees	100	.00	100	.00	100	.00	100	.00	100	.00	100	.00	1,200	.00
Repairs and Maintenance	150	.00	150	.00	150	.00	150	.00	150	.00	150	.00	1,800	.00

	1/95	% of sales	2/95	% of sales	3/95	% of sales	4/95	% of sales	5/95	% of sales	6/95	% of sales	Total 7/94– 6/95	% of sales
Telephone	1,050	.01	1,050	.01	1,050	.01	1,050	.01	1,050	.01	1,050	.01	12,600	.01
Postage	150	.00	150	.00	150	.00	150	.00	150	.00	150	.00	1,800	.00
Office Supplies	200	.00	200	.00	200	.00	200	.00	200	.00	200	.00	2,400	.00
Payroll Service	160	.00	160	.00	160	.00	160	.00	160	.00	160	.00	1,920	.00
Accounting	500	.01	500	.01	500	.01	500	.00	500	.00	500	.00	6,000	.00
Computer	350	.00	350	.00	350	.00	350	.00	350	.00	350	.00	9,150	.01
Legal	125	.00	125	.00	125	.00	125	.00	125	.00	125	.00	1,500	.00
Consulting/R&D	400	.00	400	.00	400	.00	400	.00	400	.00	400	.00	4,800	.00
Printing (Incl. Menus)	225	.00	225	.00	225	.00	225	.00	225	.00	225	.00	2,700	.00
Cleaning Supplies	350	.00	350	.00	350	.00	350	.00	350	.00	350	.00	4,200	.00
Contributions	50	.00	50	.00	50	.00	50	.00	50	.00	50	.00	600	.00
Interest Expense	15	.00	15	.00	15	.00	15	.00	15	.00	15	.00	180	.00
Cash Shortages	25	.00	25	.00	25	.00	25	.00	25	.00	25	.00	300	.00
Licenses and permits	75	.00	75	.00	75	.00	75	.00	75	.00	75	.00	900	.00
Dues/subscriptions	30	.00	30	.00	30	.00	30	.00	30	.00	30	.00	360	.00
Subtotal General Operating	14,819	.16	14,819	.16	14,829	.15	14,885	.11	14,901	.10	14,924	.09	185,561	.13
GROSS PROFIT	34,824		34,824		39,837		57,058		61,600		67,349		575,646	
TOTAL OPERATING EXPENSES	39,682	.44	39,682	.44	39,730	.41	40,825	.30	41,188	.28	41,701	.26	494,303	.34
Interest Expense	3,667	.04	3,667	.04	3,667	.04	3,667	.03	3,667	.02	3,667	.02	44,004	.03
NET INCOME	-8,526	-.09	-8,526	-.09	-3,560	-.04	12,566	.09	16,745	.11	21,981	.14	37,339	.03

Exhibit 3-8

Sample Five-Year Sales and Expense Projections

Every business plan should include a range of financial projections for purposes of engaging the investors as well as for operational planning. Typically we include a document that illustrates three potential scenarios for the first year; the first year broken down by month, for cash flow and incremental growth projections; and a five-year proforma, which takes one of the year one scenarios and projects a reasonable growth for five years out.

Since specialty food businesses are prototypically slow to break even and profit, it is especially valuable to do a careful five-year sales and expense projection. Quite often a profit doesn't generate until year two, and it can take five years for the initial investment to be paid off. Your investors will want to see how long it will take to get their initial investment back and then profit some from it. This document will illustrate the business's potential.

	Year 1	% of sales	Year 2	% of sales	Year 3	% of sales	Year 4	% of sales	Year 5	% of sales
SALES										
Retail foods	$680,000	.47	$748,000	.47	$785,400	.47	$824,670	.46	$865,904	.45
Packaged foods	136,000	.09	149,600	.09	157,080	.09	164,934	.09	173,181	.09
Office Catering	187,500	.13	206,250	.13	216,563	.13	227,391	.13	238,760	.12
Catering	424,000	.29	466,400	.29	513,040	.30	564,344	.31	620,778	.32
Hard goods (books, gift baskets, etc)	13,750	.01	15,125	.01	15,881	.01	16,675	.01	17,509	.01
TOTAL SALES	*$1,441,250*		*$1,585,375*		*$1,687,964*		*$1,798,014*		*$1,916,132*	
COST OF SALES										
Ingredients										
Retail foods	$170,000	.25	$149,600	.20	$157,080	.20	$164,934	.20	$173,181	.20
Packaged foods	61,200	.45	67,320	.45	70,686	.45	74,220	.45	77,931	.45
Office Catering	46,875	.25	51,563	.25	54,141	.25	56,848	.25	59,690	.25
Catering	46,640	.11	51,304	.11	56,434	.11	62,078	.11	68,286	.11
Hard goods (books, gift baskets, etc)	6,188	.45	6,806	.45	7,147	.45	7,504	.45	7,879	.45
Total Ingredients	**$330,903**	**.23**	**$326,593**	**.21**	**$345,488**	**.20**	**$365,584**	**.20**	**$386,967**	**.20**

	Year 1	% of sales	Year 2	% of sales	Year 3	% of sales	Year 4	% of sales	Year 5	% of sales
Payroll										
Kitchen (chef, prep, dish, porters)	$162,125	.11	$182,125	.11	$200,338	.12	$220,371	.12	$242,408	.13
Executive Chef	38,000	.03	50,000	.03	52,000	.03	55,000	.03	58,000	.03
Retail (Store mgr, clerks)	112,375	.08	114,945	.07	120,721	.07	129,958	.07	140,155	.07
Office catering (Delivery)	17,500	.01	18,375	.01	19,294	.01	20,258	.01	21,271	.01
Catering (Sales person, waitstaff)	104,811	.07	112,392	.07	120,732	.07	129,905	.07	139,995	.07
Payroll Taxes and Benefits (incl health)	72,872	.05	79,326	.05	84,613	.05	90,974	.05	97,924	.05
Total Payroll	**$507,683**	**.35**	**$557,163**	**.35**	**$597,696**	**.35**	**$646,467**	**.36**	**$699,754**	**.37**
Occupancy										
Rent $71,744	$60,430	.04	$62,847	.04	$65,361	.04	$67,976	.04	$70,695	.04
Commercial Real Estate Taxes	$700	.00	$700	.00	$1,000	.00	$1,000	.00	$1,000	.00
Commercial Rent Tax $4,305	3,626	.00	3,771	.00	3,922	.00	4,079	.00	4,242	.00
Utilities	28,825	.02	31,708	.02	33,759	.02	35,960	.02	38,323	.02
Total Occupancy	**$93,581**	**.06**	**$99,026**	**.06**	**$104,042**	**.06**	**$109,014**	**.06**	**$114,259**	**.06**
TOTAL COST OF SALES	**$932,166**	**.65**	**$982,781**	**.62**	**$1,047,226**	**.62**	**$1,121,065**	**.62**	**$1,200,980**	**.63**
GROSS PROFIT	*$509,084*	*.35*	*$602,594*	*.38*	*$640,738*	*.38*	*$676,949*	*.38*	*$715,152*	*.37*
OPERATING EXPENSES										
Insurance (property/liability)	$20,000	.01	$20,400	.01	$20,808	.01	$21,224	.01	$21,649	.01
Kitchen Supplies	15,000	.01	8,750	.01	7,500	.00	6,250	.00	6,250	.00
Credit Card Expense	7,567	.01	8,323	.01	8,862	.01	9,440	.01	10,060	.01
Bank Fees	1,200	.00	1,200	.00	1,200	.00	1,200	.00	1,200	.00
Repairs and Maintenance	14,413	.01	14,701	.01	14,995	.01	15,295	.01	15,601	.01
Administrative Salaries	108,000	.07	113,400	.07	119,070	.07	125,024	.07	131,275	.07
Payroll Taxes	16,200	.01	17,010	.01	17,861	.01	18,754	.01	19,691	.01
Telephone/Postage	9,240	.01	9,702	.01	10,187	.01	10,696	.01	11,231	.01
Laundry/Linen	11,000	.01	11,770	.01	12,594	.01	13,475	.01	14,419	.01
Garbage Removal	18,000	.01	18,000	.01	18,900	.01	19,845	.01	20,837	.01

	Year 1	% of sales	Year 2	% of sales	Year 3	% of sales	Year 4	% of sales	Year 5	% of sales
Pest Control	2,500	.00	2,500	.00	2,500	.00	2,500	.00	2,500	.00
Office Supplies	15,000	.01	8,750	.01	7,500	.00	7,500	.00	7,500	.00
Payroll Service	2,500	.00	2,550	.00	2,601	.00	2,653	.00	2,706	.00
Accounting/Legal	7,000	.00	7,000	.00	7,000	.00	7,000	.00	7,000	.00
Flowers/Decoration	14,413	.01	15,854	.01	16,880	.01	17,980	.01	19,161	.01
Equipment lease (kitchen/display)	12,000	.01	12,000	.01	12,000	.01	12,000	.01	12,000	.01
Equipment Rental (catering)	42,400	.03	46,640	.03	51,304	.03	56,434	.03	62,078	.03
Bar set-ups	14,840	.01	16,324	.01	17,956	.01	19,752	.01	21,727	.01
Printing (menus, flyers, etc)	6,000	.00	6,000	.00	6,300	.00	6,615	.00	6,946	.00
Cleaning Supplies	10,000	.01	10,300	.01	10,609	.01	10,927	.01	11,255	.01
Paper/Packaging Supplies	41,078	.03	45,185	.03	47,445	.03	49,817	.03	52,308	.03
Travel and Entertainment	7,500	.01	7,500	.00	7,500	.00	7,500	.00	7,500	.00
Security	1,800	.00	1,800	.00	1,800	.00	1,800	.00	1,800	.00
Licenses and permits (n/i liq)	700	.00	700	.00	700	.00	700	.00	700	.00
Dues/subscriptions	500	.00	500	.00	500	.00	500	.00	500	.00
Local Transportation	15,854	.01	31,821	.02	32,457	.02	33,107	.02	33,769	.02
Consulting/Management/ R&D	5,000	.00	5,000	.00	5,000	.00	5,000	.00	5,000	.00
Marketing	43,238	.03	42,805	.03	42,199	.03	41,354	.02	38,323	.02
Miscellaneous	7,206	.01	7,927	.01	8,440	.01	8,990	.01	9,581	.01
TOTAL OPERATING EXPENSES	$450,147	.31	$474,012	.30	$491,859	.29	$512,108	.28	$532,916	.28
NET INCOME	$58,937	.04	$128,582	.08	$148,879	.09	$164,842	.09	$182,236	.10
Interest Income										
Additional cash receipts (loan in, e.g)										
Interest Payment .00	44,000	.03	44,000			.03	.00		.00	
Note 1										
Note 2					25,000		25,000		25,000	
INCOME BEFORE TAXES	$14,937	.01	$84,582	.05	$123,879	.07	$139,842	.08	$157,236	.08

	Year 1 % of sales	Year 2 % of sales	Year 3 % of sales	Year 4 % of sales	Year 5 % of sales
SALES: Retail sales are based on 6 days per week/50 weeks per year. Office catering is based on 5 days per week/50 weeks per year. Other catering is based on expansion of current business.					
Retail foods	Breakfast: 150 people per day × 3.50 × 5 days	All sales increase 10% over Year 1	All sales increase 5% over Year 2	All sales increase 5% over Year 3	All sales increase 5% over Year 4
	Lunch: 150 people per day × 8.50 × 5 days	All sales increase 10% over Year 1	All sales increase 5% over Year 2	All sales increase 5% over Year 3	All sales increase 5% over Year 4
	Saturday: 200 transactions × 8.00 per transaction	All sales are 10% over year 1	All sales increase 5% over Year 2	All sales increase %5 over Year 3	All sales increase 5% over Year 4
	Supper: 50 people per day × 12.00 × 5 days	All sales increase 10% over Year 1	All sales increase 5% over Year 2	All sales increase 5% over Year 3	All sales increase 5% over Year 4
Packaged foods	20% of retail foods, added to in house sales	All sales increase 10% over Year 1	All sales increase 5% over Year 2	All sales increase 5% over Year 3	All sales increase 5% over Year 4
Office Catering	$750.00 per day	All sales increase 10% over Year 1	All sales increase 5% over Year 2	All sales increase 5% over Year 3	All sales increase 5% over Year 4
Catering	400,000 as per current trend	Sales increase 12% from Year 1	Sales increase 10% from Year 2	Sales increase 10% from Year 3	Sales increase 10% from Year 4
Hard goods (books, gift baskets, etc)	$55.00 per day	All sales increase 10% over Year 1	All sales increase 5% over Year 2	All sales increase 5% over Year 3	All sales increase 5% over Year 4

Note: Juice and coffee bar exists as a component of retail sales in this proforma. This entity could generate an additional 5–10% of sales per year and this would affect (reduce) food and labor costs by 1–2% overall.

	Year 1 % of sales	Year 2 % of sales	Year 3 % of sales	Year 4 % of sales	Year 5 % of sales
COST OF SALES					
Ingredients					
Retail foods	20% cost of goods for 80% of retail sales; 45% cost of goods for 20% of retail sales (baked goods)	20% cost of goods. (Baking done on premises.)	20% cost of goods. (Baking done on premises.)	20% cost of goods. (Baking done on premises.)	20% cost of goods. (Baking done on premises.)
Packaged foods	45% cost of goods—industry standard	45% cost of goods—industry standard	45% cost of goods—industry standard	45% cost of goods—industry standard	45% cost of goods—industry standard
Office Catering	25% of sales—taken from Catering cost of sales	25% of sales—taken from Catering cost of sales	25% of sales—taken from Catering cost of sales	25% of sales—taken from Catering cost of sales	25% of sales—taken from Catering cost of sales
Catering	11% as per current cost of sales	11% as per current cost of sales	11% as per current cost of sales	11% as per current cost of sales	11% as per current cost of sales
Payroll					
Kitchen (chef, prep, dish, porters) overall	$31,000, 2 prep cooks @ 10.00/hr, 1 prep @ 8.00/hr, 1 dish/porter @ 6.00/hr.	2 Chefs @ to Year 1's staff.	One baker added	10% overall	10% overall 10%
		kitchen salary increase	kitchen salary increase	kitchen salary increase	kitchen salary increase
Executive Chef	Owner's Salary	estimated increase	estimated increase	estimated increase	estimated increase

	Year 1 % of sales	Year 2 % of sales	Year 3 % of sales	Year 4 % of sales	Year 5 % of sales
Retail (Store mgr, clerks)	1 Store Manager @ $30,000, plus Clerks (all at $7.50/hr): 3 @ 6 hrs/day, 1 @ 8 hrs/day, 1 @ 5 hrs/day (Monday–Friday) plus 2 clerks @ 8 hours/day (Saturday)	Store manager @ 33,000 + 8% increase for clerks from Year 1	Store manager @ 36,000 + 8% increase for clerks from Year 2	Store manager @ 39,000 + 8% increase for clerks from Year 3	Store manager @ 43,000 + 8% increase for clerks from Year 4
Office catering (Delivery)	1 person @ 7 hrs a day × $5.00/hr	5% increase over Year 1	5% increase over Year 2	5% increase over Year 3	5% increase over Year 4
Catering (Sales person, waitstaff) Sales person @	$29,000, plus commission of 10% of catering food cost; waitstaff @ 17% of catering sales (Owner's figures)	Sales person @ $29,000, plus commission of 10% of catering food cost; waitstaff @ 17% of catering sales	Sales person @ $29,000, plus commission of 10% of catering food cost; waitstaff @ 17% of catering sales	Sales person @ $29,000, plus commission of 10% of catering food cost; waitstaff @ 17% of catering sales	Sales person @ $29,000, plus commission of 10% of catering food cost; waitstaff @ 17% of catering sales
Payroll Taxes	15% of all of the above	15% of all of the above	15% of all of the above	15% of all of the above	15% of all of the above
Occupancy Rent	as per lease agreement	as per lease agreement	as per lease agreement	as per lease agreement	as per lease agreement
Real Estate Taxes	as per lease agreement	as per lease agreement	as per lease agreement	as per lease agreement	as per lease agreement
Commercial Rent Tax	Standard 6% of base rent	Standard 6% of base rent	Standard 6% of base rent	Standard 6% of base rent	Standard 6% of base rent

	Year 1 % of sales	Year 2 % of sales	Year 3 % of sales	Year 4 % of sales	Year 5 % of sales
Utilities	2% is industry standard—will vary depending on airconditioning/ heating system and type of cooking equipment used	2% is industry standard—will vary depending on airconditioning/ heating system and type of cooking equipment used	2% is industry standard—will vary depending on airconditioning/ heating system and type of cooking equipment used	2% is industry standard—will vary depending on airconditioning/ heating system and type of cooking equipment used	2% is industry standard—will vary depending on airconditioning/ heating system and type of cooking

OPERATING EXPENSES

	Year 1 % of sales	Year 2 % of sales	Year 3 % of sales	Year 4 % of sales	Year 5 % of sales
Insurance (property/liability) Increases	of retail sales plus 20.00 per 1,000 of catering sales plus 5,000/year for fire/damage (non-BOP policy), includes liquor liability, umbrella and landlord's requirements	7.50 per 1,000	Increases	Increases	Increases
		proportionate to sales	proportionate to sales	proportionate to sales	proportionate to sales
Insurance (health)	No coverage for employees provided	No coverage for employees provided	Included here as an option beginning in Year 3 for primary employees (up to 4)	Included here as an option for primary employees (up to 4)	Included here as an option for primary employees (up to 4)
Kitchen Supplies	300 per week, year 1	175/wk	125/wk	125/wk	125/wk
Credit Card Expense	2.5% commission on 21% of total sales	Increase proportionate to sales	Increase proportionate to sales	Increase proportionate to sales	Increase proportionate to sales
Bank Fees	estimate	estimate	estimate	estimate	estimate

	Year 1 % of sales	Year 2 % of sales	Year 3 % of sales	Year 4 % of sales	Year 5 % of sales
Repairs and Maintenance	Industry average @ 1% of sales— would be approx. $1,200/month. This could be higher or lower depending on service contracts and age of equipment purchased.	Would increase approx. 2% per year	Would increase approx. 2% per year	Would increase approx. 2% per year	approx. 2% per year
Administrative Salaries	1 bookkeeper @ $16.00/hr × 40 hrs+ 1 admin assistant @ 30,000 + 1 baby sitter @ 15,000	5% salary increases over Year 1	5% salary increases over Year 2	5% salary increases over Year 3	5% salary increases over Year 4
Payroll Taxes	15% of Administrative Salaries	15% of Administrative Salaries	15% of Administrative Salaries	15% of Administrative Salaries	15% of Administrative Salaries
Telephone/Postage (office use only)	estimate	estimate	estimate	estimate	estimate
Laundry/Linen	kitchen uniforms, towels, aprons, as follows: 35 sets of pants/jackets @ 2.10; 100 aprons @ .60; 500 kitchen towels @ .15 per week	Would increase approx. 2% per year	Would increase approx. 2% per year	Would increase approx. 2% per year	Would increase approx. 2% per year
Garbage Removal	estimate based on volume	estimate based on volume	estimate based on volume	estimate based on volume	estimate based on volume

	Year 1 % of sales	Year 2 % of sales	Year 3 % of sales	Year 4 % of sales	Year 5 % of sales
Pest Control	estimate @ 50.00/week	estimate @ 50.00/week	estimate @ 50.00/week	estimate @ 50.00/week	estimate @ 50.00/week
Office Supplies	300/wk, year one, for set up	175/wk	150/wk	150/wk	150/wk
Payroll Service	estimate from ADP	estimate from ADP	estimate from ADP	estimate from ADP	estimate from ADP
Accounting/Legal	estimate	estimate	estimate	estimate	estimate
Flowers/Decoration	1% of total sales, based on PM's figures for catering plus $200/week for the store	increase proportionate to sales	increase proportionate to sales	increase proportionate to sales	increase proportionate to sales
Equipment lease (kitchen/display) remain constant	year terms on equipment. This figure depends greatly on capitol expenditures at start-up for equipment	$1,000/mo—5 for 5 years	remain constant for 5 years	remain constant for 5 years	remain constant for 5 years
Equipment Rental (catering)	proportionate to catering sales	increase proportionately to Catering sales	increase proportionately to Catering sales	increase proportionately to Catering sales	increase proportionately to Catering sales
Bar set-ups	proportionate to catering sales	increase proportionately to Catering sales	increase proportionately to Catering sales	increase proportionately to Catering sales	increase proportionately to Catering sales
Printing (menus, flyers, etc) 5% increase over	500/mo, after initial stock is bought	estimated @ remain the same as year 1, depending on promotions done	will probably Year 2	5% increase over Year 3	5% increase over Year 4
Cleaning Supplies	Estimated @ 175/week	1% increase over Year 1	1% increase over Year 2	1% increase over Year 3	1% increase over Year 4

	Year 1 % of sales	Year 2 % of sales	Year 3 % of sales	Year 4 % of sales	Year 5 % of sales
Paper/Packaging Supplies	4.5% of office catering and retail food sales—standard but could be higher depending on type of packaging used.	4.5% of office catering and retail food sales—standard but could be higher depending on type of packaging used.	4.5% of office catering and retail food sales—standard but could be higher depending on type of packaging used.	4.5% of office catering and retail food sales—standard but could be higher depending on type of packaging used.	4.5% of office catering and retail food sales—standard but depending on type of packaging used.
Travel and Entertainment	estimate	estimate	estimate	estimate	estimate
Security	alarm system hooked to central station	alarm system hooked to central station	alarm system hooked to central station	alarm system hooked to central station	alarm system hooked to central station
Licenses and permits (not including liquor)	does not include liquor license for catering	does not include liquor license for catering	does not include liquor license for catering	does not include liquor license for catering	liquor license for catering
Dues/subscriptions	estimate	estimate	estimate	estimate	estimate
Local Transportation	adjusted from PM's figures for 1992	Van lease @ 400/mo + insurance prorated from 7,000/yr+ driver salary @ 15,000+ gas/other expenses @2500+ parking @175/mo	2% increase from year 2	2% increase from year 3	2% increase from year 4
Consulting/Management/R&D	suggested	suggested	suggested	suggested	suggested
Marketing (includes postage for mailings)	3% of gross sales	2.7% of gross sales	2.5% of gross sales	2.3% of gross sales	2.0% of gross sales
Miscellaneous	estimate	estimate	estimate	estimate	estimate

Hints:

- Each partner or participant in the future company should prepare the part of the plan that relates most closely to his or her area of expertise or responsibility. Break the larger task of writing the plan into smaller, more manageable sections; for best results, assign topics or sections according to the individual specialty of each writer.
- If you are working in a partnership, select a team leader (or chief executive) who will be responsible for holding the team together, keeping all parties objective, and acting as intermediary, when necessary.
- Have all members of the team read and edit (suggest changes) for each section. This process will assist in elevating the quality of writing *as well as* get everybody working toward a common vision.
- Keep the plan to a maximum of forty pages, with a few more, if needed, for appendix or supporting documents.
- Have second or third drafts of the plan read by both an accountant (or financial advisor) *and* a lawyer.
- Use consultants to fill in the gaps of understanding the business, writing, researching, advising, and coaching.
- Understand and accept going into the process that business plan preparation and writing *typically* takes from two to six months.
- Edit, edit, edit, edit. . . .

GETTING PROFESSIONAL HELP

What happens if you feel that you want to a write a business plan but don't know how to do it? Or maybe you want to write a complete plan, but know that you need to hire someone, or a few people, to help you, and can't afford it. At this juncture, ask yourself this question: "Can I afford to spend between $5,000 and $10,000 to completely understand the feasibility of my 'great' idea and have a much clearer idea if it's going to work?" This is the first reality check of whether you are financially and emotionally ready to start your business, and it is blunt: If the answer to this question is "No," then you probably aren't ready to go into business at all, at least not right now. Most business consultants concur on this point.

Most business consultants also concur that you need a seasoned, dispassionate, rational ally to help sort out fact from fiction, reality from dreams. Even if you don't hire a consultant to complete your plan for you, you may want to get some "part-time" help in finishing your plan. A good accountant or food service consultant can help you polish your business plan, projections, estimates of anticipated earnings and needs for capital. Take advantage of seminars on business start-ups offered at a nominal fee by your local Small Business Administration office. (Get the names of your local SBA office in the white pages of your local phone book. You can also access them on-line at sbaonline.sba.gov.) Attend SBA workshops to get help on the basics of starting your business, financing, marketing, advertising, cash management, business insurance and law and then set up an appointment with some seasoned retired entrepreneurs through SCORE (Service Corps of Retired Executives). With their long view of business, they can provide you with some valuable insights. They should also have a look at the rough business plan you are developing and can help you refine it.

BRING IN THE EXPERTS TO BRING IN THE BUCKS— WHY BRING IN A PROFESSIONAL?

1. **To cut through the often blinding attachment or fear that prevents you from thrusting the "young bird" of your idea into the air to see how it flies.** You need to share the idea of your business with people who can help you take it to the next level. Professional help, in the form of accountants, consultants and lawyers, are the first place to test your ideas. But you need to be forthcoming with these professionals. Be secure in the knowledge that it is safe to divulge your plans, your deepest hopes *and* fears about your business. These people are in business to assist the eager entrepreneur. They are successful at what they do because they are knowledgeable, objective, *and* conservative. You are paying them to act in your best interest.

2. **Your inexperience will be counterbalanced by their experience.** Perhaps for the first time, with the help of a professional business consultant, you will be able to step out from the well-heated space behind that door and clarify and focus your concept. You will be able to expose your idea to the cold clear gaze of a professional with years of experience to back up his or her analysis (a necessary but sometimes painful process, to be sure). From that vantage point, you can better understand the role that you will play in your business for years to come.

DO YOUR HOMEWORK

All in all, when it comes to writing your business plan, whether alone, with your partners, or with professional help, you can't be too linear or rigid in your approach. Your research should encompass all of the subjects to be included in your plan. The more you educate yourself at the onset about the areas of the business you are least familiar with, the better prepared you will be to face and convince your prospective investors about the viability of your business and your degree of commitment to it.

Take your time to develop a sound and comprehensive business plan. Spend up front in the research and development phase. Don't use cookie-cutter formulas to write your business plan. Don't resort to filling in the blanks in a prototype plan or use an off-the-shelf computer program to create your business plan. Doing so robs your of the opportunity to express the uniqueness of your business. Individual business plans differ enough that there is no one "right" way to formulate the plan's language and claims. In fact, very often, the individualistic style of the business plan itself will interest potential investors. (Take another look at Exhibits 3-2 to 3-7).

It will be necessary to move back and forth between hopes and expectations, between plans and dreams to arrive at a comfortable middle ground where what you want coincides with what you can have. Even while remaining true to the spirit of your business, you have to be open-minded and flexible in your thinking.

After you have explored, written, rewritten, gotten frustrated, gotten help, written and rewritten some more, you will be ready to ask for money confidently, more knowledgeably understand how you will start up and run your business. Most importantly, you will more thoroughly understand the potential profit and other ways that going into business will fulfill your needs. Completing the business plan is a testimony to your first real test as a business person and entrepreneur, thoroughly preparing you to sell to investors.

CHAPTER FOUR

FINANCING YOUR BUSINESS

It's the old chicken-and-the-egg conundrum. You need money to open the business, but in order to convince anyone to loan you money you need a track record of success. What about going it alone, without any outside funds? The bad news? You may have blown the inheritance from Aunt Sally and you've just about given up on winning the lottery. The good news is that your savings account balance looks pretty good as partial collateral for a business loan and you have some equity in your home, which may provide the basis for a loan to capitalize another piece of the business. Even with previous experience in specialty food retailing at some level, though, perhaps working for someone else in managing *their* business, you should be prepared for a tough sell. History shows that lenders and investors more readily finance a business with a track record and a plan for growth based on experience in the industry.

To get a completely new business off the ground, the most promising place to start looking for capital would be among like-minded friends. Next turn to family—if you feel that the ties that bind would not chafe intolerably. Alternatively, you can always consider taking in partners (perhaps you already have). If none of these seem to provide a solution to the cash crunch, there's still hope.

WHERE ARE YOU NOW AND WHICH WAY SHOULD YOU GO?

If your business is a start-up and you have no previous experience as a proprietor (Stage One), then you are best advised to seek financing from informal investors instead of banks. If you have product samples but no revenue, you are considered to be in Stage Two of business development, and also would do well to seek funding from informal investors instead of banks.

You are in Stage Three of development if you have full business plans or a pilot program/current business already in place. Yet more highly evolved, Stage Four businesses are those which have been in operation for some time and show documented revenues and expenses. In either of these cases, a commercial bank or other traditional lender is an appropriate approach for funding.

Regardless which stage of business development characterizes your situation, you must first do two things: complete your business plan, and select a legal designation (sole proprietorship, partnership, or corporation) for your (new) entity. A sample partnership agreement form is shown in Exhibit 4-1.

EXHIBIT 4-1

In forming a partnership, a form such as the following may be used. This is included here only to illustrate the basic information you should expect to include. Your legal counsel should, however, have the last word on the specific language and terms you will ultimately use when forming a partnership to own and operate your business.

Partnership Agreement

Agreement executed by and between the undersigned for the undersigned for the purpose of forming a general partnership.

1. Name: The name of the partnership shall be:
2. Address: The original place of business shall be at:
3. Nature of Business: The partnership shall engage in the business of _____, and such other related activities as shall be agreed upon by the partners.
4. Duration: The partnership shall continue until terminated by mutual consent or dissolution by operation of law.
5. Capital: The initial capital and ownership interest shall be allocated as follows:

Partner	Amount	Ownership	Interest
_____	$_____	____%	$_____

   The partners shall contribute in proportionate shares any additional capital they may deem necessary for the operation of the business.
6. Loans by Partners: If any partner shall, with the written consent of the other partners, advance any moneys to the partnership in excess of the capital contributed as set forth above, the amount of the moneys so advanced shall be considered as a loan to the partnership and shall bear interest of ___% until repaid.

7. Profit and Losses: The net profits and losses of the partnership shall be apportioned amongst the partners in accordance with their proportionate ownership interest.
8. Management: The partners shall have equal rights in the management of the partnership business.
9. Duties: Each partner shall devote his/her full time and best efforts on behalf of the partnership business.
10. Salaries: The salaries for each partner shall be by agreement with the remaining partner(s).
11. Books of Account: The partnership shall maintain adequate accounting records on a cash basis of accounting, and open to inspection by each partner. The fiscal year shall end on _____, 19____, of each year.
12. Banking: All partnership funds shall be deposited with such banks as may be designated by the partners. Checks and withdrawals shall be signed by any two partners.
13. Authority: No partners, shall, without the consent of the other partners:
    (a) Borrow money in the firm name for firm purposes or utilize collateral owned by the partnership as security for such loans.
    (b) Assign, transfer, pledge, compromise, or release any debts or obligations due the partnership, except upon payment in full.
    (c) Enter into any contract, obligation, or undertaking of the partnership except within the ordinary course of business.
    (d) Make, execute, and deliver any insolvency proceeding, confession of judgment, deed, guarantee, lease, bond or contract to sell all or substantially all the property of the partnership.
    (e) Pledge, hypothecate, or in any manner transfer his/her interest in the partnership.
14. Termination: This partnership shall be terminated by death or material incapacity of any partner, mutual agreement, or upon request for termination by any one partner. Upon termination by reason of death, incapacity, or request, the remaining partners shall have the right to continue the business of the partnership business on their own behalf or together with new or additional partners, provided they pay the terminated partner the fair value of his/her partnership interest together with suitable indemnification for all their existing partnership obligations.
15. Arbitration: Any dispute or controversy herein shall be settled by arbitration in accordance with the rules of the American Arbitration association and judgment upon the award rendered may be entered in any court having jurisdiction thereof.

Partner Signature _____ Date _____

Partner Signature _____ Date _____

Partner Signature _____ Date _____

Business owners and business funders almost unanimously agree that the best tool to have in order to start looking for money and partnership interest in your proposed business is a carefully crafted, detailed business plan. Armed with such a plan, begin to shop your idea around to "informal investors." The completed business plan will be your primary means of finding funding and is the most effective form of communication between you, your investors, and lenders. After all that hard work it may be disheartening to hear that your potential investors and/or funders will probably only read a few sections, but this is fact. Getting them to commit precious time even to doing that much is a step in the right direction.

To prepare for this you want to carefully and aggressively describe your business and its potential for success in a few key sections: The executive summary and the sections on operations and financials. This last section should have enough information to communicate that you are focusing on the needs of your potential investors. This is a consistently important aspect of the business plan writing and capital raising process. To whom will you be showing the business plan for purposes of raising money? If it's the bank, you will have to demonstrate, in bankers' terms and language, why the bank is making a smart choice in lending money to you. Address why a bank (or other lending institution, including the SBA) should select your proposal over several hundred other applications. If it's a family member to whom you are pitching the plan, be equally specific about what you are asking from that family member and how much you will repay (and when) in return. Put it in writing with the help of an accountant or lawyer. Be sensitive to your family's needs in loaning you money. Family members are rarely

Places to look for money include the following:
1. Friends and Family
2. Small Business Administration
3. Local development corporations seeking to revitalize declining neighborhoods by offering funding for individuals who choose to locate their businesses there (particularly appropriate for wholesale production facilities, which do not rely on a high visibility location for walk-in trade)
4. State and local governments offering low-interest short-term micro loans for relatively small capitalization (up to $25,000, usually administered through nonprofit groups selected and approved by the SBA)
5. Private foundations offering program-related investments
6. Credit unions that feature small business lending
7. Venture capital

so altruistic that they lend money simply to support a good idea. Be sure you know what they expect.

For more anonymous investors, such as venture capitalists, be aware that these individuals are normally looking for very high return on their money in what is typically a very high-risk industry. Read up on standard offerings for venture capital investors. Don't, in desperation, offer a deal that will strangle you if profits are not achieved at the rate or level you are anticipating. In other words, don't give the store away. Push forward on the assumption that the money will be there when you need it.

A couple of other hints: To win funding, your business plan must:

- Be arranged appropriately, with an executive summary, a table of contents, and its chapters in the right order.
- Be the right length and have a professional appearance—neither too long nor too short, too plain or too fancy.
- Communicate a sense of what the founders and the company expect to accomplish three to ten years into the future.
- Explain in quantitative and qualitative terms the benefit to the user of the company's products or services.
- Present hard evidence of the marketability of the products or services. Keep your operations section shorter than the section on market, demonstrating to investors that you realize the priority of markets over products. *Investors are interested in companies that are market-driven, not product-driven.*
- Justify financially the means chosen to sell the products or services.
- Explain and justify the level of product development that has been achieved and describe in appropriate detail the manufacturing process and associated costs.
- Portray the partners as a team of experienced managers with complementary business skills.
- Suggest as high an overall "Rating" as possible of the venture's product development and team sophistication.
- Contain believable financial projections, with the key data explained and documented. When writing this section, be realistic about what you can hope to accomplish.
- Show how investors can cash out in three to ten years, with appropriate capital appreciation.
- Be presented to the most potentially receptive financiers possible to avoid wasting precious time as company funds dwindle.
- Be easily and concisely explainable in a well-orchestrated oral presentation.

How It All Works—Getting Money from a Variety of Sources

You Gotta Have Friends . . . and Contracts

Although often providing the path to capital least fraught with red tape, guarantees, and conditions, friends are also a necessary part of human survival and other consequences apply when you approach friends in a business transaction. Relationships are vital to human survival and growth, and good personal relationships are not worth risking for a business. In their blind rush to fulfill a lifelong dream, entrepreneurs often measure the sincerity of friendships by how much money these friends are willing to fork over to invest in their business. While it is not an inherently bad idea to ask friends to invest in your business as something potentially fun and profitable, it is crucial that you listen to and respect your friends' choices. If someone you know does not want to invest in your business, ask that person why and be prepared to listen. If a friend *does* want to invest, ask that investor carefully about what his/her needs and anticipated involvement will be. Don't accept the money if the conditions attached compromise your own integrity, the overall health of the proposed business, or your relationship to the investor. Don't trick yourself into "trusting" that everything will work out with a friend. Money has a way of changing the nature of all relationships not previously operating around it. Contracts are essential; they objectively spell out roles of the various players. You will be demonstrating further commitment to professionalism (and *not* insulting your friends) if you steadfastly adhere to a contract. Furthermore, remember that it works both ways: if your friend is "insulted" that you enforce a contract spelling out your financial arrangement, then possibly that friend had other intentions beyond simply investing in your business.

Ditto: Family

Family members tend to want to control things, especially when situations are bad or when the recipient of moneys is vulnerable in any way. Like government and politics, business partnerships and family relationships often make strange and destructive bedfellows. Fallings-out are commonplace. So it's always best to draw up detailed contracts with family members showing how management and decision making will be accomplished in the business, both in times of health and trouble. (You don't want to revert to having your mother, or father, tell you what to do again after all these years, do you? Some parents are just waiting to have this kind of opportunity, no matter the cost, i.e., their investment.)

Many start-up companies, however, do receive their initial seed money or start-up capital from individual investors like family and friends. Although there can be tremendous variability in the dollar value and terms of this kind of financing, these backers are more apt to expect to be paid back within five to seven years. They also tend to like to keep their investments within fifty miles of their homes and seek annual returns of between 20% and 50% on their investments. Be careful when approaching family and friends (or in being approached by them) for investment in your new business. We advise very, very strongly that these new business relationships be treated as professionally and formally as your new and pending relations with bankers and the SBA. Make sure that each of your cousins or college pals has received a copy of your business plan and a request to read it. Communicate to them how important it is *to you* that they understand your mission, your market, and your plans for operations and profit, including the time line for profitability and payouts. (Many informal investors are disillusioned when the business takes a normal amount of time, such as a year, to open and even more disillusioned when it takes two years for them to see their first return.)

As part of (or as an addendum to) your business plan, prepare an offering statement (with the help of your lawyer) that states clearly what your expectations are of the investors in terms of amount and timing of their investment and what your commitment is to them in terms of return. By treating these relationships as formal partnerships, you will minimize the risk of disappointment, lack of understanding, and failure to fulfill commitments.

Banking on Banks

Banks are notorious in their dislike of financing new business, especially food businesses, but many smaller, community-based banks today have a better understanding of the benefits of investing in the small businessperson. They have committed themselves to work in the community by aiding such entrepreneurs. No bank, however, will talk to you until you have a completed business plan to show them.

SBA Loans

Working with the government is a little like you would expect: difficult and not the most straightforward route. However, for the persistent and the thorough, going the SBA route can be a smart and inexpensive, low-risk way to get some capital. Note that if you are a woman, an individual from a minority background, physically handicapped, or socially or economically disadvantaged, chances are much better that you would succeed in getting government money in the form of loans and grants to start or grow your business. Although not available in all locations, the Women's Prequalification Pilot Loan Program enables women to prequalify for a government-guaranteed loan up to $250,000 before the business owner goes to a bank. Likewise, under the Small Business Investment Company Program, small businesses can obtain funding from SBA-licensed private venture capital firms. For socially or economically disadvantaged small businesses, the Specialized Small Business Investment Company Program provides incentives to venture capital firms to fund businesses.

The SBA has a federal loan program for people who want to start or expand their businesses. The SBA maintains local offices in many cities (See the publications, listings and material produced by the SBA in Resources, at the back of this book). The process often begins with an interview that is similar to a coaching or business consultation with one of their officers. It's important to develop good relations with people in these offices. If the chemistry is not right with the person to whom you are assigned, request to speak with another. The more questions you ask, the more information you will get. There will be applications to fill out, things to send in, and banks to contact. The Federal Government, acting through the SBA, is the guarantor of a loan from a commercial bank who is the lender.

Be sure you understand the relationships between the banks and the SBA and be sure that they are offering you every opportunity to utilize the money they are allotted by government to lend. Again, having a completed business plan will move the process along much more smoothly. (Their courses on the step by step process of writing a business plan are basic but informative for the novice. What they don't offer are insights into particular businesses, which information is often precisely what distinguishes a compelling business plan from a workaday one.)

Types of SBA Loans   The SBA provides a way for first time business owners to obtain funding. In fact, through its Guaranty Loan Program, the SBA is the largest source of long-term small business financing in the nation. The SBA guarantees from 70 to 90% of the loan value on loans up to $750,000 at an interest rate not to exceed prime plus 2.25% for loans under seven years and prime plus 2.75% for loans over seven years. (Nationally, the average loan made under the guaranty program is $210,000.)

For smaller amounts, the SBA's Low Documentation Loan Program (Low Doc) is a good place to look for funding. The SBA has made an often trying and emotion-laden process somewhat easier through streamlined procedures and less paperwork. For loans up to $100,000, you need only complete the front of a one-page SBA application. The lender (commercial bank) completes the back. Usually within ten working days after receiving a completed loan package from the lending bank, SBA will let you know whether you have qualified for the loan. For amounts over $50,000, if you are operating as a sole proprietorship, you will also need to include a copy of your US Income Tax Schedule C. If the applicant is part of a partnership, then you'll need to fill out IRS Form l065. If you are functioning as a corporation, then you will need to complete IRS Form 1120. You will also have to include a cash flow analysis (see Exhibit 4-2) and pro forma balance sheet (Exhibit 4-3), as well as personal financial statements for all named as guarantors or obligors on the loan.

Exhibit 4-2

Statement of Cash Flow

Here is an example of a typical cash flow statement for a generic specialty food store.

Cash Flow Statement
Your Favorite Gourmet to Go

	Year Ending
Cash Flows from Operating Activities	
Cash received from customers	$550,000
Cash paid to suppliers and employees	–403,000
Net cash provided by (used in) operating activities	$147,000
Cash Flow from Investing Activities	
Inventories	–10,500
Leasehold improvements	–140,000
Net Cash from Investing	–150,500
Total Net Cash	(3,500)
Opening Cash	$0
Closing Cash	($3,500)
Reconciliation of net income to net cash from operating and funding:	
Net Income	42,965
Adjustments	
Depreciation	4,650
Accounts payable	100,659
Total Adjustments	105,309
Net Cash from Operations and Funding	148,274

EXHIBIT 4-3

BALANCE SHEET

		Assets
Current Assets		
Cash on hand		−53,726
Deposits (energy, utilities, etc.)		4,000
Inventories		
Food	6,500	
Beverages	3,500	
Retail goods	4,000	
Supplies	6,500	20,500
Total Current Assets		
Fixed Assets		
Leasehold improvements		140,000
Furniture, fixtures, and equipment		23,000
Account Depreciation		−4,650
Total Assets		129,124
		Liabilities
Current Liabilities		
Accounts payable		50,659
Note payable		31,500
Total Liabilities		82,159
Bank Account		42,965
Total Liabilities and Equity		129,124

Am I Eligible for an SBA Loan? Most probably yes. Furthermore, you don't need to be turned down by a bank before you apply for the loan. Almost any type of sole proprietor, partnership or corporation is eligible. Retailers and service businesses with sales not exceeding $5 million, certainly the focus of this book, are eligible. Landlords and nonprofits, however, are not eligible. Loans to individuals with significant personal resources may also be proscribed.

The same criteria that apply to the regular SBA Guaranty Loan program apply to Low Doc loans. Note that the SBA generally requires that business operators have one-third of the total project cost before being considered a viable recipient of government-guaranteed funds).

What Kind of Collateral Will I Need?   Like any other funding source, SBA requires that sufficient assets be pledged as collateral for the loan to ensure that the business owner has a substantial interest in the success of the business. Although SBA will not deny funding for a lack of sufficient collateral, most lenders will require a reasonable amount of collateral to provide a secondary source of repayment. Normally, business and/or personal assets are pledged. Note that in addition to the chief executive officer, all owners of 20% or more of the business will be required to personally guarantee the loan.

Under the Low Doc program, the SBA has pledged that it will rely more on an applicant's character, management experience, and credit history than on predetermined percentages of equity or capital contribution to the venture. With the Low Doc program, lenders are more willing to process applications since there is less paperwork entailed. As with any other search for funding for a new business, however, you will need to submit a copy of your business plan. So producing one is still the first step, the prelude to each and every other step in the process of making your dream idea on paper turn into three-dimensional, living, breathing reality.

What Can I Purchase with My Loan?   You can borrow through the SBA programs for almost any purpose related to starting or purchasing a business or making improvements to an existing one, including the following: leasehold improvements, working capital, equipment purchases, inventory, refinancing, and real estate.

What Can't I Purchase with My Loan?   Loans for real estate speculation or investment are not permitted. Also loan proceeds may not be used for distribution or debt payment to principals.

How Long Do I Have to Pay Back the Loan?   For loans used for working capital, you will generally have five to seven years for repayment. For loans on machinery and equipment, you can expect to have either seven years or the reasonable expected economic life of the equipment. To acquire a going business, loans are repayable within seven years. You'll have ten years to repay loans received for leasehold improvements, and up to twenty-five years for the acquisition of real estate.

What Do the Bank and the SBA Look for in a Borrower?   First and foremost, the loan officer must feel comfortable about your character—that you will be likely to repay the loan. He/she must also believe that you are capable of managing the business for which you are seeking funding. A loan officer will also want to know everything about your credit history and your experience in the business.

For a start-up business, your sales and expense projections will also be examined, along with your percentage of investment in the business (usually 25–30%), your ability to withstand expenses during start-up and the initial operating phase when the business will most likely incur losses, your revenue projections, repayment potential, and collateral.

What Do I Need to Get Started on the Loan Application Process?   In addition to declaring the specific amount you wish to borrow and the purpose of the loan, you will need:

1. Completed loan documents.
2. Business tax returns for the past three years.
3. Business plan.
4. Personal résumé.
5. Balance sheet as of the day the business starts.
6. A profit and loss statement.
7. Sales/expense/income projections for at least the first year of operations.
8. A monthly cash flow projection.

Other Governmental Avenues to Pursue

There are federal, state and local offices of economic development that also offer assistance to entrepreneurs—for both start-up and business expansions. Contact the state office of economic development in your state's capital to find out about local funding sources. You can also contact your congressperson for the names of local development corps, business improvement districts, and community banks, many of which run the economic development programs in your area.

Programs are established in the form of low-interest loans and grants. *Grants* are moneys that do not have to be paid back. Applying for a grant, however, is often more detailed and laborious. Here again, your business plan is the first step to a grant application. Most grants will be funded to entrepreneurs through local development offices, who will assist or even make the grant application for you. In return, the development group receives a percentage of the grant for assisting you in placing in sharper focus how the mission of your business fits in the larger economic development initiative. Most economic development funds are awarded to businesses that strive to enhance the overall economic growth of an area, expand in local economies, hire local workers, or start businesses in areas of industrial decline. If your business is a manufacturing or distribution business or a commercial kitchen that delivers its product to higher rent commercial areas, then you may very well qualify for such a grant to capitalize part of your operations. These grants can vary in size but typically are not less than $5,000 or greater than $50,000.

Community Development Corporations (CDC)

CDCs provide equity, debt, and grant financing to small- and medium-sized businesses. They are often more flexible than more conventional sources of funding. In addition, many prefer start-up financing and are willing to back lower upside potential, nonproprietary situations. Although CDCs are often geographically restricted, here, as elsewhere, a convincing business plan may make the difference between funding and denial.

CDCs are organizations responsible for addressing the development needs of a geographically defined community. The federal program is unique in that these granted funds are used by CDCs to make venture-capital type investments. The ownership of these ventures does not rest within the federal government, but with a private development corporation governed by a board of directors composed of local business and community leaders.

CDCs are usually located in areas that are characterized by high unemployment and low income levels. Besides providing money for businesses, CDCs located in urban, inner-city areas often provide assistance in housing development and rehabilitation projects.

Could My Business Qualify as a Potential CDC? Typically, the kinds of businesses that can be beneficiaries of such investment are less likely to be retail oriented. For example, if you were seeking to open a commissary kitchen to service the production needs of multiple retail shops or catering, you might be a candidate for some CDC funding. If you are a start-up, and your business is headed by an experienced and committed entrepreneur or team, and is involved in low to medium technology or relatively labor-intensive manufacturing or product, and if you are seeking between $150,000 and $750,000 in initial risk capital, then you also might qualify.

What Are the Advantages of Being Funded by a CDC?

- Start-ups are the backbone of some CDC's business development strategy
- CDCs are essential always on the lookout for new venture investments. Being long-term and start-up oriented, they regard economic downturns as the

ideal time to get new businesses up and ready to take advantage of better times ahead

- The backing and support of the surrounding community are automatically entwined with every CDC venture

    CDCs have virtually unlimited flexibility with respect to structuring the loan package and are prepared to handle financing in unorthodox ways. In addition, given the duality of their goals, they are likely to provide somewhat more attractive terms than a traditional venture capitalist.

- Many urban downtowns, shuttered and abandoned as the city populations emigrated to suburbia in the 60s and 70s, are currently being revitalized. These downtowns are being repopulated with younger residents (employees of newly relocated large companies that are establishing these cities as centers for particular industries [for example, Charlotte, NC, for banking and Columbus, OH, for credit card processing] and immigrants, who usually fill the service needs of these new economies.)

These urban renewal projects should not be overlooked as ripe opportunities for new specialty food businesses. Much of the slated work centers around the rehabilitation of historic and spacious office and manufacturing buildings, which make great homes for food halls, shops, and combination retail/wholesale manufacturing. In these cities lie more examples of places where government money is being funneled, and where CDCs and other urban revitalization groups are funding new ventures.

If you are unsure of where to locate your specialty food business, if you want to learn about markets that need to be tapped for convenience and high-quality foods, look for opportunities where the demographics are changing and new industries are forming. (*American Demographics* magazine is a great source of information for identifying trends, locating pockets of successful businesses, and finding nationwide statistics for the entrepreneur in development.)

The Downsides of CDCs

- Operating in underdeveloped or declining areas can create challenges: They may be inhospitable for retail operations and have higher crime rates. Although urban CDCs are close to big city conveniences, it may be harder to overcome the public's poor perception about the neighborhood or the lack of upscale image.

- Local workforces have been on occasion known to require patience before stabilization and high productivity can be achieved. As with every rule, however, there are exceptions. When utilizing the local labor force previously plagued by chronic dependence on social welfare systems, unemployment or displacement from jobs, there are notable examples of the stunning turn-arounds that can be achieved with careful personnel policy and training programs.

- In general, CDCs move even more slowly than venture capitalists. You'd better not be in a hurry to gain funding if you are trying this approach. A lot hinges on the timing of the receipt of a completed business plan, but generally a minimum of two to three months is required from the date of introduction to investment.

Something Ventured, Something Gained?

You've heard of venture capital. At the start-up phase of your business, can you attract venture capitalists for funding? If so, is it the right way to go? Proceed with caution. Says Karen Kaplan, a freelance writer who covers technology and careers for the *Los Angeles Times*, "Venture capitalists look for strong management teams with proven track records. Companies must have the potential to dominate their market segment and have a product that lends itself to cultivating long-term customers" (*LA Times*, May 6, 1996).

Venture capital is the early-stage financing of relatively small, rapidly growing companies and is characterized by high risk. This method of funding provides money in the early stages of a new business and then later rounds of expansion financing to companies that have already demonstrated the viability of their concept but do not yet have access to public or credit-oriented institutional funding. What distinguishes venture capital from other loans is that the venture capitalist becomes intimately involved in your business; other than in name, the venture capitalist is your business partner. Such investors often look for a tenfold return on their money in five to seven years.

How Will I Know if Venture Capital Is for Me?   Everyone has heard the phrase "venture capital" and most of us have an idea or fantasy about what it is: huge amounts of money available for investment in new and hopeful companies. Well, like many other things, this is only partially true. To say that venture capitalists are professional gamblers with an unlimited amount of money to invest in new businesses or ventures is not to paint an accurate picture. Venture capitalists are now associated with firms, rather than working alone, and these organizations are very professional and aggressive businesses with only one thing in mind: Making money. They do this with a combination of minimal- and high-risk companies. However, as other sources of investment (mutual funds and stocks, for example) have yielded extremely high returns in recent years, venture capitalists are much less likely to fund high-risk and start-up companies (which describe most food-related businesses). And if they do, it is not likely to be on terms favorable and affordable to the independent start-up entrepreneur.

Still, it is not unwise to look into this type of funding, particularly if you are expanding a current business or creating a franchise or chain enterprise. Growing a business exponentially requires a tremendous amount of capital that you may not be able to get from other sources. By merely talking to venture capitalist groups, you stand to educate yourself about possible ways to structure deals with more informal investment sources such as friends and family.

A Bit of Bitter Irony   Venture capitalists will not only have certain financial requirements (percentage of stock and profits that go to them for their generous contribution to fund your passion), but also will often require that they implement key management structures, which may affect management personnel. Take, for example, the story of Earth's Best baby foods, the brainchild and passion of two brothers from Vermont who began their business of making organic baby foods in a home kitchen.

Continually undercapitalized and unable to penetrate the market in a way that would allow them to achieve profitability, they "sold out" to a venture capital company. This move did indeed make a national brand out of the fledgling company, but it also caused the business to be wrested away from its founders. In exchange for a tremendous influx of capital, the brothers were ousted from management, losing all operational control of their business. While still technically partners, and having received a bit of money (in their view, not nearly enough to compensate them for all the years of hard work and personal financial sacrifice), the brothers realized that they had sacrificed *their* company for the exposure and eventual success of the brand. While the recipe and quality of the product remained intact and was widely available to a larger audience (their goal), the siblings no longer had jobs, a company to grow or a place to go to work. They made the mistake of selling out in this way. To cap things off, the venture capitalists later sold the company to Heinz, which is the largest maker of baby foods in the world.

Ways to Learn More   A recommended way to explore the possibilities of venture capital is to find out about businesses similar to yours who may have used these venture capital firms. If there is a Venture Capital Association in your city, contact them and attend some of their events or venture capital fairs. These are sponsored to engage new entrepreneurs and they frequently offer avenues to explore. With your business plan in hand, schedule a couple of meetings with representatives from these firms that specialize in food-related businesses. Whether these sessions lead to gaining some capital for your business or not, they may still be useful in helping you gain some perspective on your business projections. These are relationships worth pursuing if only to clarify that the venture capital route is *not* for you.

If you wish to pursue this route further, however, do some research. If you're attempting to float a new business, find out which firms invest in new proposals and for how long the firm has been investing in new ventures, and particularly, new food businesses. Ask how old the venture funds are. You need to know up front if the firm only funds later-stage investments. Ask about the investment range of the firm (your business may indeed be too small for them). The answers to these questions should yield a short list of venture capitalists to talk to.

Do I Go It Alone? No. Initial contact with a venture capital firm should occur through an introduction from an individual or organization that is respected by the venture capitalist (usually a banker, lawyer, or accountant who has brought the firm past opportunities for investment). Lacking that, you can send a letter with a brief summary of the business plan and then follow up with a phone call. After the phone call, the last step in the initial dealings with venture capitalists is the business plan. As in most situations where you are seeking funding, no matter the source, the business plan is the first and most comprehensive instrument to communicate information about your company. Venture capitalists who don't wish to be influenced by their initial reaction to entrepreneurs' personalities rely heavily on the business plan. Besides, they don't usually have the time to spend forty-five minutes or an hour listening to an entrepreneur describe his or her business; they are apt to learn more from spending a few minutes reading the executive summary and other key points of the plan. After this initial screening, the venture capitalist will then either reject the proposal out of hand or spend more time reviewing it. If there is interest, you will hear from them further.

Variations on the Venture Capitalist Theme

Independent and Private These are professional partnerships and corporations investing pension funds, major corporations, individuals and families, endowments and foundations, insurance companies, and foreign investors. They are the major source of classic venture development funding. They invest equity in the full range of situations from start-ups to relatively mature companies and management-leveraged buyouts.

Small Business Investment Companies (SBICs)   These are private venture capital firms principally engaged in making long-term loans to small businesses or in
making equity investments in specific businesses such as grocery markets or
movie theaters. SBICs usually provide a minimum of $500,000 in financing but
loan packages may range as high as $10 million. Because these are often licensed
through the SBA and their funding is supplemented by government backed loans,
they are usually the only venture capitalists who will invest in retail food operations and wholesale food distribution businesses.

As a rule, since these entities generally borrow a portion of the capital they
invest and this requires paying interest on the moneys lent, they usually avoid
straight equity investments in early-stage companies. Typically venture capitalists
prefer industrial rather than retail products. These are certainly not the first place
to look in your search for funding.

What Do You and Your Investors Need?

Before you raise and then spend your first dime, prior to filing multiple loan
applications and getting miscellaneous commitments from friends and family,
please remember to consult your business plan for the capital budget and consider your initial operating finances to determine exactly how much money
you will need to open and operate during the first year. Additionally, consider
your own personal resources. Consider the options for financing—including a
combination of family, friends, loans (bank or SBA), or perhaps cashing in on
a 401K or life insurance policy. Consider carefully how far you are willing to go
to realize your dream, and what makes sense from not only your personal perspective but the perspective of your family. Consider, too, the needs of your
potential investors, how much of your business you will have to "give away"
(in outside stock ownership) or whether you will need to take loans against
future revenues and profits. Think about your options—you always have
options.

Remember to value your own sweat equity and to contribute some financing
of your own, which demonstrates your commitment and willingness to risk.
Don't give it all away. It's a delicate balancing act—think about how you can meet
the needs or perceived expectations of your various investors and still maintain
the proportion of your business that represents what you have contributed in
total. Make sure your financials have complete payback projections for various
scenarios (loan, stockholders, etc.) and sit back and think about whether you can
live comfortably with those projections.

Eternal Verities Regarding Raising Capital

1. You are the prime salesperson for your idea, and as a good salesperson, you are always selling. Become and act like an investor in your own company. Having some of the your own money at stake is the first step as you set off on the pursuit of capital. Other investors, both public and private, will take you a lot more seriously if you have wagered something of your own to kick off your project. (Be sure to keep track of all of your expenses, such as classes you take, fees you pay for professionals to assist you with the start up process, product testing, trade shows, etc. Document all of this as part of your monetary investment in the business and use these as tax write-offs.)

   Say, for example, you are offering units of your business at $25,000 apiece and you put in one unit of your own. Then you will know exactly what it takes to make that commitment. Like any good salesperson, if you know the product, its benefits, and its risks, you will communicate the opportunity of these more effectively to others. Potential investors will trust and respect you more if you have worked hard to put your own money into the pot.

   At the other end of the spectrum is the entrepreneur who is willing to risk it all to realize his or her dream: house, car, family savings, other businesses; these are most apt to consider loansharking an acceptable avenue to fund the enterprise. These are the entrepreneurs who are most dangerous and most difficult to temper to rational processes. These are the people who cross that fine line between acceptable, calculated risk and foolishness and for whom business is a substitute for the human side of life in all of its complexity and richness.

2. You can't rely on casual promises of money from friends or "investors," as most of them won't come through. Talk is cheap; investors' money is not.

3. Money builds on money. Put away money you have raised or commitments pledged. Showing some money to other prospective investors makes them more interested in committing their own money to your project (no one likes to be the first).

4. You will always need more money than you think, so don't turn down additional investors, if you are lucky enough to get them.

5. It always takes longer than you think to raise the money.

6. Conventional wisdom is indeed wisdom when it comes to the reason why businesses fail: 85–90% of businesses are undercapitalized. So don't sign that lease or contract for renovation until you have in hand at least 90% of what you project you will need.

DON'T OVERPROMISE

Your investors, and even the bank, want to see you succeed, and they want to be proud and have the ability to show off their smart investment. They will be satisfied when they see a smooth-running operation, the major players meshing well and working to achieve realistic, reasonable goals in a realistic, reasonable time frame. For all types of investors, whether they are your cousins, the local commercial bank, or the U.S. Government, receiving regular and timely repayments on loans is the best proof that you're on the right track. You'll get the breathing room you'll need to operate the business as you see fit when you are able to follow an expected schedule of repayments.

CHAPTER FIVE

LOCATION AND BUILD-OUT

When considering opening a specialty food store, the first thing you need to find is a good location. Sounds easy? Guess again. When asked about the key to their success, any successful businessperson will answer: "Location, location, location."

How do you find the right location for your business? Patience and a good real estate broker are two crucial elements you'll need in the search. Be prepared to look at and reject a whole slew of superficially appealing locations in favor of the one that's the right fit for your concept and budget. Therefore, the process of thinking about a location for your business should begin when you first begin rolling your business idea around in your head.

Complete build-out and fixturizing of your space starts with the work of a number of design professionals. Typically, an architect is at the center of the design team. He or she will recommend the involvement of an electrical engineer and a mechanical engineer who will put the design package together to submit to the local building department authorities for approval (and inspections later when the construction is complete). In addition to these individuals, a kitchen designer, interior designer, and general contractor are then engaged to complete the project.

Steve Jenkins, consultant to specialty food stores around the United States, on location: "Location is key when you are outside of a city. Inside a city, people will go anywhere. . . ."

The kitchen designer works closely with kitchen equipment dealers and can then estimate your equipment costs based on what your food production needs will be. If you bring in the services of a kitchen designer (who gets, on average, $1.00 per square foot of kitchen space for design), you should expect to receive: a complete floor plan; an equipment schedule; a detailed listing of electrical and plumbing requirements to service the equipment; plumbing rough-ins for the space; an exhaust plan; details for remote refrigeration, if any, and for carbonated beverage lines; any special building requirements including wall backings, concrete curbs, or floor depressions to accommodate the kitchen equipment; and elevations of the kitchen.

It's never too early to contact local real estate brokers and to call the phone numbers listed on vacant stores, if only to get a feel for spaces, the rents attached to them, and a sense of possibility for your business. Keep a diary of your search activities, noting any impressions you may have formed after seeing particular locations (great architectural potential, poor visibility, difficult parking, great retail mix in the strip center, too many food businesses, not enough food.) Build up a file of possibilities for comparison's sake, if only to eliminate areas and particular locations. Even though you may be far from signing a lease, you can benefit from knowing what's "out there." Then as you get closer to completing all your other research and idea development, you will be able to narrow your focus to particular areas or specific types of retail configurations (strip centers, downtown shopping district, freestanding building, retail/residential dual use property, historic retrofit, etc.), remembering that the real estate market is never static and spaces that were available at one point during your search may not still be available when you are ready to sign a lease contract (and if they are, you may have reason to be suspicious of their appropriateness for your venture).

In the crucial planning stages, research is key. That is one focus of completing a feasibility study for your business. In this process you will study the demographics of your area via a study of recent real estate values, look at the transience rate of the local population, note the size of households (the number with children and those who are childless). At this early stage you should concentrate on looking for sites within the community which seem to have the requisite size, visibility, parking, and accessibility. To help you in this process, connect with a good business broker or business real estate broker, one to whom you can communicate your requirements. Get recommendations from other noncompeting business owners in the area in which you wish to operate. Interview a few agents and then choose one. After the initial tour of the area, allow the agent to prescreen locations for you and then respond to those that seem intriguing on first impression. Ask questions, take the feasibility outline with you to every site you see, get lease terms, and be sure to inquire how much the landlord will contribute to the build-out of the space (known as the leasehold improvements). Weigh the pros and cons (and dollars and cents) of renting a location already set up and operating as a food store or restaurant versus renting a raw space (an empty, clean space with nothing but plumbing roughed in and electrical service leading into the location). And then wait. Waiting is the hardest but most important step in this process. Let your head, not your heart, rule when deciding on a location.

HOW MUCH SQUARE FOOTAGE IS RIGHT FOR YOUR CONCEPT?

To begin narrowing your focus, keep in mind food industry averages for different food service applications. In an operation designed to sell foods exclusively for off-premises consumption, space limitations are more easily surmountable. If in addition to take-out business, however, you are considering one or more of the following food service variations (or a hybrid of them), you will need to factor these square footage requirements into your calculation of your store's retail area:

Type of Food Service	Dining Area Required (sq ft per seat)
Fast food	8–12
Cafeteria	16–18
Counter service	18–20
Table service	13–20

When planning how much of your space should be devoted to food production to generate the kind of sales figures that will make your business viable, consider the following rough estimates:

Type of Food Service	Kitchen Area Required (sq ft per meal served)		
	For 200 meals at peak hours	For 200–400 meals at peak hours	For 400–800 meals at peak hours
Fast food	3–6	3–4.5	3–4.5
Cafeteria	5–7.5	4–5	3.5–4
Counter service	4–7	3.6–5	3.6–5
Table service	4–7	3.6–5	3.6–5

The kitchen areas listed don't include storage and office space.

DETERMINING HOW MUCH SPACE YOUR BUSINESS NEEDS

At all stages of the search for the right location for your business, bear in mind the following:

1. How much space you currently have (if you are already in business); you can extrapolate from that figure to project how much more space you will require to accomplish expansion goals.
2. What your new needs and projections of future needs (whether start-up or ongoing business) are; where possible, build into your calculations space for flexibility, expansion, and addition of new services and products over the term of the lease.
3. Rental costs—these should not exceed 10–15% of your projected sales.
4. Improvement costs—and who will pay for how much of them, you or the landlord; these leasehold improvements in large measure stay with the property—you can't take them with you. So think carefully and try to build your lease deal predicated on the premise that the landlord will pay for these kinds of improvements to his or her property.
5. Optimal management size (how much space can you handle with your current management team as you have envisioned it? When will you have to increase management?).

WHAT ABOUT ZONING?

You have found a location you like. It has possibilities. If it's been used for the preparation and sale of foods for takeout, or better yet, has included consumption of foods on the premises, then you can reasonably assume that your concept will meet the zoning test. However, if you are bringing food use to a space that has not previously housed it, then you need to educate yourself about local zoning rules and regulations.

Zoning is a city or other municipality's way of ensuring that certain types of buildings and neighborhoods are dedicated for what they consider to be appropriate usage. The broad categories of zoning are *residential, commercial,* and *industrial.* Within these are various subcategories, each of which imposes limitations on the types of residential units, retail or office use (commercial), and types of manufacturing that can be done within these areas.

When looking at new commercial space for your venture, it is important to find out what zoning restrictions may apply to the area or building you are inter-

> **Quick Checklist for the Initial Real Estate Search**
> 1. Size of space
> 2. Condition of space
> 3. Utilities that service the space
> 4. Any building restrictions placed on space that would limit retrofitting you need to do to suit your business
> 5. Accessibility to major thoroughfares, freeways
> 6. Parking
> 7. Complementarity of business environment
> 8. Cost
> 9. Competition of similar businesses in the immediate area

ested in. Two common zoning issues arise with food service businesses. The first necessitates that you understand the difference between food processing and food manufacturing. You may begin small with a particular signature line of food being produced in your kitchens. If that line "takes off," you may wish to produce it on a larger scale, perhaps for wholesale distribution. Two questions come up: Will your space be able to accommodate increased production? Will such production cause you to cross the line from food processing to manufacturing in the eyes of the zoning authorities, thus placing you in violation of the zoning codes under which your location operates?

The second zoning issue is similar. Although you may start your business with limited eat-in consumption of your foods, the demand could grow due to increased commercial activities and office occupancy in your area. With increased demand, you may see the opportunity to expand your offerings and wish to serve alcohol (or wine or beer), which was not part of your plan when you launched the business. Will the zoning regulations stand in your way?

To address these and other issues, when going out to look for space it is important to first consider how your business may expand (from light food processing to larger-scale manufacturing, or from an exclusively take-out operation to a full service café where you may want to offer alcoholic beverages to your customers), and then communicate these business possibilities to your broker or real estate agent.

LOCATION AS MARKETING

Where your business is located is the first advertising message you put out to your customers about who you are and what kind of product or service you are offering. Think about this: would it make sense for a full-service supermarket to be located in a commuter rail station, or would a convenience store be more appropriate? The value of a product or service offered through a new business will be judged by the business' location. Think about your business goals and then think about the demographics and other obvious characteristics of the areas you are investigating. Do they jibe? If they do, you have a good shot at being successful in that location; if they don't, you could be perceived as "schizophrenic," according to Andrew M. Johnson, of Johnson Commercial Brokerage in Los Angeles, author of *Tough Times, Tough Tactics: The Tenant's Guide to Leasing Retail and Restaurant Space*, an excellent primer on finding the right location for the potential retailer.

Who Are Your Customers?

It's important to remember that your success in business depends on how easy and enticing you make it for your customers to spend money at your store. So you really want to understand and focus on their needs. Above all, you have to make shopping a convenient and rewarding part of their lifestyle. Will they enter your store having planned to come in for a predetermined list of items or will they be buying on impulse? Is the scope of your offerings large enough or unique enough to make you a destination store that attracts customers from miles around? Or are you targeting customers who are impulse driven and attracted to you because you are more accessible (better parking, faster in and out) than the guy down the street selling a similar line?

To consider the answer to these questions, think about the difference between a gas station or dry cleaners and an ice cream shop—the first two are places that people seek out for specific services; the latter largely catches people on a whim. The owners of these establishments had to consider which locations would be more likely to attract the customers they were targeting. The same holds true for the specialty food retailer, whose customers are likely to be a mixture of intentional and impulse shoppers. The main issues to consider here are visibility and accessibility. Guaranteed, the more of each of these you want to have, the higher the rent will be. Higher rents, however, are nothing to fear if they enable you to do the business you need to be doing. Conversely, the lowest rent is too high if you are not doing business.

Demographic Studies

We encourage all new business owners to thoroughly research the demographics of the potential business location. The principal questions to ask can be found in the feasibility study questionnaire in Chapter 2. Two primary resources for this information are the local Chamber of Commerce and the Department of Economic Development. There are many additional resources (both on-line and on paper) that a potential business owner can consult to assist with the demographic study. A listing of these is provided in Resources at the back of this book. The main topics to consider are:

- Overall population and breakdown by age of that population
- Traffic studies (foot, car, and public transportation) and analysis of nearby intersections
- Distance from major destinations in area (schools, hospitals, shopping centers, movie theaters, etc.)
- Current services available to the local population that are most like your proposed business
- Information about area growth
- Number of residents versus people who work in the area during normal business hours
- Average highest educational level of residents and workers in the area
- Average household income (residential areas)
- Per capita income
- Rough estimate of disposable income of local clientele (both residential and commercial)

Special Needs of Food Service Businesses

When all of the other major considerations about a prospective location are settled in your mind (visibility, image, parking/access to transportation, demographics, etc.), it is then time to consider the configuration of the proposed space to see if it is appropriate for food service. Some of the first questions to ask the broker or agent are:

1. Has this space ever been used for food service before?
2. If so, what type of food service business was here before? What did they cook, manufacture, and sell on premises?
3. If there has not been a food service business here in the past, are there zoning, fire, or landlord restrictions about what may be produced in the space?
4. If the space is either new or previously occupied by a nonfood tenant, how feasible is it to do the necessary construction, including the installation of

required equipment, that would allow the new business owner to comply with building and health department regulations?

5. Is the landlord willing to contribute to the capital improvements in order for the space to be able to be used for food service? Is the landlord willing to offer free rent for a period of six to nine months or more while the construction is taking place?

6. Are there adequate services coming into the building or space? (These include electricity, gas, water, sewer, and possible heat sources.) An architect or contractor can reliably provide you with answers to this question.

7. The most important and expensive construction/equipment issue to consider is the hood/ventilation system and ductwork for exhausting these to the outside. It is important to consult the local health department (and/or building and fire department) about regulations for this and *first* check out how much this will cost you before entering into serious negotiations with a landlord. Establishing this new service is the most challenging and, often, complicated issue of construction for a new food service venture. In buildings of more than one story, establishing hood and ventilation systems can be prohibitively expensive. So think twice before signing a lease on raw space that requires you to design, construct, and install these.

8. If you are serious about building out a previously-unused-for-food-service space, engage the services of an architect, contractor and/or consultant who comes to you highly recommended to review the space with you before any major decisions are made. In addition to the checklist of equipment and compliance issues, there are often subtleties of how a space is laid out, ceiling height, general location and visibility, and existing services that they will be able to access for you in terms of your budget, time line, concept, and target market. As a new business owner, you cannot be expected to have the expertise required to evaluate at first glance all of the interconnecting features of a space. If your gut reaction says, "Yes, this is a space that has potential for my business," overrule your heart and use your head. Rely on professionals to examine the space from all angles and let their input figure in your decision-making process.

TOURING POTENTIAL SITES

It is finally time to take a look at some of the spaces you and your broker have "scoped out" for your new business. While you need time to look at each space carefully, it is recommended that you tour many spaces and go back to the ones that appeal to you the most: Multiple visits yield varying impressions, particularly if they occur at different times of the day. A half-hour initial inspection is sufficient for each new site. Furthermore, you will not only want to get a look at the interior of the available space, but also at its locale, neighboring businesses, general traffic flow, type and number of potential customers in the general vicinity. Stake out a spot, take notes (from your car, across the street from the space, in an adjacent parking lot to "your store's" probable entrance, wherever you have the widest view of the passing scene) and literally count bodies, keeping track of how long you have been observing for comparison's sake.

Take notes throughout the whole process. What do you see as you approach the potential site? From about a half mile away, how would you describe the neighborhood? From a quarter mile? From a block? Are there significant changes you perceive as you travel these distances, and what do these tell you? Are neighboring businesses, homes, and other properties well-maintained? Is the potential site remarkable in any way (architecturally, visible from the street, freeway, or highway; is it obviously out of scale with the rest of the buildings in the area?)

If you arrive by foot, is the store easily accessible from the nearest cross street and/or street level? If you arrive by car, is it easy to park? If located in a major metropolitan center, what about the site's proximity to public transportation? How do people arrive at the neighboring businesses? Is all or most of the available parking used up by these businesses' customers? What, if any, other parking is available in the immediate area?

Is there construction nearby or work being done to the streets? If so, how long will this continue and what might be the potential benefits or drawbacks to your business during and after the work is done? If possible, talk to other merchants in the area and get a feel for how they are reacting to the construction. Is it proceeding on schedule or have there been unexplainable delays that may continue even after you have taken the space?

Consider the space itself: Is it well-maintained? What's on either side of the space if located in a strip center or row of stores? What is the space currently being used for? If is it vacant, for how long has it been empty? What happened to the previous tenant? Can you see your concept in this space? What are the entryway and display areas like? What is the accessibility for deliveries? Is there 24-hour access to the space? What's the lighting like? What about the general condition— tiles, walls, ceiling, floors, and furniture/fixtures? Look for stained ceilings and walls for potential leaks and puddles of water for potential plumbing problems. How is trash stored? What does the space smell like?

Next, look at the store's layout and customer flow. Does it make sense for the current business there? How will you adapt the space for your concept and projected traffic flow? Are there significant structural elements in the way of necessary or proposed changes (such as platforms, columns, bearing walls)? Are there enough windows to give the space some natural light? Is there ample storage and office space available within the space or nearby? What furniture and fixtures will come with the lease? Do you want these, and if not, what will it cost you to remove them?

What about the general area? Is there an active merchant's association in the area? If so, what are they doing/not doing? What are municipal plans for the area, such as road construction, economic development planned, new homes, and so on? How have the demographics of the area changed in the last five or ten years? Is it in an area that is being gentrified?

Finally, what are the operating expenses for this space? In addition to rent, you will have to consider utilities (gas, electric, water, sewer), telephone, sanitation, required maintenance, property insurance, any common charges or pass-throughs (see below). What incentives will be offered to you for taking this space (construction, rent abatement, cooperative advertising, etc.)?

Again, all the answers to the above should be kept in a notebook or on a comparative worksheet (see Exhibits 5-1 and 5-2) so that you can prepare an initial capital budget with cost-of-space figures that can be plugged into your feasibility study.

EXHIBIT 5-1

LEASING CHECKLIST AND TIME LINE

Developed by Andrew Johnson, the author of *Tough Times Tough Tactics: The Tenant's Guide to Leasing Retail and Restaurant Space*, this form can help you keep track of your location search activity over the long haul, from visiting the first potential site to signing the lease on the space you select. *Reprinted by permission.*

> **Determine Concept/Establish Parameters** *3 months–1 year*

Start-up budget: $_____   Optimal size: _____ sq. ft

Monthly budget: $_____   Parking requirements_____

Secure financing: _____

Building type preference: _____

Area preference:_____

Zoning concerns: _____

> **Site Location (compile building survey and tour available sites)** *1–3 months*

Top three location choices: 1. _____

2. _____

3. _____

> **Negotiations** *1–2 months*

	Location 1	Location 2	Location 3
First proposal date	_____	_____	_____
Final agreement date	_____	_____	_____
Build-out estimate	$_____	$_____	$_____
Effective rate	$_____	$_____	$_____

> **Lease Preparation, Review, and Summary** *1–2 months*

Base rent: $_____   Size: _____ sq. ft   NNN/CAM costs: $ _____

Increases: _____   Pro-rata share: _____%   Parking: _____

Percentage rent: _____   Term:_____   Exclusives:_____

Begins: _____   Lease starts: _____   Restrictions: _____

Statements due: _____   Free rent: _____   Business hours:_____

Improvements:

   Landlord: _____

   Tenant:_____

Signs: _____

Landlord approval required: _____

Options:_____

> **Build-Out of the Space** *1–6 months*

Plans drawn: _____   Contractor hired: _____   Schedule:_____

Permits obtained: _____   Cost estimate: _____   Inspections:_____

EXHIBIT 5-2

DETERMINING EFFECTIVE RATES

When selecting a location, it helps to see the results of your search lined up side by side. The following form will help you organize your findings. It also was developed by Andrew Johnson, in *Tough Times Tough Tactics. Reprinted by permission.*

Once you feel you have negotiated as much as possible from the landlords of buildings where you have submitted proposals, it is time to compute the economic differences between the various offers. Reducing these offers to their effective rates is the best method for making such a comparison, since the effective rate is your bottom line cost per square foot per month. Use this worksheet to accurately compare the financial aspects of each building.

	Building 1	Building 2	Building 3
Building/Center Name	_____	_____	_____
Building Address	_____	_____	_____
Size of Space Under Consideration	_____	_____	_____

Include in each total annual payment the base rent, free rent, parking costs, increases, operating expenses, etc.

	Building 1	Building 2	Building 3
Total Annual Payments—Year 1	$_____	$_____	$_____
Total Annual Payments—Year 2	$_____	$_____	$_____
Total Annual Payments—Year 3	$_____	$_____	$_____
Total Annual Payments—Year 4	$_____	$_____	$_____
Total Annual Payments—Year 5	$_____	$_____	$_____
Total Annual Payments—Year 6	$_____	$_____	$_____
Total Annual Payments—Year 7	$_____	$_____	$_____
Total Annual Payments—Year 8	$_____	$_____	$_____
Total Annual Payments—Year 9	$_____	$_____	$_____
Total Annual Payments—Year 10	$_____	$_____	$_____
Aggregate Value of Your Lease	$_____	$_____	$_____
Estimated Cost to Improve the Space	$_____	$_____	$_____
Effective Rate/sq ft/Month	$_____	$_____	$_____

= Aggregate Value

+ Improvement Cost Estimate

÷ Square Footage

÷ Total Months in Lease Term

TYPES OF LEASES

The main difference between the types of leases offered on various spaces is the participation of the landlord in paying for aspects of the building's overhead. Among the issues most linked to particular types of leases are: property taxes, insurance, repairs, management fees, maintenance, utilities, building services, and sanitation and security expenses. Who pays for what under various types of lease can be summarized as follows:

| Expense | Type of Lease | | | | |
	Full Service/ Gross	Modified Gross	Net	Double Net	Triple Net (NNN)
Taxes	Landlord	Landlord and tenant	Tenant	Tenant	Tenant
Insurance	Landlord	Landlord and tenant	Landlord	Tenant	Tenant
Repairs	Landlord	Landlord and tenant	Landlord	Landlord	Tenant
Management fees	Landlord	Landlord and tenant	Landlord	Landlord	Tenant
Maintenance	Landlord	Landlord and tenant	Landlord	Tenant	
Utilities	Landlord	Landlord and tenant	Tenant	Tenant	Tenant
Building services	Landlord	Landlord and tenant	Landlord	Landlord	Tenant
Sanitation/ security	Landlord	Landlord and tenant	Tenant	Tenant	Tenant

Typically, one-story buildings that are rented to a primary retail tenant will be leased on a triple net lease basis, and the tenant will be responsible for all of the building's operating expenses. When the building space is divided among multiple tenants, particularly with a combination of commercial and residential tenants (such as in cities and town centers), the lease terms lean toward a modified gross lease basis, where the landlord pays the lion's share of the building's operating expenses and only the *increases* in these expenses over the lease period are passed on to the tenants. A triple net lease has a lower base rent with higher pass-throughs. Other types of leases lean incrementally toward a higher rental with few to no pass-throughs. Exhibit 5-3 shows, in simplified form, what a standard lease might look like, while Exhibit 5-4 covers subletting provisions.

EXHIBIT 5-3

SHORT FORM OF LEASE

Here is a sample short lease illustrating all of the main points that any lease should contain.

Lease Agreement, made between _____ (Landlord) and
_____ (Tenant).

For good consideration, it is agreed between the parties as follows:

1. Landlord hereby leases and rents to Tenant the premises described as follows: Described leased premises, including a floor plan that shows the leased space in relationship to other leased spaces).

2. The Lease shall be in effect for a term of _____ years, commencing on _____, 19__, and terminating on _____, 19___.

3. Tenant shall pay Landlord the annual rent of $_____ during said term, in monthly payments of $_____ payable monthly in advance.

4. Tenant shall at its own expense provide the following utilities: _____.

5. Tenant further agrees that:

   (a) Upon the expiration of the lease it will return possession of the leased premises in its present condition, reasonable wear and tear and fire casualty excepted. Tenant shall commit no waste to the leased premises.

   (b) It shall not assign or sublet or allow any other person to occupy the leased premises without Landlord's prior written consent.

   (c) It shall not make any material or structural alterations to the leased premises without Landlord's prior written consent.

   (d) It shall comply with all building, zoning, and health codes and other applicable laws for said leased premises.

   (e) It shall not conduct a business deemed extra hazardous, a nuisance, or requiring an increase in fire insurance premiums. Tenant warrants the leased premises shall be used only for the following type of business (describe in detail your intended operation and be sure that both the Landlord and local fire and Building and Safety departments agree to the installation and use of all cooking equipment you will need to carry out your food preparation plans): _____.

   (f) In the event of any breach of the payment of rent or any other allowed charge, or other breach of this lease, Landlord shall have full rights to terminate this Lease in accordance with state law and reenter and claim possession of the leased premises, in addition to such other remedies available to Landlord arising from said breach.

   (g) This Lease shall be binding upon and inure to the benefit of the parties, their successors, assigns and personal representatives.

6. Additional leased terms (insert here as applicable): _____

Landlord Signature _____

Tenant Signature _____

Signature subscribed and affirmed, or sworn to, before me in the county of _____

State of _____ Date _____

EXHIBIT 5-4

ASSIGNMENT OF LEASE

As part of the provisions of your lease agreement with your landlord, you should negotiate to include a provision that will allow you to sublet your space in the unfortunate event that you (and your partners, if applicable) can no longer operate the business. Such an agreement will look something like this.

Assignment of lease by and between _____ (Tenant) and _____

(Sub-Tenant), and _____ (Landlord).

For good consideration, it is agreed by and between the parties that:

1. Tenant hereby assigns, transfers and delivers to Sub-Tenant all of Tenant's rights in and to a certain lease between Tenant and Landlord for certain premises know as: (Describe exact location; include a floor plan showing the relation of the space to other retail spaces in the building, if applicable)
   under lease dated _____, 19__. (Lease)
2. Sub-Tenant agrees to accept said Lease, pay all rents and punctually perform all of Tenant's obligations under said Lease accruing on and after the date of delivery of possession to the Sub-Tenant as contained herein. Sub-Tenant further agrees to indemnify and save harmless the Tenant from any breach of Sub-Tenant's obligations hereunder.
3. The parties acknowledge that Tenant shall deliver possession of the leased premises to Sub-Tenant.
4. Landlord hereby assents to the assignment of lease, provided that:
   (a) Assent to the assignment shall not discharge Tenant of its obligations under the Lease in the event of breach by Sub-Tenant.
   (b) In the event of breach by Sub-Tenant, landlord shall provide Tenant with written notice of same and Tenant shall have full rights to commence all actions to take over possession of the leased premises (in the name of Landlord, if necessary) and retain all rights for the duration of said Lease provided it shall pay all accrued rents and cure any other default.
   (c) There shall be no further assignment of lease without prior written consent of Landlord.
5. This agreement shall be binding upon and inure to the benefit of the parties, their successors, assigns and personal representatives' landlord.

Tenant Signature _____ Date _____

Sub-Tenant Signature _____ Date _____

Landlord Signature _____ Date _____

Signature subscribed and affirmed, or sworn to, before me in the county of _____

State of _____ Date _____

SHOULD I BUY AN EXISTING BUSINESS OR BUILD AND START ONE FROM SCRATCH?

An entrepreneur's search for real estate to establish his/her new venture often leads to finding someone else's business for sale. Although perhaps not the original plan, it is often worth a look into what could be a sound investment, leading to fewer headaches and a quicker way to enter the market. On the other hand, you could be buying someone else's problems. How to tell?

As with any planning phase of opening a business, research and dedication to finding out all you can and evaluating that information is the way to begin. As with all other significant stages to business development, there are professionals out there to help you if you feel you don't want to or can't go it alone: Business brokers, consultants, and some real estate professionals can help you evaluate whether buying someone else's business is the smartest decision for you.

The first things to consider are:

1. What is the asking price of the business? How did the current owners arrive at that price? (Be sure to ask them to back up their asking price.)
2. Will the owner finance the purchase of his/her business? If not, what are alternate forms of financing available to you?
3. What is the time left on the current lease? (One standard "knock-out criteria" is a lease length of less than five years. It is never worth it for a food service business to have this short a lease; there is just too much capital investment involved. Will the landlord give an extension or new lease upon sale to you of the business at that location?)
4. What are the business' current sales and net profit before taxes? Ask for audited records from the business owner's accountant.
5. What assets and inventory are included in the sale, and what is excluded? (Make sure you understand which pieces of equipment are owned and which are leased by the current operator.)
6. Will you have to assume the debts and liabilities of the business upon buying it? (This is often an issue that is negotiated in the making of the deal.)
7. Are you paying for the location and fixtures? Or are you paying for the current business along with a considerable built-in customer base and good will? (If you are going to establish a new concept in that location, you will want to consider carefully how much the latter is worth to you.)

Other things to ask for from the current business owner:

1. When was the business last appraised? This should be part of the purchase process.
2. Make sure you get a noncompete clause. This prevents the current business owner from going across the street or corridor (or some other specified distance from your location) to open a business that would compete with yours.
3. What are the real reasons the current owner is selling? After showing some serious interest in buying the business, you may be able to read more clearly between the lines. Don't get "stuck" on any emotional attachment you may have developed to the current business owner or the location.

What are the "standard measures" used to evaluate the asking price? This is perhaps the question most often asked by an entrepreneur looking to buy an existing business, and even a previously fixtured business that is no longer operating. As in much of business, there is no foolproof formula. Some people say to take a look at current sales and come up with a formula based on that. Others say take a look at what the cost would be to you of building and stocking a store like the one you are looking at, and add on a percentage for time and energy spent to open the doors. Some would say add on another percentage for good will and an established customer base (harder to calculate and harder still to rely on). Our recommendation is to take a look at all of the above. Lay your findings out in a chart or worksheet after thinking about this way of getting started in business. When all is said and done, do you like the idea of recreating something that had a previous life? Does the work of attracting a public who may have been turned off by the previous owner's operation appeal to you? How does the purchase of an already-fixtured business change your capital needs to get in business? Will you be compromising your concept, image, and overall vision by locating where someone else has failed or only moderately succeeded? As with other significant business decisions, seek the help of your team members—architect, consultant, lawyer, accountant. Each of these professionals has the knowledge base and experience to assist you with the objective evaluation.

Checklist for Freestanding Sites to Be Net Leased or Purchased

1. Dimensions and total square footage of site
2. Linear feet of site frontages
3. Distance and direction from nearest major streets
4. Average 24-hour traffic on each frontage street
5. Number of moving traffic lanes past location, widths and medians
6. Traffic controls affecting the site

7. Posted speed limits of adjacent streets

8. On-street parking

9. Parking requirements of proposed establishment

10. Landscaping and setback requirements for parking lot

11. Topography as regards necessary grading, slope characteristics, streams, brooks, ditches, and flood conditions

12. Type of soil (natural, undisturbed, loose fill, compacted fill, etc.)

13. Drainage and maintenance of drainage

14. Existing structures (and fixtures and equipment, if applicable.

15. Type of energy available (type of gas, electric, public services, water, sewer, solar, etc.)

16. Underground utilities

17. Present zoning classification

18. Hours of operation restrictions

19. Use and zoning of adjacent property

20. Building limitations (air rights, basement, etc.)

21. Character of surrounding area (within one mile)

22. Population and income characteristics

23. Agencies requiring plan and building approval:

    (a) Health Department

    (b) Building Department

    (c) Fire Department

    (d) Water Authority

    (e) Transportation Department

    (f) Environmental Protection Agency

    (g) Local Planning Commission (including Historic Preservation Agencies)

    (h) Consumer Affairs

24. Ability to annex existing building

25. Signage—existing and potential

    (a) Pole

    (b) Building

    (c) Electric

    (d) Remote/street-side

    (e) Billboards

    (f) Stringent restrictions on new signage

26. Building codes
    (a) Building
    (b) Mechanical (electrical)
    (c) Plumbing
    (d) Fire
    (e) ADA (Americans with Disability Act)
27. Area competition (within one mile)
28. Offering price
29. Fees due brokers or agents

EVALUATE BEFORE MAKING YOUR MOVE

Successful retailers may have differing views on which product lines to carry in their stores, how to train their personnel, or how much advertising they need to do to bring the public to their door. On one thing, however, they agree: the importance of location. No single factor in the development of your business concept and implementation of your business plan is more crucial. Your concept has no life without a location—the location makes it real. All the planning in the world about how you will display your wares or outfit your employees or equip your production kitchen means nothing if you have not matched your concept to the "right" location. Think of the right location as the very air your retail business needs to survive and thrive. Location and concept are inseparable parts of the equation for success.

After you have narrowed your selection of locations down to the top three, plug the rental figures into your feasibility study and get the opinions of professionals, friends, and family. The final decision, however, ultimately rests with you and your partners, if any. You need to know that you can live with your decision at least for the first term of the lease. You have to believe that the demographic profile you have studied makes sense for your concept. You also have to be ready to call that space you have chosen a second (in many cases a first) home, a place where you will be content to spend many hours, much energy, and lots of money to actualize your dream. After all the analysis has been done and all the experts called in, you have to feel good about the space you have rented (or the business you have purchased). Then the next step is to proceed with all detailed planning, hiring, buying and building, secure in the knowledge that your concept can now be created in three dimensions.

The initial search for the right home for your business is part and parcel of carrying out your feasibility study. It's an inseparable part of your initial business planning. Just as that famous musician, when asked how he got to Carnegie Hall, said, "Practice! Practice! Practice!" the successful retailer, when asked for a three-word prescription for success, answered, "Location! Location! Location!" Your location is very nearly the only thing about your business that you cannot change (unless you move!), and no serious compromises should be made when selecting a site.

BUILDING THE DREAM: TURNING A RAW SPACE INTO RETAIL REALITY

You can't do it alone. Let us take a look at the help you'll need (architect, designer, contractor), and at when to bring them on board.

You've found the location of your dreams, either in a freestanding structure, strip mall, or revitalized downtown district. Now the task is to turn this site into a workable space suited to the needs of your planned business. To accomplish this, you have several alternatives.

The first alternative is to design it yourself (with the help of a kitchen equipment supplier). Be aware, however, that you do so at risk to your health and sanity. Designing a retail space with food use is a tricky business with all the overlapping jurisdictions of permitting agencies, the needs to fit vital equipment into the space to accomplish profit-making centers of production. Every detail counts. All I's must be properly dotted and T's crossed. Things to consider when planning your store include: surfaces for flooring and ceilings, display fixtures (fixed vs. movable), lighting, signage, and display equipment including dry and refrigerated showcases. Those showcases, in particular, should be chosen carefully; making sure that they are easily maintained, that replacement parts can be easily obtained if and when you need them, and, perhaps most important, that sightlines are good so customers can easily see what's inside. Be aware of the position of the cases in relationship to both natural sunlight and artificial lighting within the store. Glare can be a real problem, but it's easily avoided if you plan properly. Also be sure that your selection of location for cases does not conflict with heating or air conditioning output, which can cause your cases to lose temperature and consequently affect shelf life of products contained within them.

Your second alternative is to hire a design firm to work up some rough schematic plans. Most design firms subcontract out some part of the design for the build-out. Get a clear understanding of what this firm will and will not be doing for you.

The third possibility is to hire a general contractor who takes care of hiring the tradesmen and supervising all the work that needs to be done to transform raw space into finished retail footage.

In our experience, hiring a design firm is the best way to go. The services they render can range from simple, short-term involvement in your project to full-scale design, fixturizing, and project coordination. However, no matter which route you choose, you will be confronted with the same set of issues. And these boil down to making the space work for you balanced against meeting all local building and safety codes, including access for handicapped customers and/or employees, health department regulations, life safety and fire department requirements. These two goals can often seem mutually exclusive; however, since you must resolve permit issues in order to proceed, it's best to explore up front how your plan will square with the requirements spelled out by the relevant permitting agencies. Solutions can and must be found before you proceed.

There are a few major governmental agencies who get into the act: the local building and safety department, health department, and fire department. If you're choosing to open in a historic district, the codes can often be restrictive. Likewise, opening and operating in a mall normally involves adhering to rigid design guidelines including prescriptions for signage, the overall look of your storefront, guidelines about awnings, protruding signs, allowable materials for surfaces, specifics about size and configuration of exits and entrances, and so on.

Using a designer allows you to place the responsibility on the shoulders of an individual whose job it is to navigate the shoals of design and construction, finding solutions—often compromises—that satisfy you as the client as well as your prospective landlord and all the permitting agencies involved in the process. For this service, expect to pay design professionals from $25 to $125 per hour, depending on their level of seniority in a design firm; principals and partners in a firm command the highest rate and space planners and junior designers charge the lowest hourly rate. In any case, it is money well spent.

Furthermore, if your goals reach beyond a single location, your first store could well become the prototype for others to follow, in which case appearance counts for a lot. Your corporate identity is based on a well-thought-out design scheme. Memorable graphics and a strong logo design also help to build customer identification.

Any good designer should have a track record designing successful spaces. You should interview several and get some referrals before hiring anyone. Once having hired a designer (who should at this point visit and evaluate the space you are renting or buying), you will have the opportunity to discuss your business goals, budget, and time line in depth with that person. Then, you should expect to receive some preliminary sketches which will help to focus your concept further. Inevitably many questions will be raised at this point, which will be answered along the way before firm sketches and plans are produced. Then based on further collaboration with the designer, you should begin to arrive at working drawings (see Exhibit 5-5). These in turn will lead to contract documents, which are the actual detailed plans from which subcontractors (electricians, plumbers, kitchen designers) will bid on your project. (Exhibit 5-6 shows the sort of lease agreement you might encounter at this stage.)

Once on board, your designer and contractor must draw up a plan, including a complete renovation budget and time line. It would be wise of you to give both the designer and contractor copies of your business plan, with the section on concept and capitalization highlighted. Don't forget: you have been walking around with your plan and every detail of how your business will be executed, from menu to logo to the tile on the floor, but new members of your team will not have that same vision—at least not right away. In order to get the most out of your development team, be sure to spend some time getting them fully on your side and "in your head." Impress upon them that staying on budget is imperative, and schedule bi-weekly budget meetings where progress on the build-out is compared to the project time line and budget. This admittedly often tedious process will undoubtedly get your team to focus on the parameters that you have the right, as owner, to set. These meetings are nothing more than status reports, yet nothing is clearer than dollars and cents noted in black and white: get your contractor and designer to present reports of what has been spent and what expenses are coming up so that you retain control. Undoubtedly certain projected expenses will be higher than anticipated. The purpose of the team meetings is to create a strategy for staying on budget overall and may require the team to approach upcoming tasks with different possibilities for solutions. To further reinforce the budget process, it is not uncommon to offer financial incentives to stay on budget and on time!

Exhibit 5-5

Floor Plans of Two Specialty Food Stores

The following floor plans illustrate how two different-sized spaces in New York City can accommodate multidepartment specialty food businesses. The first depicts the plan of Flavors, a gourmet take-out and catering establishment, operating out of a challenging L-shaped 900-sq-ft space. The second shows the plan for Grassroots, an upscale natural foods store with two floors of selling space; one at street level, measuring 3,200 sq ft, the other (not shown) below grade, selling nonfood items including natural toiletries, housewares, accessories, and other hard goods. The two plans are characterized by a combination of self-serve and counter service areas.

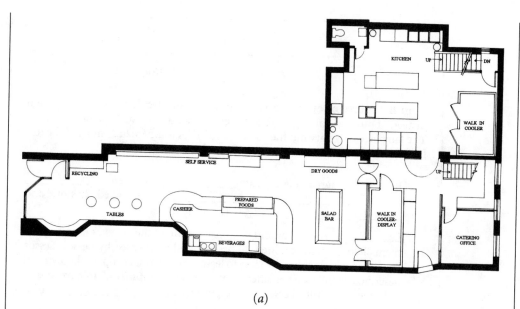

(a)

Reprinted courtesy Pamela Morgan, Flavors.

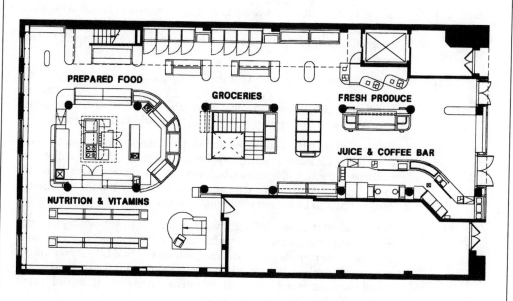

(b)

Reprinted courtesy Michael Fox, Grassroots.

EXHIBIT 5-6

LEASE OF PERSONAL PROPERTY

If, in the course of operating your business, you decide to lease equipment instead of buying it outright, you may encounter a form such as the following. The language may vary but the basic provisions should include most of the following terms.

1. Parties: This agreement is made _____, 19__, between _____ of _____, herein called "Lessor," and _____, herein called "Lessee."

2. Lease of Equipment: For and in consideration of the covenants and agreements hereinafter contained, to be kept and performed by Lessee, Lessor has leased and does hereby lease to lessee the personal property known and described as follows: hereafter designated as "equipment," to have and to hold the same unto Lessee for the period of _____ months commencing from _____.

3. Delivery and return of property: Lessee shall deliver equipment to _____, freight prepaid. At the end of the term thereof Lessee shall return equipment freight prepaid to Lessor at the place from which equipment was shipped in as good condition as exists at the commencement of the term, reasonable wear and tear in respect thereto excepted.

4. Rent: Lessee shall pay as rent for the leasing the sum of $_____ at the office of Lessor at _____ in _____ monthly installments of _____ each, payable in advance of the first day of the month beginning with _____, plus _____ to be paid as last payment.

5. Reservation of Title: Equipment and all parts thereof shall, unless a purchase thereof is made as is herein provided and until full payment of such purchase price and all interest which may be due thereon is made in cash to the Lessor, retain its character as personal property and the title thereto shall not pass to Lessee but shall remain in Lessor.

6. Repossession: If Lessee shall sell, assign or attempt to sell or assign, equipment or any interest therein, or if Lessee defaults in any of the covenants, conditions, or provisions of this Lease, it is agreed that Lessor may immediately and without notice take possession of equipment wheresoever found and remove and keep or dispose of the same and any unpaid rentals shall at once become due and payable.

7. Location and Use. Lessee shall use equipment only in _____ and shall not at any time remove the same _____ except in returning the same to Lessor or except as may be permitted by Lessor by consent thereto in writing.

8. Indemnification of Lessor. Lessee shall and does hereby agree to protect and save Lessor harm against any and all losses or damage to equipment by fire, flood, explosion, tornado or theft and Lessee shall and does hereby assume all liability to any person whomsoever arising from the location, condition or use of equipment, and shall indemnify Lessor of and from all liability, claim and demand whatsoever arising from the location, condition or use of equipment whether in operation or not, and growing out of any cause, and from every other liability, claim and demand whatsoever during the term of this Lease or arising while equipment is in the possession of Lessee. Lessee also agrees to promptly reimburse Lessor, in cash, for any and all personal property taxes levied against equipment and paid by Lessor.

CHAPTER SIX

PUTTING THE PLAN TO WORK, PART I

*Concept, Legal Structure and Compliance,
Graphic Design, Purchasing, and Pricing*

Memoir of a Specialty Food Retailer:
Back in simpler times, some of my fondest food memories from childhood involved trips to the neighborhood deli where a homemade soup or mile-high sandwich on impeccably fresh bread was served by the owner, stained apron and all, who emerged from behind the deli counter to offer up his specialties with a proud smile. The tables may have been rickety and small, but the welcome was large (the owner seemed to know all of his customers and their offspring by name) and the food was delicious. Modern day stores would do well to follow this model and many are doing just that. In a more elaborate guise, they seek to accomplish the same inviting mood and create the same level of customer satisfaction.

—Robert Wemischner

WHAT KIND OF STORE DO YOU INTEND TO OPERATE?

You've thought about, written about, and dreamed about your specialty food store concept for months and months; now comes the time when you must put the plan into action. Your task now is to physically create what you have up until this point only been able to do on paper. The first steps to this are behind you: You have come up with an idea that is realistic and gotten the money to start; you

> Marshall McKenzie, owner of the Book and Gourmet Gift Gallery, Midlothian, VA, offers this advice: "In the food business, just as in the book business, you need to always remember to not let your personal taste get in the way of being a smart business person. You should not stock products because you like the image they give to your store—you should stock products because your customers want to buy them."

> Frank Cardullo, owner of Cardullo's, Cambridge, MA, says that: "Listening to your customers is all important. You can't stuff down their throats what you want to sell. You have to sell what they want."

have selected a site and are now in the process of building it out. Now comes the nitty-gritty of drafting a menu and coming up with a complete list of offerings.

You will question whether to limit selections in your store to only a few categories, like prepared foods, salads, breads and beverages. Or perhaps you will gear up to the high traffic demands of the business lunch, sandwich, and picnic trade. Will you be more ambitious still, and include desserts, shelf items, cheese, gift baskets, cookbooks, and cooking utensils? Your space and location are certainly considerations. But more important, it is your own passion for particular kinds of merchandise that should dictate what your product line will be. Decide on those areas in which you wish to concentrate and grow those areas by devoting all of your time and energy to promotions that count.

Take your cues from the pros like West Point Market's owner Russ Vernon, a pioneering specialty food retailer *par excellence*, who says (*Gourmet News*, April 1995):

> No one person has all the ideas. After 35 years in the retail specialty business, I continue to learn new ways to compete. I remain a student of my business, always listening, reading, asking questions and traveling to wherever I might find answers. Over the years, in my passionate pursuit of those concepts, ideas and innovations, I have found the following tips to be helpful in building my business.
>
> 1. Concentrate on developing higher gross margin ideas that specifically grow your business. Those ideas may include developing a corporate gift business, new products, or a corporate catering business.

2. Move into your profit centers and dominate your market in selected product categories.

3. Sell on value, quality and "knock-your-socks-off" service. Remember, price has no bottom.

4. Develop signature products. They may be a cheese spread, a brownie, a cookie that is unique in some way. Or they may be high quality and aggressive promotion.

5. Take a helicopter view of your business and look down on the total operation. Start with a blank piece of paper. Develop the strengths, weaknesses, opportunities and threats, and work out an action plan.

6. Spend time with your customers. They will tell you what they like, what they don't like, services they would like to see, and products they would like to have. All you have to do is ask.

7. Form a food committee among your staff to dream up new products, lunch box menus, and other food-related projects. Involve and challenge your associates.

8. For prepared foods, stack your plastic containers vertically, largest on the bottom with serving sizes on each container, and pull a colorful ribbon up and tie. Place the stack on the service case so customers can clearly see what size they are ordering.

9. Conduct a simple 10-point customer survey, offered to interested customers by the cash register. Questions should ask what brings you back? What new products, services or features would you like to have?

10. Put a pre-paid comment card in all catering orders that go out, addressed to the owner/manager. Ask if the delivery was on time? How was the presentation? How did you enjoy the food, etc.

11. Make up a thank you card to be sent to customers who have favored you with good business. Thank them for their business and include your business card.

12. Shop your competition. Look for customer needs not being met in your city. Rent a van and take your key people to stores of your type outside your city. Call first, if you can; it will make your visit more informative and not waste your time if the store is hostile to the idea.

13. Have an associate who understands your needs scan the trade magazines for ideas and pass those ideas on to the appropriate people.

14. Throw a party for your staff and showcase your specialty foods for them.

15. Give your delivery van a specialty eye-catching paint job. It will turn heads.

16. Invite a local chef celebrity to your store. Let him bring his menu and prepare one or two of his favorite recipes.

17. Produce your own 90-second radio commercial and talk about what makes your store special. Give background on Balsamic vinegar, and how you like to use it. Talk about chocolates, pastas, peppers and food combinations you like. Make the listener hungry. We use National Public Radio and local classical station, WCLV.

18. Discover the needs in your community and support them. Because our customer base supports the arts, we focus on the cultural aspects of the city and the medical community. By identifying ourselves with our symphony, Ohio Ballet, Art Museum and Cleveland Orchestra, we ride free from time to time in the media.
19. Develop an in-store friendly (newsy) letter for your customers with recipes using specialty foods and exclusives.
20. Retail is detail. Carry a hand-held miniature tape records to capture ideas and note problems needing corrections. Remember the important points.

Don't try to be all things to all people or try to do more than capital or staff can accomplish well. The safest route is to position yourself as the specialist in certain areas, be the best in the field, rather than spread your resources around too thinly and do a less than credible job in product lines that are beyond your reach. Research your client base, decide on a few areas that seem to fit, and then do them impeccably well. Your customers need to know that they can rely on you for the consistent high quality of your offerings. (We prefer to think of this as a process of preselection rather than limitation). A deli case sporting a meager display of small, half-filled bowls is a turn-off to the shopper who buys with the eye first. Make a more tempting visual statement with a smaller variety of items that are abundant, bowls brimming with freshly made, popular fare that turns over quickly and is replenished often throughout the business day to keep it looking fresh and appetizing. Likewise, less than stellar products do your business no good. Don't overreach and you'll go farther faster. Add new lines and add to the in-house production load gradually. As one area is running smoothly, add another. Then revisit the first to fine-tune it and keep it current and vital.

Consider the layout and design of your space carefully; as with the many other crucial planning tests you have already successfully passed, don't overpromise to your future customers (and yourself) what you can squeeze into the store. You know where the kitchen, production, storage areas, retail selling floor, and on-premises eating space will be. You've got a chef in mind (or hired) to head the kitchen operations and have found a manager type who can be groomed to take over some of your responsibilities as time goes on. Given all the known parts of the equation, now's the time to tackle the big unknown. Now's the time to crystallize your concept. As part of that process, you need to answer the big question, "What to sell?" First, let's examine what "concept" means in the world of specialty food retailing.

WHAT DOES "CONCEPT" MEAN?

Perhaps it's easier to define "concept" first in terms of what it's *not*. It's not merely a random selection of disparate products from all over the globe. It's not a scattershot sampling of all the latest trendy "hot" items. It's not a slavish imitation of someone else's store (although there's certainly nothing wrong with borrowing the best elements from other operators around the country to create your "perfect" composite store). As Ari Weinzweig, partner of Zingerman's, a specialty food institution in Ann Arbor, MI, says: "The challenge in business is to find your own way."

Concept *is* a point of view about retailing, which implies a careful selection of products that will fill your store. Making this selection involves an intensive, and somewhat laborious, ongoing search for the best items in each genre. These items are characterized by singularly excellent packaging, flavor, value, and consistency of quality. In order to know which items deserves shelf space in your store, whether large or small, you and your staff have to taste them. Rate them and compare them with other similar items from different producers. Experiment with them so that you can recommend to customers how to use them. You need to speak intelligently about an item's origins, best uses, storage—all selling points that will help to move inventory. Avail yourself of every opportunity to use these goods by cooking with them in your prepared foods section as well.

One Retailer's View

For 14 years Barbara Schwartz has owned Gourmet to Go, a chain of specialty food stores and catering company in St. Louis, MO.

On product offerings: "You have to have enough variety so people don't get bored."

On customers: "It's more important what they get for their dollar than how many dollars they spend."

On distinguishing her business from others: "The key to what we do is that we listen carefully to our customers to learn what they want. We pay attention to their needs. In fact, before Thanksgiving, we do a show and tell where our cooks present the season's foods to our customers and sales staff. It's a win-win situation: Our individual and corporate clients are flattered to get a preview of the season's offerings (many of which result from customer requests) and as an added plus, our employees are well-acquainted with what they will be selling for the holidays."

Any number of high concept stores can be used as examples of how a well-thought-out concept contributes to the success of the enterprise. Zabar's, Fairway Markets, Murray's Cheese Shop, Dean and De Luca (NY), West Point Market (OH), Zingerman's (MI),Vivande Porte Via (CA) all make a memorable statement about quality, scope of product specialization, style, presentation, or some combination of these.

A specialty food store is so much more than a collection of bottles, cans, and packages placed on shelves in neat lines. It's also much more than thirty linear feet of refrigerated display cases filled with a tempting display of prepared foods, appetizers, soups, salads, dressings, sauces, and desserts. A limited or even a broad array of condiments, olives, oils, vinegars, and packaged goods does not a specialty food store make. One visit to the twice yearly NASFT Fancy Food shows and you will be overwhelmed and even bewildered by the staggering amount of specialty food on the market. No one retailer can hope to encompass the full range of specialty foods. Therefore decisions have to made; you as the driving force behind your store must make choices about which lines to carry and which product categories (or specific products) to ignore. With upscale supermarkets devoting more shelf space to specialty foods, it's becoming harder and harder to maintain an exclusive on any product or product line. So how do you distinguish yourself from the crowd? What will be the single, most persuasive attribute of your store that will convince customers to come to you instead of to the other big or small guy in your market area? What will be *your* "hook"? How do you bring them in and persuade them to part with some of their hard-earned disposable income? Once again, there's no straightforward answer.

But the most direct way to address that question is by making a list of the broad categories of foods you intend to sell, including foods prepared on your premises by your staff. Inventory your own expertise. Evaluate the collective strengths of your production, management, and selling team. Think carefully about what kinds of product capture and keep *your* interest. See what's out there in your neighborhood and the neighborhoods within a ten- or twenty-mile radius. Look at the capital you have allotted for inventory. Be clear about who the bulk of your projected clientele will be. Then assign rough percentages to the following:

1. How much can be made in-house?
2. How much can be farmed out or brought in for resale (include here artisanal, hand-produced items from local farmers, cheesemakers, preserve makers, specialty bakers, or confectioners, as well as hand-crafted tableware etc.)?
3. How much space can you allot for production?
4. How much space will you need for storage of inventory?

5. How much space will you use for retail—your selling floor?
   (a) Amount of space for dry, shelf-stable items
   (b) Amount of refrigerated or freezer space for display of perishables

These allotments should total 100% of the business you intend to do and the space in which you'll be working (foods for catering would not be included in your display space calculations, since they're usually not displayed but rather go out the back door). Set this breakdown aside for a few days and then come back to it with fresh eyes and clear perceptions. Discuss it with your partners, your store and kitchen designers, your chef, your manager to be. Does it still sound right and feasible to you? Of course, it can always be modified some after you open. No decision is irrevocable. But the expenses associated with reconfiguring a space can be considerable. So think carefully and long. Remember, too, that the message you present to customers from the start should be a clear one and will define you in their minds. All of the decisions you make about store layout, interior and exterior appearance, product lines, your choice of staff and their attire, logo and display materials create an impression (strong or weak, good or bad) in the minds of your customers. So think carefully about what impression you wish to make.

Let your aesthetic sense take over. How you tell your story in your own personalized way is also a big part of "concept." How you display your wares can be as important as what you are selling. Will your shelving for shelf-stable items be simple metal wiring or beautifully crafted out of wood? Are you more apt to bombard your customers with an abundance of product, stacked from floor to ceiling, with lots of signage throughout the space? Or is a clean, spare, uncluttered look more your style? Will it be a combination of these two extremes? Are you going after the European Old World market or American general store look, using all kinds of knickknacks, dried flowers, and country kitsch to round out the picture? Or do you intend to let the foods provide the color and decoration for your space? Does your budget dictate that your store will remain relatively undecorated and have the look of a warehouse? Are there some particularly unique and beautiful architectural elements (skylights, high ceilings, antique flooring, etc.) preexisting in your space that you can use as focal points for product displays and merchandising?

Concept is tied to space but it's also tied to your own personal tastes about food and your design aesthetic. It's largely dependent on your interest in particular products. Since you cannot be all things to all people, focus on the piece of the picture that you can do confidently and well and you will succeed on the strength and clarity of your vision. Your customers will perceive that you are making a statement by the choices you have made.

Make one clear big statement rather than many weak, diluted, or halfhearted smaller ones. Whether you make your statement by exemplary service, or the depth and breadth of a single product line, or one signature item prepared in-house that is your stock-in-trade, make a statement and take credit for it in all the publicity and promotion that you do. Perhaps your strong suit will be prepared foods or smoked fish or farmhouse artisanal cheeses. Whatever you choose, be the best in the category. As Steve Jenkins says, "Specialize in something." Concentrate all your resources, time, space, and staff training efforts on selling those items in the most comprehensive way possible. That concentration will include educating your consumer about these products. A well-informed consumer is a loyal customer. Impress your customers with the comprehensiveness of your knowledge about the products you sell and they will come back to learn more. That's part of your concept as well.

Are you positioned to be regarded as an authority on a particular segment of specialty foods? Is your store the source for serious cooks wishing to specialize in a particular ethnic cuisine? If you've got it, flaunt it: "We have the largest selection of extra virgin olive oils in the area" and "Our brownies are made with only imported Belgian chocolate, pure butter, and natural flavorings" are just two claims that a confident store owner can make that would set his or her store apart from others in the area.

Put your own personal stamp on the items you sell, whether prepared in-house or bought from outside sources. Wrap, decorate, garnish, be-ribbon, and label in your own way. Be consistent in your use of labels and logos throughout the store so that customers are reminded of where they are at every turn. Make sure, furthermore, that labels, logos, and signage are current, fresh, untattered, not dog-eared or food spattered by overuse.

Concept is also reflected in your attention to detail in your store. Your over-all image is tied to how carefully you can manage the details. The "big picture" is actually made up of many smaller pictures, each of which influences your customers' perceptions of how you do business. Take tours of inspection throughout your store every day at different times throughout the day. Look at the food you prepare. Look at the condition of all the surfaces you use to display and merchandise your product. Point out to your staff areas that need improvement and develop a regular but realistic schedule for maintenance of these crucial areas. Careless presentation or sloppy, wrinkled shirts or unkempt hair on your staff, "dust bunnies" and grime in those hard-to-get-at places along the base of display cases all convey the wrong message to your customers. Customers will have reason to doubt the quality of your foods if the people who sell them don't give the impression that they take pride in their work. As a matter of course, procedures should be spelled out for cleaning and maintaining your store. A regular schedule for cleaning each area in the store, from the bathrooms to the parking lot, from entrances and counters to windows and your stock room, should be instituted and strictly followed. This operational rigor is also part of your concept and makes a strong positive statement to your customers about how you do business.

CONCEPT DICTATES PRODUCT LINE

Certainly if you an ethnic store or a specialist drawing inspiration from the foods of a particular country, your product line is more easily focused and your image is more readily conveyed to the consumer. For example, consider the often stylishly reinvented Italian food stores that have proliferated around the country and are capitalizing on America's love affair with all things Italian. In these, the product line is relatively self-evident: in the refrigerated cases you will most likely find fresh pastas, sauces, pizzas and other prepared dishes hot and/or ready for reheating, prepared antipasti, cured meats (salumeria), cheeses, reworkings of the old submarine sandwich based on the three previous elements, salads, and Italian-inspired desserts; in the freezer, gelato; a self-service display of breads; and on the shelves, dried pastas, olive oils, condiments, imported preserves, and other Italian specialties, both jarred and packaged. This kind of store telegraphs its concept clearly and cleanly to its target market.

The generalist who represents many different ethnic cuisines in its product array may have a harder time conveying to the public a single identity. Think of a store selling some standard, but upscale, American fare, a smattering of Italian, some Mediterranean, some Asian influenced foods and ingredients. Its message is diversity. Which route you take depends again on the demands of your particular market, your own level of interest or expertise in a particular cuisine, and the size of your space and its location in relation to other stores offering similar lines. You may also base at least part of your decision on trends in the food merchandising world, as you perceive them in your market area.

TRENDS COUNT TOO

To a specialty food retailer, trends are not so much a thing as a feeling about what your public will buy. With your eyes and ears open, as the decision maker in your proposed business, you are free to accept and therefore capitalize on trends. However, your public may not adopt these trends with the same enthusiasm as their socioeconomic peers at the other end of the country. You can only learn by testing the waters, tentatively at first, by interspersing a few trendy items here and there on your shelves and in your refrigerated cases. If enough of your public responds by buying these items (careful tracking is essential here), then you will know how seriously you need to ride that trend.

Whether you choose to respond only to certain trends or whether your offerings reflect a response to every major trend and minor ripple in the welter of food fads from reduced fat, lower salt, and organic, to authentic ethnic, higher protein, less meats, more carbohydrates, and less sugary desserts, remember it's your call. You are free to reject and ignore what are characterized as trends in another part of the country. First, though, you need to know your audience. Before making your own statement on trends, you should gather as much information as possible about what the competition is selling. Benefit from others' experience. Read all the food magazines and food sections of your local newspapers attentively and regularly (perfect for bedtime reading). See what's happening in other food venues in your area. Above all, restaurants in your area are often a good index for what your public will buy. You can often gauge how ready your target audience will be to buy into yet another trend from yet another trend-setting part of the country far from your home base before you make the commitment in dollars and space in your store. Carefully comb the food ads in trade journals and in mass market food and lifestyle magazines; look for indications of items you may consider adding to your product line. Often you will see a particular item that strikes a responsive chord in you, appeals to your sensibility, or just seems to fit in with what you perceive reflects your image. But will it catch the fancy of your clientele? Respond by contacting the manufacturer's representative or the producer directly and then sit back while *they* court *you* with information, samples, and other facts and figures upon which you can base an intelligent decision.

As a new retailer, or retailer-to-be, you may be so involved in getting your systems down pat, filling your shelves, educating your staff while they educate your customers that you have little time to explore trends. This is a mistake. It's true that you cannot ignore your *core business*, that basic set of products and services that is your stock-in-trade. These are your bread and butter and must not be compromised for the sake of keeping up with every fad that hits the marketplace. On the other hand, if you have a chef who can make low-fat, low-salt, and low-cholesterol soups or sauces or salads, why not take advantage of that resource? Put some marketing muscle and promotional dollars behind his or her efforts and make that part of your core business also trend setting. Look at every part of your store as a potential site for setting a trend. Who knows? Your homegrown trend may launch a national trend by being the seed of a idea for a product that you manufacture (or subcontract out) and take national. Thinking big while attending to the homefront is not only healthy for a business' growth, it's essential. Balancing your core products and services with your wish to acknowledge trends as you learn about them is also essential.

Listening to customers, tracking their requests, and taking suggestions from your staff will often provide the spark you need to integrate "trendy" items into your product offerings. Then careful customer follow-up is necessary to ensure that they are aware of any new additions of products or services to your line, that they are aware of your responsiveness. This builds a bond between you and your customers and gives them yet another reason to come back to you.

How Big Is Big When It Comes to a Trend?

Sometimes a trend is so big that the influential food press in every newspaper and magazine and every other cookbook seem to be exploiting it. (Think of oat bran or fresh pasta a few years ago, specialty coffees or mesclun salad greens today.) Trends that revolve around a single item, however, are often not sustainable. These are often fad foods, such as kiwi fruit or sun-dried tomatoes, which find their way into the cuisine of every celebrated chef around the country.

At other times a trend is regional in origin at first, prevailing in only one part of the country followed by a more generalized influence later. As a retailer, you need to pay attention to opportunities that exploit trends within the context of an ongoing product promotion. For example, perhaps you have read about a new coordinated line of vinegars and oils that are beautifully packaged, taste great, and are priced competitively with others that already sell well in your store. If you have a tasting program already in place and all of your staff are prepared to promote particular products as part of their everyday routine, then the cost of adding a new line may be relatively small—no big risks and some potential gain. Furthermore, you will be projecting the image of a retailer who is at the forefront of new product merchandising.

Trends Fueled with Someone Else's Efforts—and Money

Trends in foods that cannot and should not be ignored are often catalyzed by the food boards of a particular country (i.e., the cheesemakers of a foreign country wishing to increase that country's influence in a particular market) or by a trade board rooted in a particular segment of food production in this country. In these cases, the retailer merely has to join the bandwagon by stocking some of that product. The promotional muscle of those agencies then takes over with a marketing campaign that often includes strategic placement of their product in the hands of the food press, who then stimulate interest even further. In a well-orchestrated campaign, the trade board or other commercial entity helps you to spread the word with point of purchase materials that you can use to enhance your displays. A lot of the consumer awareness raising is done at someone else's expense. These are trends that the savvy specialty food retailer can't afford to disregard.

LICENSES AND PERMITS, LEGAL STRUCTURE, AND COMPLIANCE

Next we look at the process of navigating the thicket of business licenses, permits, resale numbers, and sales and use tax regulations before you open your doors.

While specifics will vary according to your location, wherever you're opening your business you will need to apply for a business license and need to have your building plans and, later, your completed space inspected. Once you are open, you will be subject to periodic site inspections by the local health department. In the web that is Los Angeles, where one of the authors owned and operated a specialty food store for ten years from the mid-1970s to the mid-1980s, city and county officials each had permitting authority (and a hand out for licensing fees), and overlapping jurisdictions made matters even more complicated.

Beware! The service of foods for consumption *on premises,* as distinct from takeout, often requires meeting a completely different set of requirements. Be prepared to upgrade and renovate your space accordingly. Parking and bathrooms are often the key sticking points in turning a takeout into an eat-in location. Check this out with local authorities before proceeding, as violating local codes can have a devastating effect on your operations, so much so, in fact, that you could be shut down. Check and check again before doing anything to your new space. Later it is important to be mindful of tax ramifications for different segments of your business. In most states, foods consumed on the premises, whether hot or cold, are subject to sales tax.

Allow plenty of time for processing legal papers (city or county inspectors have been known to call a halt to all operations in a business that was about to open due to a missing piece of information on a business license application). Building inspectors or health department inspectors have the right to prevent you from opening (or worse, yet, close you down) if, for example, the coping on the floor in your kitchen does not conform to standards. Check and double check that all your paperwork is in order *before* opening. Much of this responsibility, of course, will fall within the purview of your designer, general contractors, and builders, but it helps for you to show these hired hands that you wish to stay on top of things at all stages of the build-out process. You don't need any surprises at this point.

Compliance: Dotting All Your I's and Crossing All Your T's

In the course of first opening and then operating your business, you will be responsible for applying for, completing, and filing in a timely manner many forms, licenses, and reports to various branches of the local, state, and federal governments. What follows here is a fairly comprehensive list of these varying compliances, when to first file for them, when regular reports will need to be filed, and the appropriate government agency with whom to file. In some cases a different government office may handle these matters in the state in which you incorporate your business. A general rule of thumb: If it pertains to daily operations, start at the local level and then inquire "up" the ladder to seek the proper filing office; if it pertains to taxes, start federal and go down to find the correct branch with which to file.

Pre-opening—Incorporation

Deciding whether your company will be structured as a Sole Proprietorship, a Sub-chapter S Corporation, a C-Corporation, a General Partnership, or a Limited Liability Corporation will be a matter of who heads your company, whether you have partners, whether you want or need the profits and/or losses to flow directly to your personal taxes, and the level of protection (against lawsuits, etc.) you feel you need to operate the new business. Consult an accountant to explain the differences to you and the pros and cons of the many different forms of business structure. It is possible to incorporate as one type of business at first and then switch later, but this almost always confuses the government and filing will become more complicated this way. Better to decide what is really best for you and your partners, now and for your projected growth, and apply as such.

The actual incorporation is in the form of an application to the state, which is a routine task for an attorney. Even if you haven't chosen an attorney to represent you in other business matters, it doesn't cost much to hire one to handle the business' incorporation, and it usually guarantees that the process will go through without a hitch.

As an incorporated business you have the responsibility to file regular tax forms with the appropriate state, city, and Federal (IRS) offices of taxation. Your local city and state may have a base filing fee, either quarterly or yearly (check with your accountant or local state and city offices) which you will have to pay, whether you are open for business or not; these are usually very minor fees. If you are opening as a sole proprietorship, you may file through your personal income tax return. In the start-up phase you will need proof of your status of incorporation for many licenses and various business applications, so it usually doesn't pay to wait to incorporate to try to avoid minor basic filing expenses.

Upon incorporation in your state, you must apply to the federal government (the office of the IRS), which will issue you a Federal Tax ID number. This is the number that you will use on *all* of your tax filings, bank and credit applications, and a host of other operating necessities. It becomes more important and useful to you as a business than a social security number is to you as an individual. You would do well to memorize this number or keep it handy throughout the start-up phase.

Needed Permits

Some or all of the following permitting agencies will need to see the plans for your business, so allow plenty of time in your preopening months for their review.

Building Department   You will need to get permission from the local building department prior to beginning any significant construction. Every locality (states and cities) has a different regulation about what comprises "significant" construction requiring a permit. Obtaining this permit is usually the responsibility of the architect or contractor. Upon interviewing and hiring these professionals, inquire as to their procedure for obtaining these permits for new jobs, and how the fee for these is handled.

Consumer Affairs, Landmark Commissions, Community Boards   In some cities and towns, building rights are restricted by the governance of other local offices, such as the ones noted above. To apply for and get a building permit may require prior application to and approval from one of these agencies. When visiting sites, inquire of the real estate broker if there are any restrictions to renovation or building in that particular space or area. If so, have them do some of the preliminary research to help you find out what you have to do to begin building. Inform your contractor and/or architect of any restrictions right from the start to avoid delays after the lease is signed.

Fire Department, Highway Department, and Transportation Department Depending on whether your store will be in a freestanding building, how far the building is from the road, and if you plan to extend the building or use an outside portion for anything other than its current use (such as for an outdoor display, sales window, or café) you may be required to apply for a special or change of use permit from one or all of the above-named agencies. Again, first check with your realtor and then with your contractor and architect.

Local Water Authority or Environmental Protection Agency   Consult your realtor first and then the agencies directly about any possible compliance issues with the sites under consideration. Communicate all issues to your architect or contractor immediately, as these will invariably affect the design and construction of your store.

Health Department, State Department of Agriculture and Markets, or USDA
As a purveyor of food you will be required to gain permission to operate from the city or county health department. As a manufacturer of food you may also be required to gain permission to manufacture from your state's department of agriculture and markets.

The city or county health department will have regulations about what types of building materials to use and may even have recommended plumbing and electrical schematics that are best suited for food service establishments. To get an application from the health department usually requires several layers of form filing and application making. Go there early in the planning stages to get the local guidelines. Some of the local restrictions and issues of compliance may help you make certain decisions about what type of operation to build and run.

If you are going to be processing meat for sale, other than in portions plated by you from your food display (i.e., packaged under your brand name and sold "off the shelf"), you will need to build and operate your "processing facility" (as so termed) according to the rules of the USDA (United States Department of Agriculture), who will, in fact, send an inspector out *daily* to inspect the quality of your operation. It is not recommended to build this aspect of compliance into your operations. If a particular meat product is your signature item and selling it under your brand (instead of behind the counter) is imperative to the business, you may want to consider having that item copacked by another USDA approved facility. This will be more economical and efficient in the long and short run.

State Liquor Authority   If you are allowed in your state to sell beer and wine (or one of these) in your specialty food shop, you will have to submit an application to the state liquor authority. Again, it doesn't hurt to inquire early, as there may be a wait for applications, or applications may not be accepted at all for certain locations. You may want the assistance of a lawyer to process this application, as it can be complicated and laborious.

Tax Issues

Sales Tax   Once you are incorporated, you can apply to your state department of taxation and finance, which will issue a certificate (or license) that allows you to collect state sales tax. You can apply directly or have your accountant do this for you. There is little to no fee for this certificate, but it could take time, so applying early gets it out of the way and then you have it when the store is about to open.

Payroll and Payroll Taxes   Once you begin to hire and pay people, either as employees or as independent contractors, you will be responsible for filing and paying regular payroll taxes. With each new person hired you must begin an employee file. Each employee must fill out an application form that contains certain information (such as name, address, social security number, emergency telephone numbers, etc.). These will be listed in a standard employee application form, which may be obtained at a local stationer's. Upon hiring each new person for employment, you are required to have him or her fill out a Federal IRS W-4 form and a US Department of Immigration I-9 form. You will file the IRS form at the end of the year, showing the total federal taxes withheld from the person's paycheck (including Social Security and Federal Unemployment Insurance). The Department of Immigration form is a proof of citizenship, requiring copies of two standard forms of identification as attachments; it will prove that the applicant can work in this country. These two forms must stay in the employee file at all times, in the event of an audit by either of these government agencies.

There is a myriad of payroll taxes that you will be required to withhold from an employee's paycheck and pay in a timely manner to different agencies; you must also contribute payments beyond what is withheld. A brief rundown of the payroll taxes is as follows:

> **Social Security Tax (FICA)—A** percentage of the gross paycheck (check with your accountant or local office of the IRS for current rate) that is *withheld* from a person's paycheck as well as *matched by the employer (you)* and made in *monthly payments* to your business bank, with whom you've established a direct deposit to the federal government.
>
> **Federal Unemployment Insurance (FUI)**—Also a percentage of the gross paycheck. This may be included in the monthly payment to the bank or paid separately. Seek advice from your accountant.
>
> **State Unemployment Insurance (SUI)**—Another percentage of the gross paycheck, paid *quarterly* and submitted with a report of all employees to the state government office.
>
> **City Tax, Disability, and Meal Allowance**—Again, a percentage of what was paid to an individual over the course of a quarter or year. Depending on the local laws, and the total dollar amount, this might only have to be filed and paid once a year.

Independent Contractors   Many employers (and employees as well) wish to avoid the responsibility of both filing and paying all the payroll taxes listed above for every employee. Many employees will have had experience working as "independent contractors" before and prefer to be responsible for their own taxes. The federal government, in recent years, has begun some serious crackdowns of what could be considered an independent contractor scam—finding people who have technically been employees yet who have been filing as independent contractors—and fining, with severe penalties, both parties for the years the person was employed. Generally, an independent contractor is defined as (1) someone who earns less than $600 per place of employment per year, or (2) works less than a certain percentage of time for any one employer.

A list of independent contractors must be kept on file in your office, the same as a list of employees. Instead of a W-4, however, a 1099 form will be filled out, indicating the person's social security number. At the end of the calendar year, this form will be issued to the independent contractor as well as filed by your company, and will show the total amount paid to the person over the year.

Beware of taking this shortcut to fill positions that you consider temporary, seasonal, or short term. It's always safer to hire "officially" all who work for you, placing them on your "books" regardless of the up-front burden of paperwork and the ongoing need to file taxes for these individuals. Get a broader perspective on this issue by talking with your accountant. If you do decide such contracting is appropriate for certain situations, take a look at the sample agreement in Exhibit 6-1.

Consultants Many consultants are actually independent contractors, and, if their business is not incorporated, you may follow the guidelines as above for tax compliance. If your consultant is incorporated, in any of the ways listed above, you need not obtain their social security number nor issue a 1099 form at the end of the year. Instead, you must obtain their Federal Tax ID number (just like the one you have) and keep it in your records. This is a preventative measure in the event of a conflict or an audit.

A Few Words of General Advice

Research thoroughly before any commitments are signed (i.e., with architects, contractors, and landlords). Apply early. Keep accurate and up-to-date records. File and make payments in a timely manner. Start and maintain a company calendar to help keep you and your managers on course. This will help ensure that you have applied for all of the above permits and licenses in a timely and efficient manner. Because of the high level of customer contact and the labor-intensive handling of perishables, the "office-like" parts of specialty food retailing often get placed at or near the bottom of the priorities list. Nonetheless, it's best not to get

EXHIBIT 6-1

INDEPENDENT CONTRACTOR AGREEMENT

Over the course of running your business, you may find it helpful and advantageous to hire individuals on a per project or per job basis. These individuals are not members of your permanent staff but rather remain as adjunct employees whose particular expertise you wish to draw upon for certain specific jobs or purposes (i.e., public relations professionals, periodic window or store decorators, product demonstrators, cooking class instructors drawn from outside of your regular staff). Here is an agreement that can be used to contract for the work of such individuals. You may abbreviate the agreement you make as you see fit, depending on the nature of the work for which you are contracting. Based on the nature and longevity of your relationship with the individual and the scope of the work you wish done by this individual, you may see fit to make the agreement less formal. Use the following as a rough guide.

Agreement, dated _____, 19_____, between _____(hereinafter "the Corporation") and _____ (hereinafter "the Independent Contractor").

The parties hereto agree as follows:

1. Employment. The Corporation shall employ the Independent Contractor, and the Independent Contractor shall serve the Corporation upon the terms and conditions hereinafter set forth.

2. Term and Extension. The employment of the Independent Contractor hereunder shall commence on _____ , 19___ , and shall continue to and including _____.. Subject to this Agreement continuing in full force and effect to and including _____, the Independent Contractor shall have the right and option to continue this Agreement hereunder for an additional period commencing _____ , 19___ , by giving the Corporation written notice not later than _____ , 19 ___ , of his (or her) intentions to do so , and upon his or her exercising such option, all of the terms and conditions of this Agreement applicable thereto shall continue in full force and effect for such additional period.

3. Duties. During the period(s) of his (or her) employment hereunder, the Independent Contractor shall serve the Corporation and shall perform any and all general _____ services required or requested in connection with their business. Within the limitations hereinabove provided, the Independent Contractor will render such other advisory services in connection with the _____ services of the Corporation as may be requested from time to time by the officers or directors of the Corporation, without further compensation other than that for which provision is made in this Agreement.

4. Time Requirements. The Independent Contractor shall devote during the period ending _____ , 19 ___ , not more than _____ % of his or her entire time, energy, and skill to the duties of his or her employment and shall periodically, or at any time upon the request of the Corporation, submit data as to the time performed.

5. Compensation. The Corporation shall pay to the Independent Contractor for his or her services sums in the aggregate amounting to $_____ or _____ % per _____ project, during the period of his or her employment hereunder. Such aggregate sums shall be paid upon satisfactory completion of any _____ project and from the proceeds received from the clients for whom _____ services are rendered.

6. Indemnification and Hold Harmless Provision: The Independent Contractor agrees hereby to indemnify and hold harmless the Corporation from any and all claims by the Independent Contractor which may arise out of and in the course of the performance of his or duties hereunder. Any and all claim for unemployment benefits and or claims for workers' compensation benefits are hereby expressly waived by the within Independent Contractor who agrees to maintain separate policies of liability, health and accident insurance as may be necessary or required by the Corporation in connection with the performance of its duties herein.

7. Relationship Between Parties. The Independent Contractor is employed by the Corporation only for the purposes and to the extent set forth in this Agreement, and his or her relation to the Corporation shall, during the period or periods of his or her employment and services hereunder, be that of an independent contractor. The Independent Contractor shall be free to dispose of such portion of his or her entire time, energy, and skill during regular business hours as he or she is not obligated to devote hereunder to the Corporation in such manner as he or she sees fit and to such persons, firms, or corporations as he or she deems advisable. The Independent Contractor shall not be considered as having an employee status or as being entitled to participate in any plans, arrangements or distributions by the Corporation pertaining to or in connection with any insurance, pension, stock, bonus, profit-sharing, or similar benefits for their regular employees.

8. Professional Responsibility. Nothing in this Agreement shall be construed to interfere with or otherwise affect the rendering of services by the Independent Contractor in accordance with his or her independent and professional judgment. The Independent Contractor shall perform his or her services in a good and workmanlike manner and in accordance with generally accepted _____ practices.

9. Entire Agreement. The within Agreement shall be construed in accordance with _____ (State) law and shall constitute the entire Agreement between the parties.

In Witness Thereof, _____ has caused this Agreement to be executed in its corporate name by its corporate officers, and _____ , the Independent Contractor hereunder, has set his or her hand and seal, as of this day and year first above written.

Contractor's Signature_____

Signature subscribed and affirmed, or sworn to, before me in the county of _____

Date _____

State of _____ Date _____

behind with these. This will only cause you to take even *more* time to catch up. Late payments may also carry with them hefty penalties and fines with interest.

A few more words: Always review your tax obligations and permit requirements with your business consultant, accountant, lawyer, architect, contractor, and realtor. Furthermore, remember that there may be other agencies to satisfy and other applications to submit specific to your type of business or prevailing in your local municipality. So ask questions of the professionals you have hired to get the complete picture. Remember that ignorance of the law is no excuse for failing to comply.

GRAPHIC DESIGN AND THE SPECIALTY FOOD BUSINESS

Up until now we have stressed to you the importance and the how-tos of preparing yourself, both organizationally and financially, to begin your journey as a specialty food entrepreneur. What comes next is the process of defining and building up your business through image and position in the market. This is important and it can also be the fun part of spending money. While exploring the range of products and services to market to your target clientele, it is important to quickly start thinking about how you will enhance your product line and/or your range of services to differentiate them from others on the market.

It often comes as a surprise to even the most sophisticated specialty food entrepreneurs (who are usually coming right out of the kitchen as chefs) that a company's graphic identification is as important as the quality of the food or the look of the store. The best-prepared owners of specialty food businesses take great pains to integrate operationally as well as aesthetically the physical location of the business, the interior design, the menu, product development, marketing and operations strategies all under one umbrella, which is called "corporate image." The corporate image begins with designing a logo and then continues by using that logo in various applications within your business, such as on a business card, stationery, labels, and packaging. The logo will also be used for store signage, advertising, uniforms and for manufacturing, as well as for anything such as T-shirts, bags, or coffee mugs that you wish to sell. See, for example, the promotional mailing in Exhibit 6-2.

Formally defined, a logo is a clearly presented graphic image that at a quick glance identifies the product and services to the potential client. A logo is often the first way your business or product is introduced to your customer. It is generally taken for granted that if something has a pleasing appearance, people will be attracted to it. If there is a name that people can somehow identify, people will remember it. When it comes to food products, good looks aren't everything but they sure can help. Attractive and memorable packaging, signage, labels, and containers all create an image for your company, and the logo is the centerpiece in conveying that image.

Creating a logo is based on much the same principle as making friends: if they remember you fondly, that is, if what's inside the package delivers what's promised on the outside, they will come back. In one glance the customer must be able to recognize the name and the position of the product—for example, not just any bread but health bread or stone-ground whole wheat bread; not just salad dressing but homemade or "lite" dressing.

TO BEGIN?

Nancy Collins, of Nancy Feldman Graphic Design in New York (whose clients include Estee Lauder, Miche, and the New York specialty food stores Mangia and Milan, and whose projects include the shopping bag programs for New York's Metropolitan Museum of Art and Museum of Modern Art) says that when creating your logo, you should "think simply and honestly about your business. " The business owner first needs to "figure out how their product or service is different from what's already on the market. At that point they have reached the first step." You need to reduce your overall business concept to its essence and then capture that in your logo. "Start the process by association," says Collins, so that the image that's being developed "looks like people's prior experience." Include an element that will be easily readable or understood by your intended audience.

As with other significant stages in the formation of your business, we recommend strongly that you seek the help of a professional for development of your corporate image. As with many other professional services, businesses owners-to-be often wish to rely on the offers of friends, relatives or "someone I know" who is a graphic designer to get the job done. Here again, using professional designers who come highly recommended to you is apt to yield the best result. You almost always get what you pay for.

Very often a new business owner will indeed start out with an idea for a logo or some logo component (a word, name, or graphic image) to which they feel quite attached. Doing some preliminary brainstorming and selecting a general style in which to work are good starting points. Taking these ideas to the table when interviewing a few good designers will quickly bring the development of your corporate image to the next level. As with the mission statement, we recommend you try your initial ideas out on friends and family first. Show a rough sketch of your logo to people whose opinions you value and ask them to tell you what impressions they form about the product simply from the logo, what they can say about the type of product or market you are attempting to attract, and what, if any, other associations they have with the preliminary image. If they respond as you anticipated, you may be ready to take the logo to the next level. If they just don't connect to it at all in the way you had hoped, step back and take a look at what they do see, and be as objective as possible. Ask your friends and your future customers what would make sense to them given everything they know about you and your business.

Here, as in many stages of the development and operation of your business, it will be necessary to learn the value of objectivity and of opening your mind to criticism. If you can learn in the start-up phase not to take constructive criticism personally, you will be well on your way to reaching your market. When testing things out on friends or relatives, it is particularly important in the beginning to remember that they are the most supportive audience you will have until you have developed a loyal customer base. Utilize these "free" resources to help you objectively define your business and pay other people to incorporate the feedback of your sounding board and your thoughts in a concise and effective way.

For people who are growing existing businesses, Collins offers the following advice: "Consistency is so crucial yet most people overlook it. Stick with what you start with, even if it is a funky thing that your brother-in-law designed. If you start out with a logo and people identify you and your company by it, stick with it. Minor updates or modifications are okay, however (if they don't change the basic essence of the design.)"

When to Begin the Graphic Design Process

When should you start thinking about a logo? Almost any designer will say "Immediately." It can take time to develop a graphic image that represents you accurately and that will not grow stale over time. It's often a trial and error process and the results should turn your plans, hopes, and attitudes about your concept into a concrete, graphic reality. Allow for some thinking time and give yourself a long enough period (several months, at least) to reflect on the rough ideas your designer presents to you.

Remember that in marketing your business, image is everything and your logo is the essence of your image. Your prepared foods may be wonderful. You may carry the most interesting array of imported Tibetan foods available in this hemisphere. You may offer every imaginable combination of precut vegetables, meats, and Asian sauces in stir-fry kits for your customers. If they don't look good, or familiar, or usable, however, few people will buy them.

What then are some of the guidelines to creating a winning corporate image? The *logo* must be simple, memorable, and attractive.

1. Think about your "*brand identity.*" This is the way company names have been associated with logos, packaging, and type over time. Some examples that define "brand identity" include Wonder Bread, Newman's Own (salad dressings, etc.), and Valrhona (epicure's quality chocolate from France). These have come to be associated with a certain image: consistency over the years, healthfulness, and luxury, respectively.

2. Think about *color.* You may not realize this, but packaging in the food industry tends to use only a few dominant colors. These tend to be on the warm side (red, orange, yellow), except for frozen foods, which rely on cooler colors like blues and greens.

3. Think about the *market,* about which customers you are trying to attract. Will the preponderance of your customers be the types who shop at a Dean and DeLuca (the *ne plus ultra,* in many people's view, of specialty food stores with locations in NYC and Washington, DC), at Trader Joe's (a national discounter of specialty foods with a lots of private label merchandise), or at Gourmet Garage (a no-frills purveyor of high restaurant-quality specialty foods in NYC)?

4. Think about the influence of *fashion*: usually the trendier you get the more subject you are to colors that are currently in fashion. In the design world, trends determine the use of color in packaging, print advertising, and store interiors. The industries of fashion and interior design are consistently at the forefront of what's "in." To keep up, read the fashion column and architecture and interiors sections in the major big city newspapers. Although graphic design is subject to the vagaries of trends, that does not mean that you need to align yourself with a trendy image. Be yourself, using your own aesthetic impulses as your guide. An old timey general store design may not lend itself to a jazzy modern logo. Conversely, quaint signage might be out of place in a spare, postmodern store. The fashion that influences the style of your stores, however, cannot be reduced to a simple formula. Just remember that if keeping costs low is an issue, the fewer colors and the simpler your design the better.

5. Think about "*positioning.*" In what market niche do you want your store, products, or services to be? Who are your principal competitors? What is *their* corporate image like?

6. Think about how your logo will translate into the many *applications* your business will need, such as business cards, signage, uniforms, and, most importantly, packaging. Make sure your logo has as much visual punch in *black and white* as in its ultimate colors. Make sure it is *faxable,* and can be *scanned into your*

computer for quick-use applications. Today the need to communicate electronically is just as essential in the food business as in any other.

What's Outside Counts Too

Packaging is as crucial as your name or logo. Think about it this way: customers have to live with the thing that they buy, that is, they have to easily store them on cupboard, refrigerator, or freezer shelves. If your products come in neat or attractive packages, then people will be drawn to them. When you think of packaging, think practical, utilitarian, and cost-effective. Be guided by what the food service industry has used successfully in the past, and what it seems to be leaning toward today, such as heat-and-serve, environmentally sound materials, and reusable containers. Form follows function, particularly in this case. When you decide on what kinds of packaging to use for the products you prepare (or repackage), give thought to what have over time become standard packaging in the food service industry (i.e., Big Mac containers for single portion hot foods, waxed cardboard containers for milk, slender-necked bottles for salad dressing). You don't need to reinvent the wheel to be distinctive. By its shape, color, graphics, and lettering, a well-designed logo can make your products stand out from the crowd whether packaged in ordinary, predictable containers or not. Remember that there is no excuse for pretentious packaging, and ultimately no use for it. A package design that looks great on the drafting table will have to stand up to much handling and use and abuse before it gets to the customer, on the manufacturing side, in distribution, in merchandising, in sales, and then in the customer's shopping cart and finally in storage at home. It has to pass this last test just in order to sell the product but you must also consider all the other handling. Great tasting food does not make up for a leaky container. It's hard for customers to get past a greasy or oil-stained label even if what's inside the container is wonderful.

HOW TO SELECT A GRAPHIC DESIGNER

As with many other professional services, word of mouth recommendations from other people in the industry work well. Also ask for names from your architect or interior designer (if you're using one) and other people on your development team. Architects and interior designers traditionally have strong working relationships with graphic designers and can knowledgeably assist you in selecting the right person to create a design that will be consonant with your business concept and within your budget.

EXHIBIT 6-2

ADELINE'S GRAPHIC DESIGN

It pays to spend some money up front to develop a strong graphic identity for your business. Adeline's Gourmet Foods, a manufacturer of a line of vinegars, dressings, marinades, salsas, and vegetable chip snacks, has successfully combined several components for its promotional mailings. The outside (Exhibit 6-2*a*) is generic enough, and is designed to be multipurpose and therefore not to grow "stale." Dated materials or limited time only promotions, such as price lists or new product information pieces (Exhibit 6-2*b*) are produced and printed separately as time and budget allow and then enclosed. "This approach," says Adeline Ashley, the company's owner and graphic mastermind, "allows us to get the most mileage out of dollars spent on advertising." With some forethought, even small retailers with relatively limited advertising budgets can benefit from this same approach. *Reprinted courtesy Adeline R. Ashley, Adeline's Gourmet Foods.*

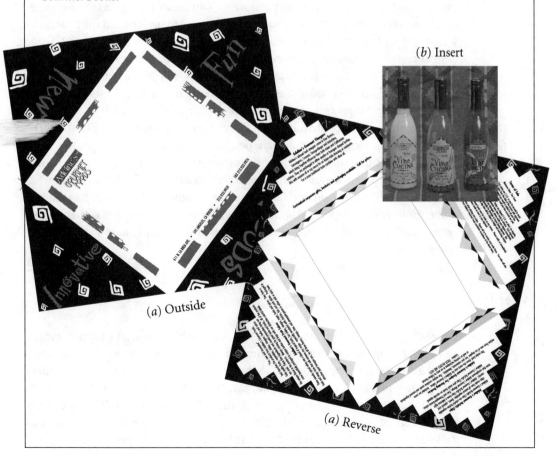

(*b*) Insert

(*a*) Outside

(*a*) Reverse

Interview a few designers. In these interviews do as much talking as listening. Tell the designers about your concept and your own perception of style and market. Ask them how they approach these types of jobs. What resources do they have and what will they have to subcontract out (which will result in add-ons to their fees)? Ask them to bring to the interview examples of their work that they think is relevant to your project. Ask about how they charge and what sort of time frame they need. Also ask about how much they involve the client (you) in the process. If you want to be hands-on, be sure you will have that opportunity. (As with all professionals, remember that you are the client and, while heeding the designer's knowledge and expertise on individual matters, you are paying him or her, and are therefore entitled to request the type of service you feel you need.) Be sure to ask for names of recent clients so you can contact them to find out directly what their experience of working with the designer was like.

After talking with at least five designers, think for a few days or a week and then contact your top three to get proposals. (You are not obligated to hire someone from whom you request a proposal, and it helps to understand the process by seeing the differences in how different people approach their work.) Some designers will enclose preliminary sketches, usually in black and white (called "thumbnails") with their proposals and these will let you see if they are on the right track. (Computer-aided design has made it much easier for designers to manipulate the design and present multiple versions of it for a client's consideration; consequently, alas, hand-drawn designs are becoming a thing of the past.) In reviewing the designer's proposals, be aware of the time line for project completion (does it jibe with the rest of the project?), what the fees proposed cover and what they do not cover (and how much this extra stuff will cost), and what interaction with your team and follow-up the designer will provide. As with any other professional, be sure you have a legal contract that spells out the work agreed upon, the time frame, fees and payment schedule, and a cancellation clause.

What Will It Cost?

Depending on where you are located, fees for graphic designers can vary widely. Some charge by the hour (a range from $75 to $150) and can usually calculate a rough estimate of hours needed to do the work you agree on in a contract; others will quote you a fee for the whole job, say, the design of a logo or store identity including font selection and colors used, and bill you for any additional charges for time spent on packaging, store signage design, private label merchandise packaging, menus, letterheads, carryout bags, and other applications. (Often designers will take out in trade merchandise from your store as part of the fee, so be sure to offer the possibility of barter if that idea appeals to you.)

It's also customary that you will be charged for print setup and other necessary mechanicals in addition to the designer's fees. Remember that the design is only useful to the extent that you apply it. Building a store's image through its logo takes careful planning and thought. Work closely with your designer ("Weekly meetings in the development phase are customary," according to Lisa King, a graphic designer specializing in logo design for restaurants and other food establishments in Los Angeles). In this way you will be exposed to the full range of the possible logo's use—you may ultimately apply it to products that are seen in your store as well as to all printed promotional literature that is widely distributed both in store and through mailings.

King also recommends that: "In the case of a partnership, or where there is more than one individual involved in launching the business, it's best to identify one person who has the direct link with the designer; in that way, decisions can be reached in a timely manner." She continues, "A complete design program can encompass everything from the design of store signage to staff uniforms. Often I select particular elements of the logo, for example, a fragment of a graphic or a type style, and apply each of them differently to each printed piece the store uses, according to how they best fit. In this way, I can tie together many disparate parts of the business for an overall cohesive design scheme which makes an impact on the customer."

There is no one "right way" to approach the sequence of engaging design professionals for specialized parts of your project. Simply do what works for you, given your needs, budget, time frame, and concept. Occasionally, the graphic designer is engaged early in the process and the logo development may drive other design considerations in the project, such as interior, signage, lighting, and sometimes even the menu.

An example of a work plan with a graphic designer for logo design and implementation within a store environment can look like this:

Meeting, interviewing, and reviewing proposals (client and designer):	4 weeks
Task list and parameters of project (client):	1–2 weeks
Initial concept (designer)—(rough, black and white sketches of possible logos, etc., secondary typography):	2 weeks
Meeting with two or three ideas (client and designer):	1–2 weeks
Client selects one or combination of these:	1 week

Designer presents almost finished artwork with color suggestions and layout for three applications:	2 weeks
Mechanicals (designer or subcontractor)—letterhead, labels, business card, hats, T-shirts, aprons, etc.):	1 week
Production (designer or subcontractor):	3–6 weeks (depending on colors, materials to be printed, etc.)

PRICING: THE ART AND THE SCIENCE

Your store is built, equipped, staffed. Now all you need to do is fill the shelves, refrigerated cases, and countertops with merchandise to sell. Easy. Now comes the hard part—pricing it right. You've done your demographic study and break-even analysis so you are well prepared to fix the right prices to the goods and services you are about to sell. Can you apply an across-the-board markup formula to everything in your store? The answer is "yes" and "no." Yes refers to the items you buy ready to sell. On these, the price you paid for the item is the chief guide to calculating the selling price. Let your invoices be your guide. Examine them carefully, figure per unit costs, and watch for gradual increases in the costs of goods you are ordering on a regular basis. (Be aware that many purveyors will "low-ball" you at first, giving you deeper discounts on certain items to gain your business, but after an initial honeymoon period will revert to standard pricing.)

Industry standard markup for packaged specialty foods (anything in its own container like pasta, olive oil, condiments, even beverages like juice and soda) is 100% to 125%. This means you can unpack that carton of pasta, where you've calculated that each 1-lb bag cost you 75¢, put a $1.65 price tag on each (using a 120% markup), put these on the shelf, and wait for them to fly out the door. In reality, of course, it is a little more complicated than this, particularly if you are in a highly competitive market and this item is available at neighboring stores.

It is crucial to know how your competitors have priced the same products, and you must use some careful judgment about how to position your products against theirs in the market. This is not only for identical products but also for similar ones. Consider your product mix, and consider that of your competition. If you have a wider selection of pasta than your competition and they have a few brands identical to yours you may want to price the identical ones slightly lower and the ones exclusive to your store slightly higher. This keeps you competitive, and because you have brands the competition doesn't carry, you will be thought of as the source for those lines of goods.

Consider, too, the prices and items sold in the large-scale discounters and price clubs, in addition to those in upscale markets that take full markup. Glean from that research not only which products you want to sell, but appropriate price points at which to sell them. Your suppliers will also probably suggest retail prices for the items they sell to you. Unless you are a big operator and are buying items by the truckload, at first it's safest to use their prices as a guide. As you get more comfortable operating your business and maneuvering in the market, you can play with those suggested prices. The wholesalers and distributors, however, are well attuned to what pricing prevails in a wide geographic range, so let their suggested prices be your guide. As an industry average or guide, strive for a 45% cost of goods sold (COGS) for your packaged products. When you comparison shop at your competitors' stores, multiply .45 by the selling price to compute the approximate wholesale cost of that product.

Pricing Your Stock-in-Trade

The tougher aspect of pricing has to do with the nonpackaged foods you will sell at your store. We're talking here about the prepared foods, whether sold for consumption on premises or as items to carry out. These are items where your involvement with the product amounts to much more than uncrating it and putting it on shelves already ready to sell. The significant difference here is that you will be buying raw ingredients (produce, meat, dairy, etc.) and paying people to transform them into the final product. For these items you have much more to consider when arriving at the final price, and you also have more leeway. In addition, these items will be unique to your store—prepared in your own way, marked with your own style and flair, and therefore ever so slightly different from similar items available at that other store in town.

So how do you figure the selling price for prepared foods? Well, thankfully, there is another industry standard to guide you. Since the labor involved to get any particular dish from produce crate to a platter in your display case is extremely complicated to calculate, consider first and foremost your food cost. Your raw ingredients should cost you between 17% and 32% of your final selling price. We know: That is a very large range. Here, too, is where some comparative shopping will also serve as part of the guide, as well as that even more key task: recipe costing. You will want to scour the market to see what prices per pound other purveyors of specialty food are charging for that Teriyaki Beef Salad or Sesame Noodles, how much they are getting for a grilled chicken and smoked mozzarella sandwich on sourdough bread. When you comparison shop, don't forget to look at the other stores' presentation and packaging. The high or low aesthetic of these can factor considerably into the final selling price, or what the market will bear. But the foremost guide is the cost to you of the ingredients, preparing all of these items according to carefully costed-out recipes, and following the recipes closely to produce each of these dishes.

Russ Vernon, the owner of West Point Market in Akron, OH, and specialty food retailer *par excellence,* has this to say about pricing:

> There will always be a better price. . . . Price has no bottom. Price is only one tool used to build business. Those who rely on price are at great risk in our changing markets. It's the sizzle that makes your store a destination and makes your store the only retailer who does what you do. Put that against price, and price will become less important.

You will not be able to assign a flat percentage markup to your prepared foods. You will want to consider, as mentioned above, your competitors' prices and presentation, the uniqueness of your products on the market overall, your biggest sellers (either known or projected, then later revised), and a gut feeling about what is an appropriate price. In all this careful calculation it may seem incongruous to you that "gut" feelings are a guide, so, to ease the potential discomfort about something so subjective, consider "what's reasonable." It might cost you $10.00 or $12.00 per pound to produce the sake-marinated filet mignon salad, but can you charge $30.00 per pound for it? Perhaps, yes, but most likely no. If this dish is a winner, a signature dish, or perhaps, a big seller, you should sell it, perhaps at a 50% or even 60% food cost, meaning at a price that is double or slightly more than double the food cost. (Remember, even with a high food cost percentage, you will have a net profit of $10.00 to $12.00 per pound with this formula, considering overhead and labor. Think about it. Are you getting that from any other salad?) Just be sure to balance this high food cost percentage with the rest of your fare, so that your menu, when taken as a whole, has an average food cost of 25% to 30%.

There are other factors to consider when creating a selling price for your prepared foods. By taking raw items and transforming them into completed ready-to-serve dishes, you are building convenience into the product and the customer is prepared to pay for that convenience. You are also packaging the products in containers that cost you money, and putting these items into bags that also cost you money with forks, knives, napkins, packets of salt and pepper or other condiments, whose cost, when taken all together, really adds up (and, with the costs of paper and environmentally safe plastics soaring each year, not getting any cheaper). All of these expenses must be factored into the cost of the raw ingredients (remember to add a buffer for mistakes and accidental overpackaging) to get to the point where you can put that price sticker on the item. Overall, you can see how your markup can be considerably higher for prepared foods.

Different Foods, Differing Pricing

There is also a different scale to use for different types of prepared foods. For salads, casseroles, sandwiches, and the like, a markup of two to three times food cost is reasonable. On low-cost baked goods (breads, muffins, biscuits, scones, plainer cookies) which you prepare, the price can be between five and six times the food cost. For baked goods such as fine desserts, cakes, and any sweet made with costly chocolate, nuts, and dairy, which will have a higher than average food cost, you need to be prepared to take a lesser markup, usually between three and four times food cost.

What About the Foods in My Café?

Pricing the prepared foods in your café (or any informal eating area devoted solely to in-store food consumption) is an extension of the process of pricing your prepared foods sold to go. The formula begins the same way, with the raw ingredient cost and how much a serving costs to prepare, from the tested recipes. You will also want to consider *how* the items in your cafe will be sold. Will customers buy goods over the counter and take them, in their disposable packaging, over to a table or counter and eat them, and when finished throw out their own refuse? Or will you sell these goods in portions other than the by-the-pound formula consistent with over-the-counter sales? Will you be serving these on plates, either paper or china? Will you need to pay someone expressly to clean up the café area? Will you have table service? If so, each of these scenarios will add your cost of selling the prepared foods café-style.

You will also want to consider *how large* the café is, in and of itself and in relationship to the total size of your store. Café seats are valuable real estate that must be paid for. Literally consider the square footage planned for your café. Calculate how many dollars of sales you must generate in that area to reduce the occupancy cost to about 10% of the sales volume. How many people multiplied by the average cost of what a person will spend in your café will have to eat there each day to get to this number each month? Is this reasonable for your store, your market, and your demographic area? Will you have to charge a little more to serve foods on premises with waiter service on china and pay a busser and dishwasher to clean up after them? Most likely. But again, you are offering convenience, and if you are offering the right thing the right way in the right place, your café can be a gold mine. Just remember to consider all the costs and calculate them into your pricing formula.

Over time, as your business establishes itself and you attract regular customers and gain a reputation for signature dishes, you will find that for certain items in your product line, you can extend the markup slightly higher. These foods carry a cachet, a certain status and exclusivity, and therefore it's appropriate to add on a premium for them—perhaps 10% higher than your usual markup would dictate. Again, there is nothing formulaic about determining when you can get a little bolder about pricing. You will want to review your sales and your costs very carefully over at least the first six months, to see how your actual costs compare with your projections. If you haven't overstated sales or understated expenses in your initial projections, then you will have room for a bit of underpricing when you open to gain a foothold in the marketplace. Undoubtedly, you will reap less profit during this period but you will be building a customer base in the meantime. Then as you progress in your menu development, make adjustments to projected selling costs, and revise your total sales to conform with reality, you will be well on your way to what your final pricing strategy will be.

Count on Vendors as They Count on You

As you develop relationships with your suppliers, both large and small, institutional and artisanal, you can become a trend-setter in your own right. How you choose to merchandise a particular product line or play up your chef's latest creations determine how much of a trend-setter you will be.

Your opportunities to start a trend are inextricably bound up with the level of trust your vendors have in you as an operator. You provide a venue for their product which is highly visible. If you educate your customers about how special certain products are, then the vendors who supply them will think of you first when they have a new product in development. Exclusive representations may result and you gain in reputation as being the first or the best outlet for certain products. You become the trend-setter.

On vendors, Steve Jenkins, a long time specialty food consultant, says: "The business of specialty food is [developing] a personal relationship with vendors. Success is measured by the people who look out for me over the years."

Similarly, when attending trade association meetings, conferences, or expositions, you will raise your visibility in the industry by making yourself known among the purveyors who are considered trend-setting or cutting edge at the moment. Count yourself in among the retailing elite (or elite-to-be) by shaking hands with the producers of award-winning products (invite them to your store to spend some time with your staff and customers). Then back up your wish to be taken seriously by asking questions that indicate that you want to become an authority on (and big seller of) a particular product or line of products. Often sampling and demonstration programs are available for the asking.

Point of sale materials are often also available. They are useful as part of displays to help draw attention to particular products you are featuring or promotions that you are running to build sales in a specific product category. Special promotional pricing is often extended to good customers, so explore that option as well. Cooperative advertising or an allowance for advertising offered as part of a deeper discount on merchandise purchased are also sometimes available. The retailer who speaks up and tells the vendor what he or she needs to sell the product often gets the best deals.

These are just three of the many software options to help the food service operator with recipe costing, inventory, nutritional analysis of food prepared, and so on:

Mastercook II (800-444-8104)
At-Your-Service Software (914-337-9030)
ExecuChef (415-383-8540)

When vendors provide sampling allowances with your purchase, take full advantage of them. Increased sales will often result if you can be more generous than is customary in your sampling. Your vendors will remember you better when you take a serious position on a particular product or product line. You are then more likely to get the kind of support you need in educating both your staff and your customers about the product. When introducing a new product, you have an opportunity to convince your targeted audience why you should be considered an arbiter of taste in your industry. This raises your profile, and higher profiles tend to get recognition by the press, which in turns raises your profile even higher. Trend-setting (and sometimes risk-taking with a new untried product line) gets you noticed and positions you to set more trends.

There are numerous computer programs that can aid and cut down the manual expense of costing out your recipes. While these require considerable up-front work (data input, recipe testing, and regular monitoring of your costs and updating based on your invoices), they are undoubtedly "worth the pain" of the diligent desk work.

A few words of very strong advice: If, after you open, you see what you are charging is not enough to make you profitable, don't make drastic increases. In a panic, many store owners make the mistake of raising prices drastically, forgetting about the competition and about what's realistic. The result is a drop in business, and even lower profits. It is crucial to consider all of the possible factors that are causing your profit or cash flow problems, such as overall high labor costs, prices to you of raw ingredients or packaging (be sure to get vendors to bid against each other for your business), insurance costs, a rent increase, and so on. Sit down with your management team to analyze the costs and sales of your business. Look at every line item as carefully as you did when constructing your first budgets. Try to get some objectivity about the issues. (Do you really need two dishwashers on each shift? Is that fancy packaging really important to your total concept and appreciated by your customers? Should you spend $5,000 or more this month on that new display refrigerator or wait?) With your team you will more easily be able to come up with a strategy for creating better profits, either by cutting expenses, changing your menu, raising prices, holding some promotions, or a

---

How to Buy

1. Know your market! Know your customers; understand their needs in the context of their lifestyle—speak with them on a one-to-one basis whenever possible and get and use their input via periodic questionnaires that promise a reward or discount or free "gift" upon completion; or scatter suggestion boxes throughout your store.
2. Be in touch with trends—read trade and consumer magazines widely.
3. Track the turnover of merchandise, seasonally and throughout the year.
4. Don't overbuy.
5. Buy in time to meet projected demands for seasonal products; buy enough to keep merchandise well stocked through peak periods; recognize fast sellers early so you can be sure to reorder in a timely fashion before the vendor runs out.
6. Markdowns are costly; overbuying ties up much needed capital that could be used in other areas of the store; slow turnover of inventory can impact negatively on profits.

combination of these. If you see pricing as an organic part of the larger picture, rather than an isolated issue, you will increase your potential for a successful and long-lived business. When a doctor treats the human body or the artist creates a painting, they are both mindful that each part affects and is affected by every other part of the total picture. Operating a healthy business is really not very different from this.

CHAPTER SEVEN

PUTTING THE PLAN TO WORK, PART II

Hiring and Training, Store Policies, Cash Management, and "A Day in the Life . . ."

You're almost there but hold that sigh of relief for a while longer. With the lease long ago signed, the build-out almost finished (except for a few minor touchups of paint and floor tile), the bulk of your products selected, the menu complete, and perhaps some of your key staff in place, you may be ready to breathe the sigh of relief (and of preopening exhaustion), but hold on, it's not quite time yet. It's time now to sit down to draft the guidelines, policies, and procedures for how to operate your store.

This preliminary work—designing systems to manage all of your resources, both human and material, to maximum effect—will pay off when you open in helping you maintain standards and consistency in all areas of your operation. As an enhancement of that process, we suggest you write a training manual for your entire team to refer to for job descriptions, policies and procedures, background information about the company, menus, uniform requirements, and the like. For your staff this document is their bible, as the business plan is yours. On the daily operations side, you will quickly find the need to systematize inventory and create cash controls with people-run and computer-run software. You will design forms for order taking, by phone or by fax, for staff scheduling, and for equipment and space maintenance. These will help make a multitask, multiproduct, detail-laden business manageable.

To organize the overwhelming responsibilities of day to day operations, you may want to create a master calendar. With the great multitude of details that make up the running of a business, it is impossible and foolhardy to attempt to commit the multitude of important dates, deadlines, and events to memory. Get a giant wall calendar and note on it all promotional events, holidays, staff birthdays, vacations, publicity deadlines, and tax payments. Equipment maintenance schedules should be noted too. Color code them by category to make them easy to distinguish. And then revisit the calendar frequently to update it and to remind you and your staff of coming events.

BUILDING A STAFF

Your primary focus, once the construction is well underway and you have selected your product line and begun to purchase your inventory, will be your staff.

Hiring and Firing—The Importance of Building and Maintaining a Healthy Staff

Many to-be store owners scramble in the two to three weeks prior to opening to hire and train their staff. With all the careful planning you have been doing all along—from writing a mission statement to performing a market analysis and feasibility study to writing a business plan to seeking out and hiring the right team to build your dream store—there's no need to skimp and cram now as the final weeks tick away before the store is physically ready to go.

About six months prior to opening the time is ripe to search for and hire your key managers and chef, those top positions that will not be filled by you or your partner. You should plan in your budget to have these key players on board two to three months prior to opening. In addition to creating and testing your menu, helping with selection of your product line, assisting with designing the flow of operations, selecting small equipment, and getting point of sale systems and accounting/bookkeeping systems in place, one of the most important preopening tasks your key managers will have is the hiring and training of your staff. For this, you will need to create an operations manual and fill in the details for all job descriptions. This is work that can be done at any point prior to your store opening; it should not wait until the intense few weeks just before showtime. It takes time to write a good and thorough operations manual, and it's a good idea to have your entire management team involved in the process. So start early, and as always, allow for time to edit and reedit as you go along. You do not have to create the perfect manual on the first try, but you do need a good solid foundation on which to build. In fact, as your store matures you will want to update the manual to reflect your actual business.

Consult your time line (or checklist) to opening often, particularly as the major aspects of construction and licensing and buying equipment are well underway. At weekly meetings with your contractor, architect, and consultants, discuss the completion of the major phases of build-out. Consider that they will probably have a margin of error of at least three to eight weeks (given the scale of your particular renovation). Six to eight weeks before opening your doors is the time to put your general staff hiring and training plan into action.

Where do you find the best individuals for the job and build a team for the front as well as the back of the house that works well together? How do you train them to make the most meaningful contribution to help build your customer base?

Russ Vernon on building a winning staff

When interviewing for a job at West Point Market (which often involves three interviews for each applicant and long discussions designed to ferret out the best applicant), I always ask the prospective employees to tell me about the best boss they ever had and what they expect to learn. I also ask "Why would you hire you?"

On maintaining the excellence of his staff, Vernon continues:

Our training programs provide a clear advantage over competitors who don't. We prepare our people to become customer obsessed. A challenged, educated, empowered employee, who has been given the freedom to create, innovate, and achieve personal growth is our best resource against increased competition.

The Organizational Chart

When faced with the request (by their consultant, new manager, or investors) to create an organizational chart, many new business owners simply scoff. This is understandable: to draft an organizational chart it is necessary to analyze the labor needs of your business, assign specific roles and hierarchies to staff members, and commit to a structure—all things inherently distasteful to the creative entrepreneur. Think of it as a mind map to guide your decisions about staffing, staff assignments according to the strengths and background of the individuals you hire, and the interrelations between employees and their functions. The act of constructing a chart should be a road to clear thinking.

Steve Jenkins on owner's roles in their stores: "You've got to have your own butt on the counter. Don't count on managers and staff. Keep your hands always on the product."

Although an organizational chart is indeed another thinking task you need to do in order to start a healthy business, once finished, it will be a useful instrument to help guide your staffing needs, your own role in your business (and, therefore, daily and yearly tasks and goals), and because of the effect of the prior two, your budget and financing needs. Now there, doesn't it sound more enticing already?

Like other structures and formulas, your company's organizational chart will grow and change as your business does, but this doesn't mean that you shouldn't draft one now and keep it with you as a guide to be changed as the roles and needs of your business change.

To craft this valuable tool first think about *your* role and the role of *your partner* (or partners), if appropriate. Go back to the beginning of your conversations with prospective partners and simply separate "active" (or working) partners from nonworking partners. The active partners, in order of their daily role in managing the business, get placed at the top of the chart. (Nonworking partners, if they form an advisory board or have some voting control of the business, are also placed on the top of the chart, often off to one side.)

Usually the roles of partners are divided into the following three categories: front of the house—service, on-the-floor marketing, selling, and operations/ management; back of the house—kitchen and production; and back office— administrative, which comprises mostly the financial and accounting functions but also the entrepreneurial functions such as marketing, advertising, and other big-picture planning. If this is how you are structuring the working relationship with your partner(s), be clear where lines are drawn between the segments of the business.

For example, will the chef be responsible for food cost, inventory, and menu pricing? If not, then these functions will be done by the management staff, perhaps in some partnership with the chef or his/her staff. Bear in mind, however, that there are no absolute rules about what functions should be performed by which division. The needs of your business and talents of your staff will dictate this as you move along. However, once the strengths of your team members becomes clearer, it is a good idea to designate authority in broad terms to keep the boundaries clear so no one steps on anyone else's toes.

Begin with the top and work your way down. The organization chart helps you, in the business planning stage, determine how many staff people you will need to run your business. Think about scheduling, hours of operation, and all the bases that need to be covered. Do you need telephone salespeople and administrative (secretarial) staff? Do you want to designate one job as that of a purchasing agent? Will your store manager also be your financial controller? Who will report to whom? (When this is spelled out on a chart, then any problem that comes up in operations will be more easily answered.) Share your ideas of how the organizational chart is structured with your partners and, if you have them already, managers. Do their ideas match yours? If so, move forward from completing the chart to writing job descriptions; if not, it is probably a good time for a partner meeting to discuss the functions of the business and the staff needs for these. Exhibit 7-1 shows an example of an organizational chart.

E X H I B I T   7 - 1

ORGANIZATIONAL CHART

An organizational chart is first drafted when the business plan is written, both as a way to begin to describe to investors and your partners what the hierarchy and management structure of the business will be as well as to begin to project staffing needs.

Prior to hiring your staff it is time to revise the organizational chart. At this time you will have more or less figured out the roles of yourself and your partners, if any. You may have also already hired your key manager and/or chef and designated their roles, which is a way to begin to draft the chart.

The organizational chart will lay out the number of staff people as well as the reporting structure of these future employees. Further, you and your key management staff can begin, with the head start of the organizational chart, to write the staff manual, assigning tasks and responsibilities to each level of employee. The organizational chart can also function as your first tool to calculate payroll.

We have constructed this sample chart based on a model of a 2,500-sq-ft store with a 500-sq-ft kitchen that produces food for (1) retail and cafe sales, (2) platters such as for lunch and business meetings, and (3) custom catering such as weddings and other social events, the three main revenue sources of the business. The nearly 2,000-sq-ft store sells predominantly prepared foods, mostly during the lunch hour. There are packaged food items available, but these sales make up a very small percentage of total sales. A core team, comprised of the owner, a silent partner with financial oversight, and a full-time bookkeeper, drive the three business sectors. Each of the sectors has a manager that reports to the owner, and subsequent roles follow as per the chart.

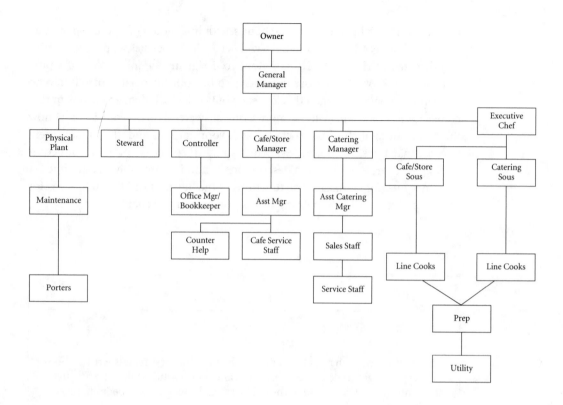

Putting Names and Faces to the Outline

Once the outlines are done and your proposed schedules are complete, once you know what your needs are, the search for a staff begins. Depending on the demographics of your store (i.e., how many other stores around are like it) and the experience and network of your managers as well as yourself, you may have some idea about who and how many experienced food service workers are available and/or looking for new work. It's a fact of business life that ambitious, hard-working and motivated people are always out there looking to move to the next rung on their career ladder.

Culinary schools are one logical place to start; it's often a win-win situation where individuals who have already declared an interest in food service benefit from gaining experience in a real world situation and you as the employer gain by hiring people who know their way somewhat around food. (An internship can often be arranged where work hours are flexible; these limited internships can lead to a full time positions if there's a good fit between employer and employee.)

Empty nesters, both women and men, also make good employees, as long as they are up to the physical demands of the job. This category may include early retirees or change-of-career types, as well as homemakers who never worked during their child rearing years but who pride themselves on their cooking abilities and depth of interest in food. As an added bonus, with maturity often comes reliability. You as the employer need dependable workers to handle the day-to-day, detail-laden business of running your store, whether you are present or not.

Also look to professional organizations and current employee recommendations for leads to possible candidates.

You can't completely rule out hiring employees away from other businesses in the area. We do not advise outright stealing of employees from your competitors, however gently scoping out the possibilities will most assuredly prove beneficial to your staffing needs.

Next, a sign in the window of your shop-to-be announcing your opening and staff needs, "Now Hiring for the Positions of . . . ," will certainly glean potential staffers. Don't overlook the local unemployment office or labor department office, which often houses a public employment service. There you will find a pool of people who are guaranteed to be looking for work and can start right away. If the option is open to you, try to establish a relationship with a counselor at the unemployment office who can write a careful and detailed job listing that clearly explains what your needs are. A face-to-face meeting with a job counselor will help to establish the standards you are looking for in a staff and may eliminate a flood of underqualified referrals from that office showing up at your doorstep for interviews.

Nongovernment employment services are another possible resource for your new staff but be prepared to pay a hefty placement fee for the service. Prescreening at these agencies can be widely variable so investigate thoroughly the agency's track record before exploring that route. Try to get recommendations of agencies from your manager(s) and/or other shop owners. You can always try to strike a deal for their fees. Perhaps you can pay only if the employee stays working for you for a set period of time (say three or six months), or perhaps the fee can be reduced based on the number of people you hire through that agency. In most large cities, there are specialized agencies that may prove to be useful, continuing sources of employees for your business.

Finally, the broadest outlet for hiring is to put an advertisement in one or several local papers. Generally speaking, the more skilled or sophisticated the job (e.g., assistant manager or higher level cook), the more important it is to advertise in the newspapers with the largest circulation in your area. For counter staff and utility positions the smaller, more local papers are your best outlet. Of course, for initial and general staffing needs your ad might read: "Specialty Food Store/ Gourmet to Go Hiring for all Positions. Relevant experience or culinary school grads preferred. . . ."

Remember that, once you're up and running, the best time to look for workers is when you don't need to fill any positions. Keep a current file on prospective employees so that you may turn to it when you need to find a replacement or an additional employee.

It will be most helpful to establish some internal structure for interviewing prospective employees, starting with guidelines about accepting applications, phone calls (or faxed résumés) or walk-ins. You may want to note the following on your signs and in your advertisements:

"Accepting applications Mondays through Wednesdays from 3:00 to 5:00 p.m."
"Call so-and-so (manager/chef) from 9:00 to noon."
"Fax your resume to. . . ."
"Walk-in interviews every afternoon from 2:00 to 4:00 p.m."

While you may feel like you need to see everyone who may walk by or read your ad, you will be happier not being bombarded by calls and walk-ins, which will undoubtedly take you away from other important and timely tasks. The mere act of setting down specifics about when and how you will take applications and/or interview potential staff will help you see how your prospective employees can follow directions. If they are detail oriented and understand rules and structure, they will most likely comply with your guidelines for interviewing and hiring. Candidates who show up for a walk-in interview in the late morning or after 5 p.m., when you indicated interviews would be held from 2:00 p.m. to 4:00 p.m., may be revealing more about themselves than they realize and may be offering you an indication of how they will handle customers and what their relationship to their manager will be while working for you. (To be sure, some worthy candidates may experience scheduling conflicts with a limited interview period. Calling ahead to explain that and requesting another interview slot is a very different scenario from that of an individual who shows up at the wrong time and still expects to be interviewed.)

Out of One, Many

While there are different technical or skill needs for different positions within your specialty food store, it's still advisable to create a standardized interview form for all employees, perhaps augmented by a few specialized questions for each key position (i.e., questions about experience of service for counter help, a request for more detail about cooking skills for kitchen help, etc.). By establishing a standard interview form you will have a single, objective criteria for selecting whom you want to hire and train. Of course, you will also have subjective impressions of the individual gleaned from the interview to bolster the more objective information. Acknowledging that your candidates' responses to technical questions may not vary much, you may be still be able to differentiate one interviewee from another by their degree of confidence, general demeanor, self-possession, or dress, all factors that will influence your decision whether to bring that person back for a second interview or to be trained. Conversely, someone of whom you or one of your managers takes a dim view may in fact be a perfect candidate for the manager or head of that department, and based on their answers to a standard interview, may later become a great employee. Predicting who will turn out to be assets or liabilities in your organization is not a science, but starting with some broad guidelines helps to increase the likelihood that you will pick more winners than losers in the hiring game.

What's the First Step?

First, the application: All stationery stores carry packets or pads of a standard application form. These are perfectly acceptable and also include questions that, by law, must be asked of potential employees, such as Social Security number, and so on. If you decide to create your own form, use the samples in Exhibits 7-2 and 7-3 for a start. They have been adapted from a standard application form in New York State and have the state-required questions on them. You will want to consult your state's department of labor to confirm what information you are required to ask from prospective employees in your state. The government sets these standards for its regulation of unemployment insurance and to monitor the job-hunting efforts of unemployed persons. (Be aware that the labor department may also require you to keep *all applications* on file for a certain number of years in case there is an investigation into someone's unemployment case.) Prior to beginning your interview process, find out this information from your local office.

What Should Be Included in This Interview Form?

A standard interview form can be comprised of anywhere between ten and twenty questions that range in scope from asking about a person's pervious work expe-

EXHIBIT 7-2

GENERAL STAFF INTERVIEW QUESTIONNAIRE

Name: _____

Phone: _____   Date: _____

1. Suppose you begin by telling me about your previous jobs. I'd be interested in knowing your salary, your duties and responsibilities, your likes and dislikes about the job, and any special achievements along the way.

   _____
   _____
   _____

   To what extent did you feel limited in your last position?

   _____

2. Can you fill me in on the gap of time between your last position and today?

   _____

3. How long have you been actively looking for a job? _____

4. When would you be able to start working for us full time? _____

5. What kind of salary are you seeking? _____

6. What are some of the opportunities you are looking for in your next position?

   _____
   _____

7. Do you prefer to delegate responsibility or perform tasks yourself?

   _____

8. What do you consider your strongest qualifications?

   _____

9. And your weakest?

   _____

10. What would you do if you noticed that a counterperson who has worked for us for several years has put a pound of coffee in his/her bag to take home?

    _____

11. What would you do if you noticed a new employee do it? _____

12. What can you tell me about some of your other interests? (What kind of music are you interested in, what do you spend time doing when you're not working?)

_____
_____

13. Do you have any questions?

_____
_____
_____
_____

E X H I B I T   7 - 3

SUGGESTED QUESTIONS WHEN INTERVIEWING INDIVIDUALS
TO FILL A MANAGERIAL POSITION

Manager Interview

Name: _____   Phone: _____

Date: _____   Interviewer: _____

1. How many people were you directly responsible for in your last position? _____ Were you solely responsible for hiring your staff? _____ And firing them? _____

2. What was the greatest managerial/organizational challenge you have ever met? _____

    How did you approach it and what were the results?
    _____
    _____

    How would you approach that same challenge now?
    _____
    _____

3. What are you committed to?
    _____
    _____
    _____
    _____

4. What would challenge that commitment?

_____
_____
_____
_____

5. Where do you see yourself in five years?

_____
_____
_____
_____

6. Let's say you begin working for us and everything's working, you've settled into a routine with regard to your tasks and have completed some projects. What's next for you?

_____
_____
_____
_____

7. What are some of the things about yourself that you would like to improve? (Note: You can say, "What about tact? Do you have as much tact as you'd like?" Or "Improve your attendance record," "Self-confidence," or "Controlling your temper")

_____
_____
_____
_____

8. Is it possible that you may be somewhat oversensitive to criticism?

_____
_____
_____
_____

9. How far are you willing to go when it's not working?

_____
_____
_____
_____

10. What about how long you've stayed at each job?

_____
_____
_____
_____

11. What's your role vis-à-vis kitchen staff?

    _____

    _____

12. What is the chef's job in the front of the house?

    _____

    _____

13. Given your past experience, I suppose there are some aspects of this job you would be looking forward to. What are these?

    _____

    _____

    _____

14. I suppose, on the other hand, there are some aspects you would really be "stretching" yourself to handle. Can you tell me about these?

    _____

    _____

15. (If applicable) What prompted you (or will prompt you) to take a cut in pay in order to work for us?

    _____

    _____

    _____

16. Where do you see yourself in five years?

    _____

    _____

17. Do you have any questions for us?

    _____

    _____

18. Do you have any special schedule requirements?

    _____

    _____

19. Three professional references.

    _____

    _____

    _____

rience, to what they liked the most/least about former jobs, to what their plans for the future are, to how they might define certain concepts that are important to the specialty food business (i.e., "What do you define as 'good service'?" or "When is the customer *not* right?" for counter staff and "When is it okay not to follow a recipe?", or "How do you determine if and when a perishable food should be discarded?" or "How would you sanitize a cutting surface in the kitchen?" for potential kitchen workers).

You will best be served by designing questions that do not inspire a simple "yes" or "no" answer. Try to formulate questions that begin with "What can you tell me about . . . ?" or "How would you respond to . . . ?" or "How did you handle . . . at your last job?" These are not trick questions; they are simply ways to establish the individual's perspective and way of thinking. This is your first chance to assess the values and attitudes of the people who may come to work for you and how those values and attitudes mesh with your own and complement the goals of your business. It is often the most time you will have to speak to each of your potential employees individually prior to opening, so we recommend that you use the time to get a good sense if these potentially talented and often nervous people are going to represent your vision and be creative and effective ambassadors for your business products. You might even wish to think of the potential candidate as a newly arriving member of your family. Can you see living with him/her day to day? Answers to these, in combination with the candidates' technical skills, will indicate who to select to be trained.

At the interview, know in advance what set of general skills you are looking for. Then set out the broad outlines for what the job entails. Define the job loosely, allowing for employees to promote their talents outside of the strict job definition.

In the interview, ask leading questions and trust your instinct about interpersonal chemistry. How does the interaction between you and the candidate feel? Accounting for an understandable amount of nervousness or diffidence on the part of the interviewee, how comfortable is the exchange between you? Are the respondents' answers adversarial in tone? Does the individual make steady eye contact with you? And what about the attire and overall appearance of the individual you have in front of you? Think long and hard before making a commitment. You are hiring nothing less than the ambassador of good will for your business. Take your time to find what seems like the right person for the right job. It's easier to hire the right person in the first place than attempt to remake the "wrong" person into the kind of individual who will best represent you to your customers. Don't count on things to change much once the individual has been offered and accepted the position.

Getting Through the Interview

First, don't underestimate the job interview as a crucial part of the process. Asking tough questions and listening carefully to your candidates' responses is the first step to finding the right individuals for the job. Think carefully about what each of your jobs requires in terms of the personality profile of the person filling it. Individuals who tend to be more people-oriented will naturally do better where they can interact regularly with customers. Others who are more analytical, disciplined, and introverted will no doubt do better in support functions in the back office, such as bookkeeping, accounting, and purchasing.

Read between the lines when you evaluate the responses to questions about past work history. Don't hesitate to ask about the applicant's first job and what he or she learned from the experience. The answers are often illuminating. Pose "either–or" and "why" questions that afford the candidate some latitude in answering and demonstrate an ability for critical thinking. Isolate his or her preferences for working with a well-defined job description versus a position that requires more self-starting, initiative-driven work, and act accordingly based on their answers. Hire attitude first; product knowledge and the details of the job can be taught to a person with the right attitude, even if he or she does not have culinary background. In the interview, look beyond first impressions to see the potential of each candidate.

Rather than have to screen responses to a newspaper want ad, advertise your positions in trade journals and local culinary association newsletters to target a more narrowly focused readership who are more apt to have the background and interests you require.

If you are using résumés to make the first cut, read them carefully and ask for details on the past work history noted. How did the candidate feel about past managers and co-workers? How does the individual feel about your checking his or her references—what will the references say?

What Is the Best Plan for Hiring and Training?

It's not as scary as you think, because you have already created a framework from which to start to build your staff. Remember the organizational chart you wrote for your business plan? Get it out. Sit down with your key manager(s) and/or chef (who should have been on board by two to three months before opening) and review it. Review your projected sales and the divisions in which you expect to generate those sales. Take out that employee schedule you wrote to help figure out staff costs for your Profit and Loss statement that went into the business plan. With all of these as guides, begin to scrutinize and edit the organizational chart and the payroll schedule and budget. They are helpful reference points that you already spent valuable time creating.

If you are working with both a chef and a general or operations manager, ask them to outline schedules for their departments (Exhibit 7-4 shows a sample). From these schedules ask your team to determine how many people they will need to fill that schedule. To this add between 30% and 40% and use that as a guide for how many of each position you will need to hire by opening day. The buffer is for people who are hired and trained, but for many reasons don't make it to the show. Also, you will want to overstaff a bit at first (which, remember, you have budgeted for) to weed out some folks who are just not up to snuff and to allow for any gaps or oversights in scheduling. While your new staff will most likely be looking for full-time work, or to make the most money as possible, it is not advisable to overbook your newly trained team, overtax their capabilities while still green at their new jobs, or in any way doom them to an early failure.

EXHIBIT 7-4

STAFF SCHEDULE

The following is a simple grid that can be used both to schedule your staff and to project weekly payroll. Often a manager may be inclined to overstaff to protect him/herself from an unexpected rush, or understaff to protect a tight budget. Usually his/her actions are taken out of excitement or worry, and meant well in either case.

This schedule should be done weekly in a new operation, and then perhaps less frequently once a pattern of business and regular staff is achieved. It can be very valuable to save every week's schedule and, when the week is completed, make a note or two as to how the schedule met the needs of the business that week. A manager should always calculate the weekly payroll when drafting up the schedule and compare those figures to the budget. If there is a large variation, especially in the direction of spending more than budgeted, your managers should be instructed to have a conversation with you so that a strategy can be made to keep the overall budget in line.

STAFF SCHEDULE

Name	Monday	Tuesday	Wednesday	Thursday	Friday	Saturday	Sunday	Total Hours	Pay Rate	Total Payroll

TRAINING

Calling potential employees in for training, after the application and interview process, is the next step to hiring them. Remember: a person in training does not have to have been hired by you. There are rules and regulations set by local labor departments about training periods. Be clear in your operations manual (discussed below) that just because a person is brought in for training doesn't mean that he or she is guaranteed a job. You should make it clear that, even after bringing someone on board after training they are in your employ on a trial basis for a specified period of time (say, three to six weeks) before being fully considered "on board." This will relieve you of the laborious warning period if you see that a person is just not going to fit into your organization after working for you for only a couple of weeks.

Whatever the local laws is in your state, be sure to comply with them to avoid repercussions and a bad reputation in the industry later on.

With your management team, determine a training schedule for each main group of employees (i.e., kitchen and counter/floor staff) separately. Let your managers create the training schedule and propose a training budget to you for approval. Decide which team member will be responsible for which aspect of training for each group. (The kitchen staff should have some training in salesmanship and the counter/floor staff should have some training in the menu and at least a nodding acquaintance with actual kitchen skills and procedures.) As the owner, you may want to design and implement a general training session or two on work ethic, the background and purpose of your concept, business goals as related to your expectations about staff, and team-building strategies.

With your management team, design a training program and schedule that fits your needs (e.g., when construction is nearing completion and your hired staff can begin to work in their new "home" and perhaps later when there are people invited to attend a tasting of your wares). Make sure the training regimen includes all aspects of the job for every position being trained. Also make sure that all prospective employees have gotten a copy of the employee/operations manual prior to the first day of training (creating this manual is discussed in a later section). Reviewing it with them might be a good way to begin the first day of training (assign a more detailed reading of the manual as homework).

How to Structure Training

Each job should be divided into small units of tasks; training is then structured around those units, or modules, which will later be strung together to comprise a day in the life of each employee. Basic modules might include the following:

Kitchen Staff—Food sanitation and handling, knife skills, food storage and inventory practices, sauces and dressings, basic grilling, braising, frying, baking, and so on.

Counter Staff—Basic customer service, familiarity with operations of equipment (coffee, espresso, juice machines), sandwich making, packaging (wrapping, boxing, and bagging), cash register training, returns, floor maintenance (lights, dusting, stocking shelves).

Training is done this way for the following three reasons:

1. Starting people off slowly and deliberately, task by task, skill by skill, will give each of your new team members the best opportunity to succeed in their training, and, later, on the job.

2. You can conserve training time (and dollars) by combining skills or modules that need to be learned by all staff, regardless of position. (This intermingling in training will help foster team spirit as well as give you another opportunity to see how each team member gets along with each other team member and adapts to a variety of personalities.)

3. When it comes down to the nitty-gritty and fine-tuning the specialized aspect of the positions at your store, you will have already weeded out people who are not quite right for you at this time. You will then have a slightly smaller pool to work with in the key training periods. By focusing on the most promising individuals, you stand to be able to give more valuable instruction and get more to those who make the cut. In return you will probably get more indication from the trainees that what you are imparting is getting through to them.

Have Some Fun Before the Curtain Goes Up

You may want to create a celebration as the finale to the preopening training period, somehow capping all the hard work that's been done so far in a way for everyone to see the results. Perhaps this is in the form of a trial run, a day when the store is open to friends and family only, and everything is free or half price. Perhaps it is a series of role-playing exercises where one set of trainees cooks and serves to the other set. You will all want to have a few dress rehearsals before the curtain goes up!

Based on the performance of your team in training, your managers will create an employee schedule that best utilizes the talents and skill levels demonstrated. Mix your talent up and don't put all your best performers on one shift; mix the leaders (or stars) with the base support. Think of the lineup of a baseball team and create your schedules as a mix of what will best serve your needs at different times of the day, week, and season.

All in all, the message about training is: give your prospective staff the best opportunity to succeed. To do this you must structure the hiring and training process in a way that's equitable, that fully communicates who you are and what this business is about, and that offers as much technical and team-building training as required for you to get optimum results.

THE FLIP SIDE: FIRING AN EMPLOYEE

Dismissing an employee is the one aspect of store ownership and management that truly could be called a necessary evil. Sometimes the actions, attitudes, or codes of behavior of an employee are such that firing is the only recourse an owner has. The decision to fire an employee is usually based in part on demonstrable facts of behavior or wrongful actions and in part on a strong gut feeling that that employee is not acting ethically or in keeping with your store's stated mission. Whatever the reason, chances are that, as the owner, you will know when an employee needs to be reprimanded or fired.

First, the Warning

Before taking any definitive action, check with your local labor office to learn about your employees' rights about being properly notified prior to a firing (or layoff). If you are working with union members there will certainly be a specific procedure that you will be required to follow. Get to know these rules first, include them in your operations manual (discussed below), and go over these in training with your staff. Above all, *communicate with the employee as soon as a problem arises.*

Use your operations manual as the source of all information about how you will handle employee behavior. Here you can outline how and when a warning system will be utilized to notify employees of a problem with management. With these policies spelled out in black and white, it's far easier to implement them. It's also easier to reprimand an employee for violation of a company rule or code of behavior if that rule or code of behavior has been well delineated in your operations manual. Holding *all* employees accountable for proper behavior, compliance with rules, and policies makes it easier to be objective when dealing with an employee whose actions call for a reprimand. Enforcing policies across the board will help to reduce the temptation to take each case individually. Being dispassionate is easier said than done when dealing with an employee whose performance does not measure up to your expectations or whose behavior is less than salutary, but it is the necessary part of the "necessary evil" noted above. Bear in mind that projecting an image of indecisiveness can end up costing you time, money, and the loyalty of good employees in the long run.

Three Strikes and Then Out

If you utilize a simple system of three warnings accompanied by some moderate measures of discipline (losing a shift or two, not getting priority scheduling, giving up opportunity for a raise for a certain period of time), you will avoid undoing all of the hard work you have done to build and maintain an effective staff. Even with careful consideration and thoughtful review of each employee's performance, you are bound to make some mistakes or wrong judgment calls. Sometimes, there is no clear culprit or a series of events that led to a mishap (e.g., the wrong date or time for the delivery of catering order).

> Mark Goldberg, a builder of food service operations based in the Bronx, New York, relates the following scenario: A corporation ordered a lunch for thirty-five. Fifteen minutes after the order should have been delivered, the customer called the caterer to ask where the food was. The catering manager was thoroughly surprised, since the lunch was noted for the following week on his calendar. The client was understandably annoyed and resorted to ordering in pizza. The next week, a lunch for thirty-five appeared at the client's offices. When the client called the caterer, this is what he had to say: "Last week I thought you were just stupid, now I think you're really stupid."

These and many other things can and do happen, so a "three strikes and you're out" policy gives you the opportunity to establish a pattern of suspect behavior and also offers the employee an opportunity to make a turnaround. In the long run, this can save you money (key staff replacements can be painful and costly in finder's fees and training).

In a larger operation, warnings may be issued directly to the employee by their supervisor or by the manager on duty. In smaller operations, it's usually a case of sitting down and talking with the employee in question, in private, either before or after a scheduled shift. In either case, be sure that you (or the individual on your staff to whom you have delegated the responsibility) make it a point to set aside uninterrupted time to discuss the situation with the employee. Get the employee's feedback and document the exchange fully.

Warnings should be written by you or the supervisor/manager who issues them and signed by the employee and a member of the management team. Once signed, the employee should be reminded what the warning means, which warning of the three this is, and what he/she needs to do to maintain good status with the company. It's up to you (in concert with your management staff) to decide whether warnings may be erased from the employee's record after a period of time (say, six months) or if they are retained as part of a permanent employee file. As a responsible employer, you will want to take a little extra time with an employee who has been issued a warning to offer him or her some more training, some time off, or some coaching in general. It's important to remember that many of your employees have gone through a long and arduous route to be part of the team that represents you and your vision; you have an investment in them. This investment will, from time to time, take nurturing, which is half of the "contract" you negotiate with your employees. Just like children in a family, employees who "act out" are often signaling that they need a little attention. They wish to get some feedback about their performance and need to hear that they are valuable to you. You're still the boss, and you have instituted rules and regulations and when these are broken you will issue warnings. After the warnings, however, there may be some education needed on your part or the part of your managers to help bring the employee back to the fold, and, perhaps, get him/her to the next level.

What About Serious Infractions?

There are some kinds of behavior or some rules broken that are more dire than others. Mishandling of cash and physical violence are the most obvious examples of these. You may state in your operations manual that any events related to either of these (and others that you choose) are equivalent to three warnings in one. In other words, you may maintain the right to fire someone *on the spot* if his/her actions or behavior result in hardship or danger for the company or another employee. As with the other warnings, write this one up too, keep it in the employee's file, and keep the file on premises for as long as the labor department deems necessary. Disgruntled employees that you fire may file a complaint with the local labor department, claiming you mishandled their employment; such claims might be efforts to get even, or to get their jobs back. By knowing and following the rules and keeping accurate and tidy records, you will avoid a lot of backtracking if this happens.

Effective systems of both hiring and firing will help establish you and your business as well run and will also assist in time and cost-saving processes. Utilize your key management staff to design and build the structure of your rules and regulations, interview forms, training period, and actions of discipline. They will be, after all, the ones who are responsible for carrying out the bulk of this work. Keeping this in perspective and devoting resources to the development and maintenance of your employees, you will have a head start toward running a cohesive organization and a profitable business.

THE OPERATIONS MANUAL

It's to be expected that you will have to lay a certain amount of track while the train is moving, that you will have to fine-tune your operations after opening (at least several times). Before the doors are open to customers, however, and while there still is the luxury of planning time (and we know that it won't feel that way) you would do well to prepare for opening those doors by creating a thorough operations manual, set down on paper in a readable, accessible form. If your key personnel are already in place, utilize their expertise in combination with your own to set the tone for the way the operation is to be run and organized; have them help write your operations manual.

The operations manual is a document that will manage all of your resources, both human and material. It is a guide to operating your store, written for your personnel. It is organized in sections that cover the concept and history of the business as well as the background of you, the owners, and other key personnel (perhaps the chef and manager). It is a checklist of store facts. It acts as a directory of basic functions and procedures, and, most importantly, it is a resource book with menus, product listings, and prices of goods sold as well as an outline of policies and procedures for your staff. All of the preliminary work preparing it will pay off when you open by providing a consistent resource to helping you maintain standards in all areas of your operation. The operations manual is a training tool and the bible for your business.

What will your book of rules be like? How will you convey your corporate vision clearly and persuasively to everyone from the highest level of management to the maintenance staff and all layers in between? Depending on your management style, your business' operations manual or store bible may vary in content and degree of specificity.

Think about what it takes to operate a great store. Refer to the store comparisons you wrote for your feasibility study, honing in on particular attributes of stores you have visited that you would like to incorporate into your store. Identify what your store's strengths and areas of special interest will be in the key areas of quality and variety of products, service, display, store layout, services offered, merchandising, and so on. Together with your manager(s), define the concept of the store, and set about identifying daily procedures and staff policies based on that concept and nature of your store. Again, objectivity is your best vehicle to effective and responsible communication. Create rules you can live by and grow with, rules that reflect the intent of your key managers. Make sure the carrying-out of these rules will yield consistency, as well as the best possible service and follow-through for your customers. Remember, *consistency* is the number one element that cements customer loyalty. If customers know what to expect, even if it isn't "the best . . ." or "the most . . ." (but, of course, with all this careful planning it will be both), they will return.

As with the feasibility study and the business plan, the task of writing an operations manual will be easier if you use an outline, which we provide below. To customize this outline to suit your business emphasize the nature of your business, in its organization and content—service, product, or a combination of both.

Begin by casting your mission statement in terms that will make sense from the eyes of an employee. This statement should include your purpose, your goals, your concept, and somehow communicate your business ethic. Your vision of the business needs to be understood and adopted by all who work for you. You can use slogans, which become statements of your corporate culture. If you believe them (and you must), your employees will catch some of your fervor. Phrases like "Do it right," "Be the best," and "We stand behind everything we sell" can be effective shorthand to characterize your commitment to the success and growth of the business. Try to come up with one or two original phrases that capture who you are and why you're different. One of our favorites is a clever adaptation of a well-known slogan: "The customer may not always be right, but he/she must be satisfied." These, as written in your manual and read by each of your staff members, become a mantra for your business and an anchor for your employees' everyday dealings with customers and products.

Next, create a table of contents for the manual. Then, with your management team, begin to fill in the sections. One successful outline for an operations manual includes the following:

1. **Store Concept and Mission Statement**—Adapted for the eyes of your staff and including concept, goals, and sense of place and team

2. **Owner's History**—General background of owner(s) and what led up to this point

3. **Store or Business History**—When the business was founded, built, and opened, how it has grown and so on

4. **Store Details and General Information**—Address; telephone, fax, and e-mail; store hours and days of operation; store size; number of employees; range of

products and services (in brief); payment methods accepted; services available; information about specials and/or advertising

5. **Product Line**—Update regularly with current product list and menus with prices

6. **Store Policies and Standard Procedures**—To include: clocking in/out; uniforms, cleanliness, jewelry, and so on; vacation and sick days and pay; payday, paycheck cashing, and so on; how to answer the phone; how to handle queries/complaints by customers (more on this in service); discipline, rules about behavior, and causes for dismissal; staff discount

7. **Organizational Chart**—This should include all owners, management, and staff positions and define their roles and interrelationships in the business' hierarchy

8. **Job Descriptions**—Include one for each position

9. **Service**—This should be the largest section of the manual, and we offer some specifics in Chapter 8 on key issues of service.

More Tips for Writing the Operations Manual

Some topics, and our suggestions for handling them, to include in the operations manual:

Absences and Tardiness—Set a clear policy about paid sick days and make clear from the start your dependence on your employees to be on time, ready to work. Make it clear that their late arrival puts an undue burden on their fellow workers and neither you nor your staff like a latecomer, with or without an excuse. Employees who are frequently absent or late (or both) are rarely an asset to your business and, lacking any compelling reasons to the contrary, should be promptly dismissed and replaced. There is no room in your organization for individuals who can't (or won't) pull with the team.

Appearance of Hair (Also Facial Hair for Males)—Explain required use of hair restraints for longer hair (male and female), both for front of the house and for kitchen workers. (Health department codes provide good third-party back up for your prescriptions for behavior.)

Bonus Based on Performance—A general statement will back up your verbal assurances that you are the kind of boss who will recognize outstanding quality of work and reward it accordingly

Dress Code—State here your broad preferences about employees' attire; also include requirements about employees wearing aprons, hats, T-shirts, or other apparel emblazoned with your logo during their shifts; kitchen employees must be separately addressed with clear, professional standards of dress. Include here suggestions for proper, comfortable nonskid footwear (kitchen and behind-counter floors can get slippery; standing on one's feet for prolonged periods of time also is more easily accomplished with good support from proper shoes).

Free Foods or Some Fair System of Discounting—This should be clearly spelled out , applied to all personnel equally, and leave no room for misinterpretation; include here a policy about discounts for foods purchased by employees' immediate relatives as well.

Illness—Be safe rather than sorry; let your employees know that being sick on the job is a hazard to the health of other employees and also a hazard to customers' health. Insist that sick employees stay at home to recuperate. Doctor's release should be required for absences longer than two days. Spreading germs spreads no goodwill for your business.

Jewelry—Cover here your thoughts about earrings, nose rings, and other body piercing; set a standard and stick to it. What's tolerated in one employee sends a message to all other employees. You need to be consistent here; take a stand and stand by it. Again, in food service, less is more. So use good common sense here and think of the customer when setting down rules about what's appropriate in your store.

Overtime for Hourly Employees—Set forth a policy; this is standard and can be lifted verbatim from the Department of Labor's Fair Labor Standards Act. Note that although the provisions of this act are explicit about minimum wage and overtime, they do not require that the employer offer vacation pay, holiday pay, sick pay, severance pay, jury duty pay, voting pay, premium pay for weekend work, premium pay for daily overtime work, shift differentials, rest periods, coffee breaks, or meal breaks. These are all at the discretion of the employer.

Overtime for Salaried Employees—Define here in a short statement your expectations that salaried, exempt employees are contracted to work until the day's work is done. On especially busy days and during peak holiday periods, all efforts will be made to make the workload manageable, hiring extra help to relieve undue burdens on these individuals. Annual bonuses and/or profit sharing programs, as tokens of your gratitude for a job well done, usually go a long way toward keeping these employees happy. Employees who are exempt from overtime, and are therefore considered salaried, must be employed in a bona fide executive, administrative, or professional capacity, or as an outside salesperson.

Paid Vacations—Set up a clear schedule of eligibility for paid vacation time based on term of service: one suggestion is a day for each two months of service after the first three months of probationary employment, or a week for each full year worked. Set a maximum allowed on length of vacation accruable.

Personal Hygiene—Here is an area where it is often easier to state in writing what you expect. Employees who seem to violate written prescriptions for personal cleanliness can be urged to read this section as a discreet reminder of your standards. Each employee, whether working in retail or production, is your ambassador, whether on the front lines in direct contact with customers or in direct contact with the foods you are selling; state the need for clean nails and no offensive body odor or bad breath. Use of strong perfumes or colognes is often taboo in an environment that should engage all of the senses, including the customer's sense of smell. In a food store, the foods and preparation of the foods should provide the aroma; appealing to your customers' senses with enticing aromas helps to sell your food; perfume and cologne tend to get in the way here.

Raises—These should be given in response to outstanding performance over a reasonable period of time (to be defined in personnel interviews, and then in twice yearly reviews after working a probationary period of say, three months. This should be a general statement that expresses your views about rewarding good work, a restatement of what you have said in person during job interview and any follow-up interviews prior to hiring.

Sick Days—Here you need to spell out your policy on paying employees for days missed due to illness. Impress upon your employees the importance of notifying you if they will be out sick by calling you either the night before they are due to report for work (if they feel ill then and will probably not make it in the next day) or in the early morning of the day they will be missing. After missing a certain number of days, employees should bring with them a doctor's note on the day they return to work, stating that they are released from the doctor's care and free to return to work. Hourly employees should be addressed separately from those who are salaried and exempt from overtime. Although not required by law, sick pay may be extended to your hourly workers as a sign that you value the good work they do and recognize that their attendance record is otherwise unblemished.

Zero Tolerance of Theft—It should go without saying that stealing by one's employees is an owner's worst nightmare. An employee's trustworthiness is usually sensed upon meeting and interviewing that individual. Good, checkable references, both work and personal, also help to establish that this individual is someone worth hiring. Incidents of theft by employees can be difficult to prove (in the case of accountability for cash, unless you set out clear shifts during which only one employee has responsibility, you will have no recourse if the cash drawer comes up short). Product inventories are harder to track with 100% accuracy, even using computer inventory programs. If you have suspicions, however, that an employee is pilfering shelf items, you are probably right, and if you can pinpoint the disappearance of foods during that individual's shift, then you should confront that individual and put him or her on notice first, probation next, and then discharge him or her. Profit margins are small enough in the specialty food retail business without reducing them further by shrinkage at the hands of your employees, who are supposed to be looking out for you, keeping an eye on customers who may have sticky fingers.

Zero Tolerance of Alcohol or Drug Abuse—This applies to use on the job or to an employee's arrival at the workplace having used alcohol or drugs prior to coming to work. This says it all.

By the time you are finished with the operations manual, you will have:

1. Reexamined both your short-term goals (getting open, staffing all positions, producing lines of product to sell, systematizing order-taking, delivery, basic staff training on the job).
2. Thought about your long-term goals (growth, mobility, flexibility, and promotability of staff).
3. Determined how many people or positions there are to account for in job descriptions and considered their interrelationships (for a graphic approach to this, see the making of an organizational chart, Exhibit 7-1).
4. Decided the most important elements of your business and given your future staff tools to communicate these, to sell your products, and to help you reach your goals.
5. Designated a person on your team to demonstrate, teach, work through problems, and set an example for every procedure you wish to institute among your staff. It is unfair to expect your staff to carry out tasks and procedures that management is unable or unwilling to do. The operations manual is an active tool at creating the spirit and message of team work—from store maintenance to merchandising, from cooking to selling.

Lastly, remember to update your operations manual regularly so that employees coming on at regular intervals get the current information. Reviewing the manual regularly yourself will help you to keep in touch with the basics. You can become so mired in the details of day-to-day operations that you lose perspective on the business as a whole. In order to lend direction and focus to your business, you not only need to be constantly aware of how all the little details are being handled but also see the big picture as well. Your operations manual can, therefore, function as the fullest expression of your hopes and expectations for the business. Therefore, it deserves a lot of thought on your part and the on the part of your key personnel. Nothing less than a clear-eyed, dispassionate, and comprehensive view will guide your business in the direction you wish it to go.

CASH MANAGEMENT IN THE SPECIALTY FOOD BUSINESS— KEEPING TRACK OF WHAT COMES IN AND GOES OUT

Cash management is one of the most important things about operating a retail business. After all the work you have done to establish the business, from feasibility study to business plan to getting financed to build-out to opening, this single aspect of daily operations can be the make-it-or-break-it aspect of your success as a specialty food entrepreneur.

Considering its crucial nature, the subject of cash management could fill an entire book. First-time retailers who have many other issues to address when running a new business are often plagued by the question: "How do I set up cash controls that will be thorough and really work?" As the owner of a business that is about to open, you should not let fear get in the way of effective decisive action.

As with all of the other essential elements of planning your business, the mystique of careful cash management is best addressed with research, a comprehensive approach to understanding your needs, and staying committed to your decisions.

First, the research: The written materials you will find on cash management rarely describe the day-to-day actions of ringing up sales, making change, getting change from the bank, reconciling the cash drawer at the end of the shift or the end of the day, the counting and recounting of piles of small amounts of cash, or making bank deposits. Textbooks used in restaurant and hospitality are a good source of information for the accounting perspective of cash management but the practical side is largely ignored.

Do Some In-the-Field Research

Take a tour of the competition or model operations upon which you will base your store. Pay particular attention to how they handle cash. How many cashier stations does each store have relative to the size of the store? Is there a central cashier station and checkout, or is there one at each department? Does more than one person have access to the cash register at a time? How does the manager interface with the cashier, if at all? How much volume (in numbers of customers if not dollar volume of sales) does each register handle per hour, or per quarter hour (send a "spy" out to get the scoop if need be)? Are the cash registers part of a computer network (if so, jot down what brands you see)? Do they appear to be independent units (write down the names of these)? Take a note as to whether the stores you visit accept credit cards, checks, and/or have house accounts.

See What's on the Market

The second mode of research is to contact a few point of sale computer companies and ask to have a demonstration of their retail systems. Also visit a vendor of cash registers to see the variety and complexity of what is available in an independent cash register system. Additionally, you may want to seek out point of sale vendors (both hardware and software) at restaurant/hospitality or specialty food trade shows. In this forum you can see (and, ultimately, may be overwhelmed by) the wide variety offered on the market. Then you can begin to understand the virtues and differences of each kind of system and also get a sense about how much you will need to allot in your budget for these systems.

Salespeople for cash management systems are usually extremely knowledgeable about the benefits of their products. These benefits are measured largely in the ways that the various machines record sales transactions in detail, in how they later break the data down for analysis, in how they integrate the sales with other important business functions such as inventory and payroll, as well as in how they protect owners from employee theft. The most significant difference between a cash register, even a fancy electronic one, and a point of sale computer system is the level of integration the cash register function has with back-of-the-house bookkeeping. The general rule is, the more involved and integrated the system, the tighter the cash controls are going to be. This is only logical: A point of sale computer system, with electronic and software ties to the back of the house, connects the selling functions to the other management functions of the business.

It pays to do this systems research early on in the business planning phase. The system you select to manage the cash in the front of your store will affect the design and construction of your selling floor (and power needs as well), and will determine how your bookkeeping and accounting will be handled overall.

Simply stated, a point of sale computer system is a combination cash register and computer system in one. To the counterperson and the customer it looks and acts like a cash register, ringing up sales and making change. With this kind of system, however, you have the capability of seamlessly processing sales using cash, credit cards, checks, and house accounts. For the manager, the point of sale computer system is a tool that calculates inventory and compares it to sales, can aid in determining and maintaining food costs and payroll costs, and minimizes the managers' own contact with the cash on an hourly basis. For the store owner, it is a system that does all of the above to better manage the business as well as act as a minimizer of theft.

Point of sale systems are the best minimizers of theft. As cash registers and monitors of inventory and stock simultaneously, the computer functions as a recorder of transactions, numbering each in an internal system. Transactions can only be deleted by a manager who has the secret code allowing him or her to do so. Even then, these transactions are coded by the ID number of the person initiating the function, so that every transaction, whether regular sales, voids, account transfers, discounts, or giveaways, is recorded in the machine.

The appeal of a largely cash business is largely obvious; however, there is a downside. In a business where many people handle the cash coming in, there are at least as many opportunities for mishandling and theft as there are cash handlers. It's only logical that the tighter the system, the more controls and checks you have built into it, the fewer the opportunities for theft. You will want to (and have to) engage your key managers in establishing and maintaining controls. You will also want to establish and maintain your own set of controls that no one else in your business is privy to.

What's Next?

Once you've researched cash management approaches, the next and very important stage in selecting one for your business is evaluating your budget for potential systems. As expected, the more complicated and thorough point of sale systems will indeed cost the most. The hardware consists of actual cash register units as well the back office computer, which a manager or bookkeeper will use to process all the information generated in the front of the house. In addition, for all the functions to be available, and for the hardware components to "talk" to each other, software will be needed. The sophistication of software packages varies, but every point of sale computer will at least need the basic cash tendering function and the ability to transfer information and collate it in the central office. What you do with the information once it gets there (from inventory to payroll to general ledger functions) are the optional add-ons, quite costly to buy and to be trained in (i.e., having high "up-front costs") but definitely useful.

By doing your cash management system research and "shopping around" up front, you will be better equipped to make a decision about what your business' needs are. There is no absolute rule of thumb about the ratio of projected sales to level of sophistication of the cash management system, but one thing is clear: Buy as much as you can afford. In addition to their antitheft features, the more expensive systems will reduce the amount of time a manager will have to spend calculating and coordinating the sales and inventory records of your business. This means that your key personnel have more time to be training your staff and to commit to sales and marketing overall—the aspects of your business that often get put at the bottom of the list when day-to-day details need to be attended to. Think also about your business' growth: Even if one cash register is sufficient today, will it still be enough in a year or two or five? If you plan to add different segments to your business, such as mail order, catering, delivery, will you be able to integrate controls for these into a relatively unsophisticated manual cash management system? Business owners who have opened small and upgraded later will most likely tell you that they regretted not having placed a higher priority on acquiring a more sophisticated system early in the game. Aside from missing certain crucial information while starting up and running a new business, and sustaining possible losses of cash from mishandling and theft, contracting for and installing a new system while you are operating can be cumbersome. It can be stressful to switch gears in midstream, and it often forces management to oversee the running of two systems simultaneously until the kinks in the new system are ironed out.

Okay, now that you get the point about point of sale systems, what do you do with the cash every day?

Just as you have control systems for other day-to-day operating functions, it is recommended that you have a list of checks and balances for the cash management function of your business. Begin by thinking about the flow of cash on a daily basis, beginning with where you will keep cash secure on premises. You may want to discuss with your contractor various types of safes that can be built into the floor or walls of your back office. When thinking about the kind of safe to buy and install, think about who will need access to it, for depositing money, retrieving money, or both.

The cash you will need on premises daily includes your cash drawers (a "bank" of between $150 and $300 per shift, per register is recommended); additional change stored in a secure vault (up to $500, chiefly made up of singles, fives, and quarters); bank deposits ready to be made; and whatever petty cash you feel necessary to have on hand to pay bills. (Petty cash, that is, hard currency on hand for cash purchases, should be kept to a minimum, and the actual funds should be taken from your checking account so that you have a record of all purchases to be included in your expense reports.)

It is most important that cash amounts in your cash drawers, change reserve, and petty cash box be kept consistent from day to day and week to week. The actual cash you use for the cash drawers and change reserve, because it stays consistent, does not ever have to be calculated with your other cash assets; that money is there only to assist you in doing business and will itself never be used for anything.

Whether you choose a "manual" cash register system (i.e., one, two, or more independent units) or a point of sale system for your business, you should establish a checklist for the beginning and end of the shift/day functions, including the actual handling of cash.

Start with the store opening; The procedure we outline here is a common scenario used by many small to medium sized businesses. The opening manager comes in to open up the store. He or she takes from the safe the cash drawer(s) that have been set up (i.e., with proper change amounts, always verified by the new manager) the day before by the closing manager. Using these, the opening manager sets up the registers for the new day's sales. Bank deposits that were also set up by the closing manager are recounted for verification, and then they are brought to the bank, along with any big bills from the change reserve that need to be cashed into smaller bills and coins, and a check to replenish petty cash if that reserve is low.

When the cashiers report for work, at the beginning of their shift, they too should verify the change in their cash drawers by reading the drawer and signing a calculator tape or receipt to confirm the amount that's there. When working with a "manual" or independent cash register system, it is recommended that only one person have access to a cash drawer during any given shift. Of course, the reason for this is that it minimizes potential for theft and pinpoints who is responsible for transactions during that period. With a point of sale computer system, each employee who wants to enter the system has to sign in to gain access, and thereafter each transaction is coded by employee. It is easier in this case to track missing money, but it is still recommended that a separate cash drawer be issued to each employee at the start of his or her shift.

During the course of the day the kinds of transactions a cashier will have to make will include cash sales, credit card sales, house account sales, sales by check, returns for exchange or credit (for various reasons), and voided sales. Sales and returns will usually be coded by department (i.e., cheese, produce, cookbooks, etc.). The cashier may also be responsible for making payments to vendors from the till (and, again, we advise keeping these to a bare minimum). So, money is coming in *and* going out from the register during the course of the day. Even manual cash register systems have a variety of keys that will keep track of the various transactions, and each system will come with a complete set of instructions for this. Take the time, or assign your managers to take the time, to fully understand the capabilities of your cash register or point of sale equipment. The functions were designed to aid the managers' and owners' ability to track cash transactions, the lifeblood of your business.

During the course of the day the manager may be called upon to assist the cashier with certain aspects of the cash management. Most often this involves either a customer complaint combined with a return of merchandise, or a replenishment of the register's change. Issuing credit for returned items will typically need a manager's approval, and it's up to you to determine the policies that work best for your store. Restocking the register with change simply involves replacing larger bills (from the cash register) with smaller bills and coins (from your reserve in the safe). This and all other cash register or point of sale system processes are simple as long as one cardinal rule is always obeyed: Every transaction, going in or out of the register, must be balanced with a record of the same on the other side. For example, when getting change, what comes out of the cash drawer in larger bills must be replaced to the penny by smaller bills and coins. This keeps the cash drawer balanced, and also keeps your change reserve balanced. When making petty cash payments from the cash drawer, a legibly written receipt for a particular amount of money replaces the money that has been taken out of the drawer. Adding a further dimension to the management of your business overall, a point of sale system will automatically remove an item from your store's inventory when a sale for that item is rung up.

The closing of the shift or day's sales is often referred to as "Z-ing out" the register, since the register key must be aligned with the Z position. (It's best to issue a Z key only to staff members with authority to perform this function.) This is when the tally of sales is calculated and the balancing of the day's cash is done. Each cashier's sales summary (Z-report, "deposit" and worksheet of the day's transactions, created in-house to provide you with information you may want to track such as weather, store specials, and other events or particulars of the day) will be verified by a manager prior to depositing it in the safe, then to be processed by the opening manager. Because a variety of transactions occur on a particular day or shift, this can be a rather complicated process. Many store owners have devised simple enough systems to enable the cashiers themselves to do the tallying. These computations are later verified by a manager and the moneys are then usually deposited into the bank by a manager.

As noted above, some store owners prefer to have the managers take total responsibility for the cash at the point when the register is being "Z-e'd out," minimizing the cashier's ability to know certain details of the business such as sales volume. There are no hard and fast rules about this. However, through strong team building your sales staff (including your cashiers) can be engaged as your partners in business. The more they know and can be responsible for, the more they can feel themselves a part of a growing entity, reaping the rewards along with you through promotions, bonuses and raises. With strong controls in place it may be beneficial to delegate as many tasks as possible to lower rank employees, thereby freeing your management staff for more of the sales-building work that will grow your business.

We have included a sample cashier's report worksheet (Exhibit 7-5), which can be used with any type of cash management system you choose to employ in your store. The information on this sheet can be then input into a computer system, or even a manual bookkeeping system. Reports, such as the ones shown in Exhibit 7-6 through 7-8, can then be generated to assist you in monitoring your business.

Planning for effective cash management is one of the things that often falls through the cracks when starting up any new business. After all, it is not the sexy, fun, or tasty part of the specialty food business. It is, however, essential to every other aspect of your business (from buying to merchandising to hiring and paying your staff to planning menus and creating recipes to effective sales and customer satisfaction) since cash, at the point of entry to your business, must be closely tracked. What comes in and goes out of your business determines what directions your business can and will take in the future. Admittedly, before opening, when the cash seems to be flowing in only one direction out, it's difficult to think ahead to opening day when cash will start flowing *in* to your business. Yet again, however, proper advance planning will ensure effective management of the cash in your business once you have opened. If you set clear rules and routines about the handling of cash from the start, you will reap the benefits later when your growing responsibilities as the owner prevent you from having first-hand involvement in this aspect of operations.

EXHIBIT 7-5

REGISTER RECONCILIATION SHEET

Cash management demands accuracy and consistency from shift to shift. If you provide a detailed and easy-to-use form to each of your staff who works the cash registers in your store, you will be able to keep close tabs on the flow of cash, check, and credit card transactions through your business. Here is a suggested format to follow.

Your name _____

Day/Date _____

Shift   AM   PM

Weather

Itemize

payouts

$ _____

$ _____

$ _____

$ _____

$ _____

$ _____

$ _____

$ _____

$ _____

$ _____

$ _____

Total _____

Checklist
• Use all change possible in bank!!
• Make sure all money is facing the same way
• Wrap up batches of 50 singles w/ rubber bands
• Sign your name above and on deposit envelope

Starting Bank	
	+
Prepared Food Sales	
	+
Packaged Food Sales	
	−
Payouts	
	−
Subtract Coupons, etc.	
	=
Cash You Should Have	0
Total Cash You Have	
Over?	0
< Short? >	
	−
Minus Bank	
	=
This Shift's Deposit	0

Checks

Notes/comments:	
	100's
	50's
	20's
	10's
	5's
	1's
	0.25's
	0.10's
	0.05's
	0.01's
	Total

Keeping Track of Sales Leads to More Sales

Adding one more layer of usefulness to the point of sale system, you can capture information about your customers' buying habits by creating a database from your register. If your point of sale system is linked with a database, you can track valuable information such as frequency and dollar volume of each customer's buying history. Knowing what they buy, how much they buy and when will give you a good idea of how to stock your store. Creating a database of information about your customers will enable you to target your mailings or telephone communications about specific product promotions. You can also produce mailing labels, personalized letters, telemarketing cards, and promotional mailings from your customer database. It stands to reason that if you know what your customers buy, you can develop stronger relationships with them. Personalized service based on your customers' demographic, biographical, and sales profiles can go a long way to strengthening the bond between buyer and seller. If your customers feel they are special and receive information from you that suits their particular lifestyle as defined by what they buy consistently from you, they will in turn make a stronger commitment to your business. Using a well-designed database can give you the edge over the competition. It will also let you focus limited marketing resources on a precisely pinpointed target audience where your efforts will produce the most profitable result.

As with any other system purchases, you need to examine the options carefully. Be confident that you can afford a system that will work for you. Allow for

EXHIBIT 7-6

SALES JOURNAL

The simplest manual bookkeeping system will include a sales journal (to track sales on a daily/weekly/ongoing basis) like the one shown here.

Week Ending—> [   ]

	Mon a.m.	Mon p.m.	Tues a.m.	Tues p.m.	Wed a.m.	Wed p.m.
Starting Bank—>						
Food						
Beverage						
Other						
Payouts—>						
Cash—>						
Checks						
Coupons						
Comps						
Total on Hand—>	0.00	0.00	0.00	0.00	0.00	0.00
Over/Short	$0.00	$0.00	$0.00	$0.00	$0.00	$0.00
Deposit Amount	$0.00	$0.00	$0.00	$0.00	$0.00	$0.00
Sales Tax	$0.00	$0.00	$0.00	$0.00	$0.00	$0.00

XYZ Store

Week Ending Jan 01
Sales:

		Percentage of Sales
Packaged Foods	$0.00	
Prepared Foods	$0.00	
Total Sales	**$0.00**	

Revenue:

Cash	$0.00	
Checks	$0.00	
Card	$0.00	
Cashiers Errors	$0.00	
Sales Revenue	**$0.00**	**0.0%**
Sales Tax	$0.00	
Net Cash Flow	**$0.00**	
Total Deposits	**$0.00**	

Thur a.m.	Thur p.m.	Fri a.m.	Fri p.m.	Sat a.m.	Sat p.m.	Sun a.m.	Sun p.m.
|0.00	|0.00	|0.00	|0.00	|0.00	|0.00	|0.00	|0.00
$0.00	**$0.00**	**$0.00**	**$0.00**	**$0.00**	**$0.00**	**$0.00**	**$0.00**
$0.00	**$0.00**	**$0.00**	**$0.00**	**$0.00**	**$0.00**	**$0.00**	**$0.00**
$0.00	$0.00	$0.00	$0.00	$0.00	$0.00	$0.00	$0.00

Exhibit 7-7

Cash Disbursements Journal

The following is a prototype document to help the start-up specialty food store owner track his/her expenses on a daily basis. This form was designed many years ago, prior to the days when every small business owner had a PC on site. But the document is valuable even today, as a way for assistant managers or shop stewards to record the daily flow of invoices and checks in and out of the company. It can also be entered onto a personal computer in database/accounting software such as Lotus 123 or Microsoft Excel, from which entries can be cross-referenced to other documents.

Date (week ending)	Vendor	Invoice #	CK#	Amount
Weekly Totals				

The structure of this document is such that a manager/owner can have, "at a glance," an overview of the day's/week's spending. This is the information to the left of the bold line, where data, invoice number, amount, and method of payment are entered. To the right of the bold line, the payment is broken down by category so that, by totaling these categories at the end of each week, totals spent for each category of operating expenses can be easily calculated. The categories of your cash disbursement journal should correspond to the categories of your profit and loss statement (see Kitchen/Market P+L, Exhibit 7–8, for structure of the profit and loss statement) so that your information remains consistent. Please remember that *every* payment made from your company, whether by cash or check and from whatever source, should be entered into this log so that all of your operation's expenses can be properly tracked.

Food	Liquor	Paper	Cleaning	Payroll	Utilities	etc.

future growth in whatever system you install. Be sure that your staff can easily input the information about your customers that will be necessary to build an accurate database. Check that the system can accommodate the specificity of data that you wish to capture about your customers. Above all, be sure that you are ready to take full advantage of the information generated by such a system. Knowing your customers is one thing; reaching out to them with well-targeted promotions based on that information is another. Instituting a customer database system is only the first step. Analyzing and acting on the findings is when the investment can begin to pay off.

EXHIBIT 7-8

KITCHEN/MARKET P+L/BUDGET PROTOTYPE

This operational profit and loss statement is a user-friendly tool to determine the health of a specialty food business on a weekly or monthly basis. This document, when filled out completely and accurately, will offer the entrepreneur and his/her key staff a clear idea of what aspects of the business are going well and which are warning signs for trouble.

For new businesses we recommend that this be completed weekly, summarizing after each four-week period, since certain expenses, like rent and utilities, are only paid once per month. The top section of this document is most useful to get an overview of the food and payroll costs on a weekly basis. These are the areas that a new entrepreneur must be vigilant about in order to build a healthy business. You can easily fall off target in these areas, so watch your purses!

	Budget—Period Ending _____	% of sales	Actual—Period Ending _____	% of sales	Variance—Period Ending _____	% of sales
Sales						
Bulk items						
Packaged foods						
Produce						
Hard goods						
Total Sales						
Cost of Sales						
Ingredients						
Bulk items						
Packaged foods						
Prepared foods						
Produce						
Hard goods						
Total Ingredients						

	Budget—Period Ending _____	% of sales	Actual—Period Ending _____	% of sales	Variance—Period Ending _____	% of sales
Payroll						
Management						
Clerks/cashier						
Kitchen						
Administrative						
Payroll taxes						
Total Payroll						
Occupancy						
Rent						
Comm rent tax						
Utilities						
Total Occupancy						
Total Cost of Sales						
Gross Profit						
Operating Expenses						
Insurance (property/liability)						
Insurance (health)						
Kitchen supplies						
Credit card expenses						
Bank fees						
Repairs and maintenance						
Telephone/postage						
Laundry/linen						
Garbage removal						
Pest control						
Office supplies						
Payroll service						
Accounting/legal						
Flowers/decoration						
Equipment lease (kitchen/display)						
Cleaning supplies						
Paper/packaging supplies						
Travel and entertainment						
Security						
Licenses and permits						
Dues/subscriptions						
Consulting/management fees						
Marketing						
Miscellaneous						
Total Operating Expenses						

	Budget—Period Ending _____	% of sales	Actual—Period Ending _____	% of sales	Variance—Period Ending _____	% of sales
Net Income Additional cash receipts (loan in, e.g.)						
Repayment of loan(s)						
Distribution to shareholders						
Income Before Depreciation and Taxes						

Reprinted courtesy Stuart Tarabour, Kitchen/Market.

KEEPING ORDERS IN ORDER

There is no turnoff for a customer greater than to receive the wrong merchandise in an order, or worse yet, receive a delivery on the wrong day or at the wrong time. All of that slowly built-up good will goes out the window with one stupid, avoidable mistake like that.

The customer who gets home with appetite keenly geared up for a particular salad or entree or dessert and unpacks the order only to find items destined for another customer, or substituted items about which he/she has not been consulted, has grounds to be irate. The good retailer needs to avoid this at all costs with a detailed order form (see Exhibit 7-9). During an especially busy holiday period or weekend, things can and do go wrong. So it's best to fill in the blanks fully to keep everyone happy and take care of the bottom line. Check and double check the information as it is being filled in. Then, before the customer leaves the premises or hangs up the phone, go over it once again. You can never be *too* accurate.

A DAY IN THE LIFE OF THE SPECIALTY FOOD STORE

As in any other business, there is no typical day in specialty food retailing. The day is made up of many elements, some small, some large, some fixed, others highly changeable. To get a sense of what it's like behind the counter, on the sell-

EXHIBIT 7-9

SAMPLE ORDER FORM

NAME OF COMPANY

Address _____

Telephone number _____

Today's date _____ Time _____

Customer's name _____

Address _____

Telephone numbers: Day _____ Eves and weekends _____

Date of order: _____ Ordered by _____ (specific individual who placed order)

Telephone number if different from above: _____

Number of people intending to serve: _____ Adults/kids _____ / _____

Occasion: Birthday _____ ; Anniversary _____ ; Baby shower _____ ;

Engagement party _____ ; Graduation _____ ; Other _____ ;

Is it a surprise for individual at this address? _____

Name of contact person with whom to check on order, if necessary

_____

Delivery: yes ____ no ____ Approx. time of delivery _____ Address _____

Directions to that location

_____

Pick up: yes ____ no ____ Approx. time _____

Items ordered: [Insert normal order form with space for amounts, quantity, price per pound, totals for each item. Also include a general guideline about the customer's flexibility in amounts being ordered; is it okay to go over by a few ounces, or do the amounts need to be precisely on the nose?]

After each item insert: May substitute if necessary with _____

Total amount of bill:		
	Merchandise	_____
	Tax	_____
	Delivery charges, if any	_____
	Rental fees	_____
Method of payment _____	Total	_____
	Less deposit, if any	_____
	Balance	_____

Any special handling instructions _____

Any equipment (bowls, platters, baskets, props, miscellany etc.) to be returned to _____

by _____ (date)

Name of individual who took order _____

ing floor, and behind the scenes, let's peek in at a prototypical store that has been up and running for about six months, sized about 2500 sq ft (2000 sq. ft. retail space, 500 sq. ft. production kitchen). The owner (a businessman first, a foodie second) is a hands-on type who likes to keep involved in all aspects of the business. All systems are in place, staff has remained unchanged from opening day (one head chef, two prep cooks, one dishwasher, one store manager/head counterperson, one assistant counterperson, and one delivery person/driver). The weather is good and the time of the year is mid March, a midweek day (no major holiday, no major vacation exodus). Store hours of operation: open seven days, 9 a.m. to 7:30 p.m.

Note that the following is just one scenario among the many that are possible. It's just one shake of the kaleidoscope. It's included here to give the flavor of the fragmented, often frenetic life people in food retail lead from the time they unlock the back door until all doors are locked, the last light turned out, and the alarm is armed.

7 a.m.—The owner walks in to find his answering machine blinking; plays the message to find that the head chef has called in sick. There are two medium-sized lunch parties (one for twenty people, the other for thirty-five) to go out on the catering truck. Luckily most of the foods have been prepped the night before; what has not been done can be pulled from the day's retail production. The prep cooks are fairly well-versed in the preparation of the foods that are required for the lunch parties. Still, without hesitating, the owner puts on his "just-in-case" chef's "whites," and, leaving nothing to chance, plunges into the preparations at hand (the lunch parties happen to be two frequent and loyal customers, but all customers count, so there's no room for slack). His literally hands-on involvement derails his plan of having some thinking time in the office to map out summer promotions and to start work on summer hiring strategies. Those will have to wait until after the lunches go out and the store lunch rush is over. Always alert to the unexpected, he's unfazed and, together with his staff, gets the job done. The lunch foods are ready in time and the platters prepared and decorated, if a bit more labor intensively than is usual. (After all, the boss is pinch-hitting here; his routine usually consists of approving completed trays before they go out, not making them up.) All in a day's work. What counts is that the customers will never know that Chef _____ called in sick that day. They will have their orders on time, done to a turn. The head counterperson and the second-in-command arrive and set about cleaning the display cases, inside and out. They then begin to assemble the appetizer and cold deli meat sections, replenishing where needed.

8:00 a.m.—The produce delivery was due a half hour ago. Ten minutes later, it arrives without the special lettuces that were promised to the customers who ordered the lunches for delivery. The boss sends one of the prep cooks out to the nearest upscale grocery to buy the lettuce at retail (the produce company will allow the store an adjustment for their mistake).

8:30 a.m.—The phone rings and there's a new customer who was referred by a regular wishing to place a lunch order (cold poached salmon) for a business lunch to be delivered by noon. The owner checks inventory on fresh fish in the cooler, hesitates for just a minute, and then graciously accepts the order. Back to the kitchen for some more heavy-duty cooking. The salmon needs to be poached, *the sauce verte* needs to be prepared, but everything else is under control. The two retail salesclerks arrive, ready to start tackling the large shipment of shelf-stable items that arrived yesterday. Shelves need to be dusted and displays taken apart to give a fresh look to merchandise. The owner hands the clerks a list of markdowns, and they begin repricing and displaying some of this slower-moving merchandise to make room for the new items. An appointment with an advertising salesman, scheduled for this morning at 10:00 a.m., has to be postponed until tomorrow.

9:00 a.m.—The prep cooks are busily engaged in preparing the day's salads for the showcase. The cheese purveyor has just arrived with the weekly delivery. With the head chef out, the owner checks in the order and assigns one of the counterpeople to store and display the new merchandise.

10:00 a.m.—Desserts for the day's orders need to be completed. The pastry case needs to be cleaned and stocked. Bread display needs to be done. The owner pitches in where needed, keeping an eye on the front door, greeting customers by name as they come in, all the while taking phone calls from vendors and a member of the Philharmonic soliciting foods for a benefit event. The window display artist is due in to change the winter motif to something that says "spring." She and an assistant arrive and need the owner's input periodically during the half day they are at work on the windows. The delivery man arrives, goes around the corner to gas up the delivery van, and returns to get instructions about the three lunchtime deliveries. The three "catered" lunches are ready. All components are labeled clearly, stored separately on different shelves in the walk in box. The order tickets are prominently displayed with the number of pieces each order should contain clearly marked on them. All of the components of each order are boldly marked with a large number (1 for the first order to go out, 2 for the next, and 3 for the last) and grouped so the delivery man can differentiate the orders easily. In the store, the display cases are filled, ready to go. Breads are in place, the sandwich station mise en place is set (meats and cheeses are sliced, main dish salads and dressings are ready, condiments refilled; all is ready for the lunch-time onslaught). The counterpeople have been doing this routine for enough months that they are right on target in their preparations but can fall back on a master checklist (see a sample task list following this "day") as the ultimate reference to be sure all the details have been remembered (this is also used as a training tool during the summer to keep temporary employees on track).

11:00—The phone is ringing continuously. Customers are placing lunch orders for pick-up, mainly at 12:00 noon. The fax machine is purring, spitting out more orders for lunch. The counterpeople, helped by the boss, have begun to prepare the sandwich and salad orders, boxing them and attaching the clearly written order tickets to each, with a time for pick up prominently written at the top of each order. They are then refrigerated until pick up time, arranged in alphabetical order by the last name of the customer. Pulled from preparing the bank deposit, the head counter clerk is pressed into service to help with the assembly of the trays for the order that just came in this morning. She will have to return to the bank paperwork after the lunch rush.

11:30—The three catered lunch orders are being loaded into the delivery van. The delivery person drops the container of *sauce verte* destined for the salmon, which splatters an area 4-ft in diameter (no extra was made). The dishwasher is pulled from prepping vegetables to mop the floor. The driver then reports the mishap to the owner, who has to think quickly on his feet. He scans the shelves of the bottled merchandise on display in the store and finds four jars of an imported mayonnaise made with good olive oil, and deems it a reasonable substitute. He then takes the premade sauce into the kitchen, doctors it with fresh herbs, tastes it, pronounces it fine, and then asks the delivery man to package it carefully. The delivery man tapes down the lids of each container, bags them, and adds them to the order waiting in the truck. With a quick, but thorough double check *against the written orders* (having learned the hard way that a mere visual check of the walk in box isn't enough to be sure that no stray components remain), he is out the back door and on his way to make deliveries 1, 2, and 3. He needs to collect the balance of payments on each, so he is prepared to give change of $100 if need be. He returns; the deliveries have gone well. He's ready to take a few more as soon as the sandwiches for these orders are complete.

12:00 noon—The lunch orders that were phoned in are starting to be picked up. Five customers come in to order some take-out items. One is looking for recommendations on a new chutney to serve with the chicken salad she is purchasing for a spring picnic supper. Another wants to sample the new feta cheese from Denmark that has been widely advertised in the monthly newsletter. The pace quickens. Phones are ringing. The cash register hums. The owner is greeting customers and taking orders at the same time. It's a busy day (the first nice weather after nearly a week of rain).

1:00 p.m.—The lunch rush continues until 1:45 when one of the counterpersons take his lunch break while the other holds down the fort. Then the prep cooks and dishwasher take their lunch breaks. With the chef out, the boss needs to take a quick inventory and then call in the produce, dairy, bread, and meat orders for tomorrow. First he checks the order board for items that will be needed on hand for orders through the weekend, making sure that all categories are accounted for.

2:00 p.m.—The boss eats on the run—just a quick sandwich and a taste of that new marinated Italian salad, a work-in-progress that the head chef began working on two days ago. There are phone calls to return (and one last look at the spring windows for final approval before the window dressers present their bill and depart). Drafting the new summer store promotions and the new picnic menu for the outdoor music season at the amphitheater will both have to wait until tomorrow.

3:00 to 7:00 p.m.—The remainder of the day proceeds smoothly with the display cases being replenished with freshly made prepared entrees for the afternoon and predinner take-out rush. All foods are properly labeled, dated, and stored as they are prepared.

7:00 p.m.—Closing involves a thorough cleanup of the retail space. The kitchen and production areas are swept and mopped. An inventory of basic salads and dressings reveals that the chef will have a big day tomorrow when he returns. Meats need to be marinated for the pâtés for the weekend. Cheese spreads need to be replenished. Pita crisps need to be baked and packaged for the weekend.

7:30 p.m.—After the doors are locked and the front lights turned out, the counter manager counts the cash drawer in preparation for the deposit, places it in the safe, and heads for home.

Well, what a day! A day in which both a lot and very little were accomplished. A lot went into simply maintaining the status quo, attending to the details to keep the steady flow of customers served and satisfied in their transactions with the staff. It was a day with very little future-oriented planning. It was a day of keeping up with the demand that good food and good service and a growing reputation have created. But was it a day of breakthrough ideas, launching into new directions? Hardly. These moves are harder won, but not impossible.

With a key employee out, the dynamics of the store operation are changed considerably (and this is not the first time this has happened, nor will it be the last, to be sure). What is there to learn from the experiences of this day? Several questions are certainly raised. The answers are not always easy.

1. How do you set up a routine and be prepared to veer from it?
2. How do you make a schedule and stick to it?
3. Are you well enough staffed to cover absences of key people? Can the business afford to support another person, perhaps a part-timer to fill in on the heavier prep days, toward the weekend? Are you better off increasing payroll a bit to enable you, as the owner, to be free to attend to the planning agenda which will yield growth for the business?

Here's what is indisputable: The only way long-term planning will get done in the course of a day on which the business is fully operational is if it's put on the larger schedule as an integral part of the day's work. Put aside an hour each week (or more, if feasible) to pull back from the store operations and do the creative thinking alone (or with your partner(s)) and perhaps another hour more each week to do some brainstorming with key staff in an informal, lull-time afternoon meeting. Appoint someone to take notes at the meetings and then post the notes so the whole staff can review them. Schedule regular staff meetings to discuss and remedy day-to-day problems. Keep track on paper of all suggestions that arise from the ranks as well as those from your customers (empty those suggestion boxes frequently and read the contents carefully and diligently). Discuss the suggestions at the next staff meeting (and the next and the one after that, as need be). Involve your staff in arriving at new ideas, streamlined procedures, and promotional tactics. Don't discount any idea, however lame or far-fetched it may sound at first. Then follow up by offering a reward for the "best idea of the week" (or month)—a dinner at a neighborhood restaurant for the winning employee and a guest, perhaps, or a gift certificate at the local music or video store. Tap into your staff's particular interests and reward them accordingly.

Manager's Daily Checklist

Helping managers and other key personnel get used to a routine can be facilitated by using a concrete list of tasks for reinforcement. Accounting for individual store differences, here is a checklist of daily tasks to use as a basis. Use this as a guide to build your own daily regimen.

Opening the Store

Turn lights on

Turn security/alarm off

Check all refrigeration, stoves, and ovens for operating ability

Turn on coffee pot (a must)

Boot computer system

Check cash registers

Read manager's log for notes from closing manager

Check with any employees who are already in for problems (mechanical or staffing); check with chef for daily specials

Check daily staff plan (employee schedule) to know whom to expect when

Check answering machine or voice mail

Make bank deposit from previous day

Get change

Pay bills

Set up cash drawers

Establish appropriate environment (including lights, temperature, and music)

Hold preshift staff meeting (front of house), including daily specials and theme for the day

During Operations

Check regularly on cashiers, counterpeople, and kitchen staff

Check maintenance of selling floor, display cases, shelves (cleanliness, orderliness, and quantity of stock)

Maintain environment (including lights, temperature, and music)

Maintain staffing according to schedule

Gather sales statistics regularly (hourly? per shift?) for information about trends and flow

Review kitchen (staffing, food waste, storage and handling of food, equipment)

Set aside time for paperwork, correspondence

Spend time on customer service and personal salesmanship

Close-out

Lock doors and put security in place when store is closed and customers are out; dim outside lights

Close out registers

Shut down all equipment possible

Verify cash drawers and shift deposits

Handle any paperwork compliance needed

Oversee staff sign/punch-out on time!

Check maintenance and restocking (where appropriate) of all areas: selling floor, display, shelves, lights, walls, floors, and so on

Check kitchen maintenance (equipment, storage, labeling of prepared foods, etc.)

Turn coffee machine off

Turn lights out

Team up last people to leave for security's sake

At the back of the house, where details abound and not everything can be committed to memory, your kitchen manager or head chef needs some firm reference points to operate smoothly. A list such as the one in Exhibit 7-10, from a takeout/café with Southwestern-styled cuisine, enables all kitchen personnel to plan ahead. All of the items that need to be on hand, prepared, and ready to go into the dishes that this kitchen produces are noted, with par amounts (basic minimum established after the business settles into a routine), amounts needed daily to bring the amount up to par, and shelf life, where appropriate. In this way, the discovery of last-minute shortages and other crises leading to serious gaps in your product offerings can be averted. Your customers count on you daily to have on hand the dishes which have built your reputation. Disappointed customers can soon become lost customers. You can avoid shortages and reduce spoilage and waste by insisting that your staff make use of such a prep list. After a few months of operation, you should be able to create one tailored to your own menu and volume.

BACK-OF-THE-HOUSE PREP LIST

Par refers to the amount normally held on hand of each item, given as a guideline to kitchen staff. The information in parentheses indicates how much or how frequently the item is made or made ready to be used as a component in a dish. If your operation requires two shifts, then good communication is essential between shifts so each can prepare for the other. A form such as this can help to communicate the information necessary to running a smooth back-of-the-house operation, which in turn impacts on the retail, or front-of-the-house, operations.

Par	Item		Tues	Wed	Thur	Fri	Sat	Sun
	Chicken stock (1 week—freeze)							
	Rice (4 days)							
	Frijoles (red) (4 days or freeze)							
	Black beans (4 days or freeze)							
	Chop garlic							
	Chop onion (white)							
	Chop onion (red)							
	Grill onion (1/4's)							
	Lime juice							
	Guacamole (every day)							
	Salsa verde (2 days)							
	Salsa rosso (2 days)							
	Tortilla chips (1 week)							
	Clean parsley							
	Clean cilantro							
	Clean spinach							
	Cook spinach (2 days)							
	Grill zucchini (1 day)							
	Grill yellow squash (1 day)							
	Grill corn							
	Roast peppers (3 days)							
	Grill chicken breasts (3 days)							
	Vinaigrette chipotle (5 days)							
	Ranch dressing (5 days)							
	Soak chipotles (5 days)							
	Clean lettuce—romaine (1–2 days)							
	Clean lettuce—iceberg (1–2 days)							
	Clean red cabbage (1–2 days)							
	Grate jack cheese (4 days)							
	Grate cheddar cheese (4 days)							
	Fry tortilla baskets (1 week)							
	Roast tomatoes (2 days)							

CHAPTER EIGHT

CORPORATE CULTURE, DISPLAY AND MERCHANDISING, AND CUSTOMER SERVICE

DEFINING YOUR CORPORATE CULTURE

Beyond the numbers, projections, costs, and budgets, as part of your business plan, you need to sketch out your vision for the company—put into words what defines your company. This has become known as corporate culture, the new buzzword in the food service industry (with the accent on service).

What does it mean? The intangible yet all-pervasive feeling a customer gets when entering your store is a prime example of what corporate culture means. It has to do with how your store looks and feels, how your selection of merchandise is displayed and offered for sale, and how your staff functions within your systems and with the customers. It starts with you, your vision and planning, and the way you communicate your concept. It works its way down to your key staff, and even to your lay staff. How have you selected the merchandise and trained your staff in the verities of the stock and your prepared foods menu? How have you emphasized the overall aesthetic of your store? How does your team interact with you or other upper management in the organization? And you with them? What is the demeanor and tone of your interactions with your staff, upon whom you depend? In seeking to emulate your behavior, employees are conveying your corporate culture to the customers.

Corporate culture encompasses all the attitudes, values, beliefs, customs, policies, and traditions that define your business. More than rules, policies, charts, and organizational manuals, corporate culture connotes the extent to which the work environment encourages or suppresses personal and professional growth, employee morale, and productivity. As the owner or manager of your store, you set the tone for all business transactions carried out within that store. You are the living, breathing role model for your employees about customer contacts, personal appearance, hygiene, and manner of communication with others (both in-store and on the phone). As the owner or manager, you are the embodiment of your store's corporate culture. How you act sets the example.

Since crafting your business plan, you should be able to explain your vision and goals for the company in a matter of minutes. This same vision should then be communicated to employees or prospective employees. When in full operation, your store will tell volumes about your corporate philosophy daily. If you exhibit flexibility in your interactions with employees, you lead the way for others on your team to show a willingness to change. Although leading without ego is easier said than done, remaining aloof from your employees will do your company no good. In a service-oriented business, where each member of the staff plays an important part in delivering exemplary service to the customer, there's little room for egotistical, self-centered behavior on the part of manager or staff. High turnover can result from employees' frustration, from their inability to reach you, from their working at cross-purposes, from their feeling overworked, or from lack of recognition; any of these will affect your organization's culture (and ultimately, its success). Unhappy or dissatisfied employees often move on (or, if they do stay, they undermine other employees in a downward spiral). If you as their leader have no time for anything but "putting out fires," jumping from one crisis to another, products and services are bound to suffer and the future of the business can soon be in jeopardy. Taking time out from a busy schedule to compliment an employee for a job well done can pay off many times over in increased employee productivity and high morale among team members. Happy employees and high morale help to ensure success for you and your business.

What Kind of Workplace Will You Provide?

Is your store a high energy place where customers (and employees) come to have a good time? Do the employees have fun at work? (Happy employees tend to be more welcoming to your customers.) Or is your store a low-key, serious, we-mean-business kind of place, where the staff extends a formal, but cordial welcome to the customers? Will your corporate culture encourage high employee absenteeism, low morale, employee compliance through fear? Will it be an environment where praise is rare and employee grievances are common? What policies can your employees turn to for guidance about how to treat customers? Do you have a formal, detailed employee manual, including an explicit section on customer relations? Or do you expect to provide formal or informal training programs to equip each employee with the means of contributing to your bottom line? If your employees don't know what you expect from them, how can you expect them to help you achieve your goals, either short-term or long? You'll need to put into place high quality service standards and systems that spell out in detail how customer transactions should be accomplished.

It is important to have a training and *re*training program in place to help employees meet your specific standards. Each of your selling and production staff should have well-defined daily sales and production goals, with their performance evaluated frequently.

To generate a positive corporate culture, experts advise strong interemployee communication with regular, motivational feedback including recognition, comprehensive training where possible, and follow-up. By your actions and words, you can encourage teamwork, honesty, and ethics. Underpinning all of this should be a clear mission statement that employees identify with and a feel a part of. If possible, include your key personnel in the process of its formation. However, no mission statement should be so rigid that it ignores the need to change, switch gears, strike out in new creative directions, even take some calculated risks to improve things. There has to be room for members of the team to express their opinions openly to influence the direction of the organization. Leaving room for dialogue between employees and management is a crucial first step to building a committed staff, thereby reducing employee frustration, stagnation, and turnover.

As an owner your actions, appearance, and behavior set the standards for what you can expect from each of your employees, from top management on down. Based on what they see you do and how they see you behave, they will duplicate the behavior and attitudes during the course of their workday in your store. By taking the time and the care to write an operations manual, you are already communicating to your staff that you take your business seriously. By clearly outlining what is important to you about your business, about how you want your staff to behave, and how you will all treat your customers, you are one step closer to running a smooth and profitable business. To enhance your hard work at writing this manual, we advise you to build into operations channels of communication between your staff and your managers and your managers and yourself. Post a suggestion book for staff members. Make sure your managers read it daily. Hold weekly management meetings to discuss operations, sales, customer feedback, and staff issues with your key management. Make sure they hold regular meetings (even daily preshift pep/sales-boosting talks are good) to keep the streams of communication open. Once a month or so, hold full staff meetings as well, where key issues from the smaller meetings are brought up and addressed.

A staff newsletter is another possible form of staff communications. The example in Exhibit 8-1 will give you a clear look at what's possible.

MERCHANDISING YOUR WARES

Now that your dream space is just about open, it lacks one major element—product on the shelves. You've selected them, and ordered them, and now they have arrived. Slowly and carefully you will fill up the shelves and display cases with all manner of sparkling and inviting comestibles, some of which are made on the premises in those health-, fire-, and building-department-inspected and approved kitchens. Opening day is at hand. Should you open quietly without fanfare, and let the public find their way to your door? Or should you open with a bang, inviting friends and friends of friends, the food press, local community dignitaries for a night (or series of opening night) shakedowns before opening? You will execute your first promotional plan in just a few weeks. It's time to figure out just how the stock will be arranged, your selling space configured, and your signage aesthetic.

Coming up with a general philosophy about and specific idea of how you are going to sell the merchandise you have so lovingly assembled, purchased, prepared, imported, and displayed is essential. Do you display passively and wait for people to discover just how wonderful your offerings are? Or do you embark on an ambitious and often expensive plan to advertise your operation in the local papers and through other media outlets? Your own style and budgetary allotments will provide most of the answers to these questions.

Some people confuse marketing with merchandising. Here's the difference: Marketing is the message you send out into the world to get people to notice you and come into your store. Merchandising is the sum of all messages, both subliminal and obvious, that you send to people once they are in your store. In the coming sections and in Chapter 9, we examine both marketing and merchandising to help you develop the tools and plans to get your store noticed and to keep the customers coming into your store, as well as enticing them to do more than just look admiringly at the wares you offer.

Building sales through cross-merchandising your products would seem to be an obvious concept, but it does take some forethought, lots of effort, and a bit of creative spark. Customers may enter your store looking for one thing and leave buying that and more, but it all depends on how you display your wares.

Exhibit 8-1

Zingerman's Staff Newsletter

In larger retail operations, keeping a staff abreast of everything from new products and sales goals to departmental performance, special events, and staff meetings is accomplished as shown in this excerpt from Zingerman's (Ann Arbor, MI) newsletter, *Workin'!,* The newsletter is published monthly (with contributions from staff members). "Ideas of the month" are noted, along with recognition of superior performance by employees. Zingerman's acknowledges service and innovation with gift certificates and cash awards.

2nd Quarter
DSE Award Winners!

Best Service Improvement wins $250:
Mail Order for their new E-Mail Order Taking System
which has provided many customers with a convenient no-cost, quick way to communicate during any time of the day or night. We are now involved in ongoing food and service conversations with a number of customers who find it very useful and convenient.

Best Merchandising Work wins $350:
Goes to jointly to ZingNet Graphics & Mail Order
for the 1996 Zingerman's Catalog. It was more logically presented, products were effectively "bundled" for better sales, graphics were neater and more effective. The payoff? Sales for Dec. up 55% from last year!

3 Special Merchandising Runners Up - Each wins $75
1st Runner Up - Jointly to the Deli's Merchandising, Perishables, Dry Goods and Next Door Departments for their major improvement of the overall look of signage and handouts throughout the Deli. More color, more energy.
2nd Runner Up - The Sandwich Line for their Sing For Your Supper Promo.
3rd Runner Up - Jointly to Deli Dry Goods and Merchandising for their new olive oil tags.

Best ZCoB Community Service Project wins $250:
Goes jointly to the Deli's Lively Goods and Dept. of Atmospheric Conditions
for organizing the regular promo, "What's New at Zingerman's" where customers can learn about new and noteworthy products from the entire ZCoB. They sent out an easy to use form to help *all ZCoB businesses* use this event to effectively promote their products.

Best Quality Improvement wins $250:
Mail Order for their radically improved 1996 gift basket selection
They've completely revamped their selection from 1994/5. Improvements include new baskets, Zingerman's wooden crates, more popular choices, and better packaging. Results include a huge shift from more difficult to make "custom" baskets to customers happily ordering the new offerings.

Best Profit Generating Innovation wins $250:
The Practical Produce crew for their Great Avocado Adventure
In less than ten days in December Skip and the ZPP crew turned a mere $100 worth of ripe avocados into amazing $3000 in sales (an incredible .033% food cost!) while still passing a good deal and good food on to our customers. Avocado alchemy at its best.

Honorable Mentions: + ZingNet Info Services for saving a projected $2500 a year by switching long distance phone companies from MCI to LDMI.
+ **Mail Order** for their new and very popular Bread Club.

Congratulations and thanks to all of the above folks for their innovative actions.

Wondering why your department didn't enter the DSE Awards this quarter? Me too. To enter have your department fill out an entry form (on "file cabinet" on the Main).

Winners happen 4 times a year. Deadline for the next quarter's entries is April 20, 1996.
Not available in stores.

WORKIN'!

A Staff Guide
to
Food, Fun &
Flavor
in the
Zingerman's
Community of
Businesses
February, 1996
Vol.III, No.2

© 1995 Zingerman's Delicatessen, Inc.

1

Reprinted courtesy Ari Weinzweig, Zingerman's.

Think of each display in your store as a mini-merchandiser, a boutique within the larger store layout with the potential to separate more cash from your customer's hands. Never miss an opportunity to increase the customer's bill by opening his or her eyes to a new condiment that you have featured as a special pairing with a particular meat. Make it a special of the week, or month. By all means, offer a sampling of the two items together. Nothing will sell it faster or better. Of course, wines or other beverages you recommend as the perfect accompaniments to your foods are a natural add-on sale. Don't forget to offer the cheese to end a meal, and to display a basket of some beautiful fresh fruit beside your ripened cheese display. You're not only building up sales, you're building up your customers' confidence in your ability to educate them about the best way to eat and serve the foods you sell.

If you're selling prime quality cured meats, be sure to have an irresistible display of mustards and other condiments right beside them. If you're selling a curried dish, why not suggest a wonderful bottled chutney to go with it (or bottle one of your own if fruits are plentiful and the chef has time . . .). Be sure to sell the dill mustard sauce along with your house-cured gravlax salmon and your own special cranberry conserve along with the roast turkey.

Merchandising Strategies: Where to Sell What?

Merchandising means display—both small and large—the details of your store and the overall look and feel of the place. To find your own style and what works best in your store, you will need to experiment with many different kinds of displays, both self-serve (illuminated by much printed informational materials) and those manned by a knowledgeable staff member. Assess the results and sales resulting from each method and then experiment some more. You don't need to commit to any one style of merchandising your wares. Change your displays frequently; don't be limited to seasonal groupings. You can build a themed display around any item. Read the literature from your vendors (and don't hesitate to ask for more information). Anything that helps you to sell more of a vendor's products should be free for the asking. The history of the item, its production, method of processing, classical and nontraditional uses can all contribute to a better display, one that will better sell the product. It's a win-win-win situation; you, the vendor, and your customer all benefit. The more information you have about the products you are selling, the more targeted can be your sales effort. The items themselves (and the vendors too) often dictate how products are best displayed.

Flexibility Is the Key

Freestanding shelf units with movable shelving lend flexibility to your displays. Built-ins are good but often limiting—odd package sizes may conflict with your shelf heights. Once you are open, constantly track the "footprint" of your customers as they enter and shop your store. What section do they gravitate toward first? If enough of your customers go to a certain section of your store first, then you should carefully consider what you are selling in that area. Are you making the best use of the space there? Could the area use a face-lift? Or can you re-create what draws them to that area in other areas of your store? Is it a focal display piece, or is it the items sold in that spot that draws them, or both? (Look at the lighting in that area and in your entire store. Look at the aisle space between areas—do customers feel relatively uncrowded if they wish to stop and linger in a certain area?) What gives customers a feeling of comfort in that particular area of the store? Does the layout of that area make your customers feel like browsing at a leisurely pace? Or is the space more apt to compel your customer to flee once they've found the item or items they are looking for (and is that your unconscious intent)? How can you make the area more hospitable or welcoming for your customers (and their children, if yours is a family destination)? A bit of character and folksy charm can go a long way to making your displays work. Mix and match the streamlined rectilinear displays of product with the more homespun piles of product in a basket.

Always be on the lookout for some all-season props. A fresh coat of paint or a colorful backdrop cloth or piece of brightly patterned yard goods can often turn what might look like an unpromising thrift-store discard into the perfect vehicle for your themed displays. So think beyond the current condition of a table, a chair, a shelf, or even a wheelbarrow. You may be surprised at how well they can bring focus to a display at low cost. (You may have to look for some dry storage area to keep your growing stock of props, but you can't make compelling displays without a few impressive centerpieces).

Display: Showing the Goods

Is there any one "right" way to set up your deli showcase displays? Looking at stores around the country for many years, from the smallest to the largest, the answer would appear to be a resounding "No." What about displays of shelf-stable items? For these, eye-level visibility is key. Flexibility also helps. If you can use freestanding, easy-to-roll around display units with adjustable shelves, you're apt to get best mileage from the space you have to devote to these items. The same holds true for refrigerated display cases. Those with adjustable shelves for multiple configurations will enable you to build displays of food that jump out to your customers and say "Buy me." Use many different materials as the base in your perishable displays (thin marble slabs, bamboo mats, mirrors, iridescent cellophane, colorful cloth, leaves, flowers, etc.) To create a distinctive and memorable look, you might want to use a specific backdrop to identify each of your food categories, such as entrées, salads, soups, and sauces. Once again, an unswerving attention to detail, essential in itself, is also the best way to put your own stylistic imprint on the merchandise.

Raise Your *Profile with High Profile Displays*

To make your displays reach out and grab the customer, make use of the vertical space in your cases with a liberal use of risers (standard glass block, old bricks with character, or other easily cleanable, durable material—check tile stores and stone quarries for inspiration). "Flat" is just that, and it just doesn't sell. Just be sure your counterpeople can reach the foods for easy and quick service and that the props and supports for your containers of foods are easily removed and cleaned. Remember this is a process that must be done daily to put the best face on your offerings.

How to Organize Your Offerings

Grouping merchandise by category is one way. Grouping items from broadly related categories (i.e., vinegars on the shelf close to oils, mustards, herbs, sauces, condiments, etc.) that cook-enthusiasts would use in combination is another. Help the customer save steps in your store by grouping items conveniently.

Specialty foods sell best when you can associate them with other products. To make a vinaigrette dressing, you need a good quality olive oil, a flavored vinegar, and oftentimes mustard. So there are three items that should reach out to customers in one quick scan of your shelves. Or how about massing out a display of your recommended brands of this common triad of ingredients? (A sampling station staffed by a salesperson would be a logical extension of this kind of display.)

What will bring you customers is a matter of your own individual product line's strengths, the physical layout of the retail store space (look for any particularly unique architectural characteristics that you can play up to accentuate your displays of goods), lighting, signage, and flow. How a customer feels when he or she enters your store will impact heavily on what that customer buys. Is the customer's eye overwhelmed upon entering or is there a central focal point or display that catches his or her attention, an uncluttered place of relative calm where the customer can linger before being plunged into the thick of your retail space?

If you use such a welcoming display near the front door, don't place it too close to the door. The customer who wishes to stop and browse or read a label should not feel rushed by others who enter the store shortly afterward. You need to allow breathing room. Customers need to feel that they have a sense of privacy even in a very public environment. They need to feel free to browse, to take an item off a shelf, read the label, and then replace that item on the shelf if they choose, without anyone judging their actions or hovering over them during this period of indecision. If the customer wants help, he or she will ask for it; then a customer service person can offer suggestions to help make the decision easier for the customer—but only if asked. Many customers will look at another item, perhaps from the same category, and then return to the first item before deciding which to buy.

These are some of the factors that may influence the way you display your wares:

- What space is devoted to shelf-stable items in relation to the space for perishable items that require refrigerated storage?
- How high is the ceiling? What are the acoustics of your space? What's the proportion of hard surfaces to soft ones?
- What are the sources of light for your store? Are you able to capitalize on a dramatic architectural feature such as a skylight? Or is the area windowless except for the storefront glass?
- Where is the check-out counter in relation to where the customer enters?
- Is there more than one way to enter and exit the store? (Parking is *the* factor here.)
- Do you have enough space to divide your showcase displays by course or by product type—appetizers, main dishes, cheeses, desserts; fish separate from meat, pastry separate from cheese?
- Can you make room for permanent demonstration stations throughout the store?
- How accessible is the backup supply of perishables (prepared foods, smoked fish, appetizer items, meats,) and nonperishables? Are they in another building or on another floor or far away from the display case area?

- How many people will be working behind the counter at one time?
- How much vertical space do you have for stacked shelf display?
- Does the height of your showcases allow for top of the counter displays in order to maximize opportunities for cross-merchandising?
- Does the height and configuration of your display cases allow counter help to hear customers and be heard by them easily?
- Can you hang signage or floating displays from the ceiling or from metal bars that hang below the ceiling for product tie-ins and special promotions?
- Have you given thought to the floor behind the display cases in terms of cleanability and how it affects the backs and legs of your counter staff?

When a customer or potential customer enters your store, he or she should get a clear and quick message about where they may expect to find which categories of foods. Don't waste a single opportunity for cross-merchandising. Use items that will bridge one section with another, such as dry goods (crackers, condiments) that go well with either cheese or deli meats.

Take a good look at stores you visit for ideas. Look critically at the width of aisles, lighting, signage, eye-level merchandise (jars, bottles, breakables) versus items that are closer to the floor (usually bigger, bulky goods).

What Makes a Good Display?

When you set out to bring customers to a particular segment of your product line, your best tool is a compelling display. Whether you have the budget to hire an outside professional to create your displays or rely on an employee in-house who demonstrates a flair for visual drama, here are some general guidelines to follow when creating product displays:

1. Find the focal point.
2. Limit the number of competing elements; your eye should be quickly drawn to one main part of the display.
3. Design your display around only one dominant motif.
4. Select a prop that has a logical tie-in with the products you are trying to sell.
5. Don't let the prop overwhelm the product; it's product you are trying to sell, not props; mass product abundantly in the display, whether shelf-stable or perishable.
6. Make use of colors that are appropriate to the season and to the theme if there is one.
7. Stand back and see if the displays "calls" to you and your staff; see if it sells.

What Makes a Bad Display?

1. Too much product, backdrop, or too many props can confuse the customer rather than stimulate interest in buying.
2. Too little to look at in a display sends the message to the customer to "move on quickly."
3. Inappropriate use of props is just as bad as no props at all; the props are merely vehicles to bring the products you wish to promote to the fore.
4. Lack of theme (Mediterranean, Italian, ethnic, summertime fare, holiday specialties, etc.) does not compel your customers to stop and take a second look.
5. Staying around too long or staying in one place too long makes a display "stale" in the eyes of regular customers.
6. Lack of attention to detail—if your display is collecting dust, harbors dead bugs, features product with soiled labels, or simply if the amount of product is sparse—sends the wrong message; rethink your display strategy (staffing, placement, maintenance); review "What Makes a Good Display?" above.

CUSTOMER SERVICE—THE FINAL KEY TO GREAT SALES

While creating an operations manual will directly benefit your staff, this part of the preopening preparations will also confirm several important aspects of your business and help you to see them through the eyes of the people who will work for you, carrying your message to your customers.

Distribute your operations manual to all personnel in training. Perhaps, at the end of their training, where reading the manual cover to cover is mandatory, offer a short quiz on what they've learned so far. This will help in accessing the potential staff member's level of seriousness about the job as well as how effectively you have communicated what is important to you about your business. You cannot be too detailed when it comes to stating expectations about employee behavior or performance. It's easier if your employees know up front what you expect of them. It is always harder to bring them around to your way of thinking after they have had the chance to slip into what you consider bad habits.

Other Customer Service Tips:

1. Develop a basic script for the way you'd like your staff to interact with customers, and then allow each employee to tailor it to his or her own interpersonal style. Some role-playing exercises before opening provide a good way for you

and your staff to get comfortable with the interactions. It may also help you head off potential problem areas in your business. (These dress rehearsals for success may also reveal that someone who has been hired for a behind-the-scenes position is a natural-born salesperson. Store that bit of information in your memory for that day when your prime counterperson is unavailable.) Remember that what will help to build your business is communicating information effectively to customers and sending the message of sincere, thoughtful service with each transaction. Attitude is key. This can be conveyed in many different ways. Being friendly without being intrusively personal or obsequious, being professional without being condescending are the attributes to prize and cultivate in those employees who interface with customers.

2. Think through the customer's experience as he or she enters your store. Write into the script which becomes part of your manual where you and your staff can and need to impact on that customer's experience. Without doubt, first there should be a brief greeting, sincere and attentive. A smile and eye contact are the essential parts of this first exchange.

3. Decide what message(s) about your store you wish your customers to take home with them, along with their purchases:

- Consistently high quality merchandise
- Highly ethical business practices
- Quick and courteous service
- Depth of product knowledge displayed by you and your salespeople
- Responsibility to larger community—contributions to local charities, donations of foods at the end of the business day to homeless shelters and anti-hunger food distribution channels
- Your business' commitment to social action (hiring and training minorities, multiethnic, multiracial composition of your staff)

How to Handle Complaints

How much latitude for personal discretion will your employees have when it comes to resolving complaints? In the initial stages of the business, when your overriding goal is to please customers and gain and keep every customer who walks through the door, you may be more generous in bending over backwards to keep the customer happy. As you gain some market share, you may find that you do not have to give in to every unreasonable demand a customer may have—but this is best determined on a case-by-case basis. Listen attentively, then pause to think about the best way to handle the complaint before offering the remedy in a calm and low voice. You need to be objective: consider who the customer is, size and frequency of his/her purchases, how much influence that customer may have in the community, and who else may be listening before defining a hard-and-fast rule about customer adjustments. When offering adjustments to remedy customer dissatisfaction with a product or service, you and your employees need to remember that:

- The customer must be satisfied.
- The customer is literally paying everyone's salaries.
- One should never challenge or disparage a customer.
- If in doubt, your employees should always consult you (if available) or your next in command for suggestions on how to handle complaints, returns of foods, anything at all.
- Unresolved complaints fester and lead to ill will—it's best to resolve the complaint during the first conversation if at all possible.
- Word of mouth about unresolved complaints travels quickly and can undo all of the goodwill you have been working hard to build up among your customer base.
- Never be diverted to do another task or handle another customer while you are in the middle of resolving a complaint; this can exacerbate the situation. Until the situation has been resolved, your attention should be focused on the customer who has lodged the complaint.

Some Breakthrough Dialogue for Achieving High Customer Service Standards

How long should you or your employees wait before offering assistance and how do you go about it? "May I help you?" just doesn't cut it. Any question that can answered in one word ("No" or the frequently resorted-to "No, I'm just looking") makes it difficult to establish a connection with that customer. A better set-up to a positive response would be: "Have you seen our new line of _____? Let me show you and you can have a taste on us."

What questions should the salesclerk or counterperson ask first to make contact and break the ice, questions to help steer a customer to finding what he/she wants in a timely way (and also give the salesperson a clue as to which direction to take the customer next)? Such questions might include, "Are you looking for a particular kind of mustard?" (if the customer is scanning the shelves where the mustards are), "Are you in the mood for pasta tonight?" as opposed to "What do you feel like having for dinner tonight?" which might simply yield an "I don't know"—an answer that gives the salesperson no clear clue about the next question to ask). Be specific, not too general here. Other questions might zero in on new products such as, "Have you tried our new house-made chutney?" or "Did you get a taste of our new rustic loaf?" Wait for an answer and then proceed with some more leading questions or comments that express approval of the customer's level of knowledge about your foods. Never talk down to the customers or assume that they are ignorant about the kinds of foods you sell (experience shows that consumers are more knowledgeable and sophisticated now about more kinds of foods than ever before).

A good salesperson moves seamlessly from the general to the specific, from asking about the customer's familiarity with your products to what kinds of foods they like. The next questions should focus on specifics about customer's preferences for spicy foods, rich foods, diet-conscious foods. Are they buying for an occasion, or just for a fuss-free dinner tonight? How many are they buying for?

How aggressive can the salesclerk or counterperson be when serving a customer who has come in to your store knowing what he or she wants to buy? How soft should the soft sell be? That is determined by your style, personality, personality of your staff, and may vary from customer to customer.

What It Takes

Communication skills are paramount; anyone you hire needs to be able to convey clearly and persuasively an excitement and enthusiasm about the foods they are selling. People who work in a kitchen are more apt to describe how a dish is made, what ingredients go into it, and why it is special and worthy of the money and palate of the customer. If convincing words don't roll off the tongues of your employees, provide them with a script, a guide to your spiel and your patter. But let your menu, both in its content and in its graphic presence, communicate your message and be your primary marketing tool and money maker.

Use role-playing as a good way to discover areas of strength and weakness in an employee. Give all of your employees a first-hand experience to see your store from the customer's side by giving each of them a fixed amount of store credit to spend. Encourage them to buy a broad range of merchandise in order to experience each department of your store, and then arrange a meeting to discuss the experience. In this way, you allow them to vent their feelings about how the store is running. From such a meeting may flow some interesting and ultimately revelatory information, which you can use in implementing changes in problem areas, whether operation, product line, display, style, whatever. Teach your staff to listen to what the customers are saying and to convey the customers' messages back to you. At regular meetings, invite all of your staff to contribute their take on how store operations are going, incorporating their own and customers' comments, opinions, and suggestions. Use the information that emerges from these meetings, and demonstrate your responsiveness to employee input and implement those changes, however subtle, as you see fit. Seeing your store through new or different eyes often can be illuminating, and hearing from your employees in this way cements the bond between management and labor in a way no other interchange can.

A NEW DYNAMIC

How about treating your employees more like customers? With quality of service becoming more and more the only factor that distinguishes you from others in a highly competitive field, employers benefit if they maintain a nurturing and respectful relationship with their staff, their number one asset. Training can be costly but little or no training on the job can be more costly, despite an often high turnover rate. The individuals who have the most contact with your customers are often the individuals who are least prepared or compensated. Robert Christie Mill, a hospitality management professor at the University of Denver, states: "Service leaders treat employees the way they want the employees to treat the customers. They (the service leaders) realize the world they create for their employees is the world their employees will create for their customers." Show your staff you appreciate their good work; Exhibit 8-2 highlights one entrepreneur's method.

Good service depends on well-trained, well-placed, and well-respected staff. As the owner, you set the tone for how your customers are treated. With a good training program in place (whether formal or more on-the job, seat-of-the-pants), your employees will deliver your products to your customers in a friendly, nonthreatening manner. Good service should flow in one seamless stream from the owner-operator down through the layers of management, from store manager to department managers (in a multidepartment store) to counter clerks, floor clerks to check-out workers, cashiers, baggers, and custodial staff. Enlightened management knows that the ethics and attitudes they express when dealing with their employees will be projected in the employees' dealing with customers. According to Bill Fromm, from the book, *The Real Heroes of Business . . . and Not a CEO Among Them* (Doubleday, 1994): "Managers have no right to expect that the quality of the work being done will be any better than the quality of the environment it's being done in." You as the owner create the environment the work will be done in.

Build loyalty of your staff by showing them that you, the owner, care about how they feel about their job. Speak to your employees regularly, either informally one on one, or at regularly scheduled staff meetings as a group. They have to know that you care. Question your employees pointedly: "Are you happy here? If not, why not? What changes would you like to see implemented?" Keep lines of communication open in *both* directions. A directive-driven business will tend to

---

EXHIBIT 8-2

"MUNCH MONEY."

Employees like to know that their efforts are appreciated. What they find in their paycheck is often not the sole motivator for good work. Russ Vernon, the innovative owner of West Point Market (Akron, OH), has devised a plan for recognizing and rewarding employees with "Munch Money," coupons redeemable at his store. These are distributed to department managers to dispense at their own discretion to staff members who have gone beyond the call of duty in their jobs. *Reprinted courtesy Russ Vernon, West Point Market, Inc.*

---

alienate all but the most passive, sleepwalking, do-the-job-by-rote employee. With those kinds of employees you will be on the fast track to failure, struggling every inch of the way and getting nowhere fast.

Remember that retaining customer loyalty resides in the hands of your employees. Make them part of the family by introducing them to your customers. This encourages your customers to regard your staff as friends and as trusted sources of information. Realize that the cost of replacing employees due to turnover is high. It's far better to spend money up front on training. This takes time but the time and effort are worth it. As Mill states: "What happens if you train people and they leave? Consider this: What happens if you don't train them and they stay?"

Include employees in any newsletters or other store publicity you use as a marketing tool. Invite the employees to write about a particular product or event in which they are involved (or simply write a short article in each issue of your newsletter highlighting the background and accomplishments of a different employee, and over a period of time highlight every one of them). Show the customer how a particular employee has successfully interacted with other customers. Emphasize how the customers will benefit by becoming acquainted with a particular employee whose special talents or responsibilities relate to serving the needs of that customer. Be sure to include how you and your staff help to save the customer's time through the goods and services which are your stock-in-trade. Affording greater leisure time in a time-pressured existence is apt to be a compelling selling point. You add value to products sold by offering how-tos such as recipes, menu ideas, or serving and storing tips. Your employees need to be able to give the assistance your customers require. Cultivate an open line of communications between customers and the employees with whom they come into contact regularly. Loyalty then builds on *both* sides of the display case.

Here is a thought-provoking letter which appeared in *Progressive Grocer* (January 1996), making a compelling case for good service. *Reprinted by permission.*

Silent—but deadly

Sometimes what we don't hear can have the greatest impact. Read this letter and see what you think.

Dear Deli Manager:

You'd better remember me. I'm the nice guy who shops at your deli. When I get bad service, I never complain. I never yell, I never criticize, and I wouldn't dare make a scene. I'm one of those "nice" customers.

But I'll tell you what else I am. I'm the customer who won't come back. I'll take whatever you hand out because I know I'm not coming back. Oh sure, I suppose I could tell you off and complain or argue, which might make me feel better, but in the long run, I think it's better just to leave quietly.

You see, a nice, quiet customer like me, multiplied by all the others like me, can bring a business to its knees. There are plenty of us all over your town and if we get pushed too far, we'll go to your competitor down the street.

So take care of me, and don't take me for granted And don't think that just because I don't cause a racket every time I'm in your store, you can take advantage of me. You'll also find that, if you treat me right, I'll be the most loyal customer your department every had.

Signed,

The Quiet One

Courtesy Larry Partridge, Jonesco Enterprises, Dallas.

The Suggestion Box

Use a written suggestion box, which resides in one department for a time and then moves to another, as a good way to gain a view into the operations of a particular department. Get and use customer feedback. Institute change incrementally. Monitor the effects of such change on your operation, on your employees, and on your bottom line. Then act accordingly.

From Reactive to Proactive

As employees grow into greater responsibility, allow them the room to manage, to be proactive, to solve problems quickly and on their own. Allow them to go beyond merely acting to accomplish a finite group of tasks. Relinquish your control over small areas, gauge how things are going and then gradually cede larger and larger amounts of power, shifting more responsibility, and hence accountability, to your most promising employees. Allow employees to reach their potential. The best employees are those with multiple skills. It pays to rotate employees among a variety of positions to keep both their level of interest and productivity high. Offering employees the opportunity to tackle new challenges lets them know how you feel about their work—as long as the compensation attached to those new responsibilities is commensurate. When discussing new responsibilities, talk about increased compensation at the same time, laying out a range of salary increases tied to a pre-set calendar of performance reviews. Be prepared to answer the employee when he/she asks: "Where will I be in three months . . . six months . . . a year . . . two years?"

How Much Should It Cost You to Sell?

The cost of retail sales help should hover around 7.5 to 10%—payroll higher than that should be carefully reviewed; individuals who cost more than that should be reviewed and they should be closely worked with to remediate their low productivity (or be discharged after a specified amount of time if things don't improve). Sales staff compensation should be kept in line with each individual's performance, where practical. Inspire the less stellar retail staff to learn from the example of your "star sellers."

SERVICE—INSEPARABLE FROM STAFFING AND TRAINING

Ask any regular customer to prioritize what brings him or her back to their local gourmet to go and the number one answer is unfailingly and resoundingly, "Service."

Let's face it. The gourmet food retailing industry is a service business as much as if not more than any other food service business. As a retailer, you are providing foods with a gloss of romance attached to an upscale, mostly discerning audience who is willing to pay good money to "dine out" at home. The irreproachable quality of your food is taken for granted—the customer expects good value for the hard earned money he or she spends. But, above all else, the customer also expects and deserves good service.

What is good service? It begins with a respect for the customer, an acknowledgement that the customer pays the salaries of every individual in your organization. Good service encompasses having your employees address customers by name whenever possible. It also includes keeping your customer aware of new products and trends. Sell by educating the consumer. Talk up the products by talking *up*, never down, to your customers. Never insult customers with a condescending attitude. Exude confidence in the quality of your product line. Be enthusiastic about each product you sell, whether it is an old standby salad or the newest pâté or cheese spread to enter the market. Sell to each and every customer (whether first timer or long-established) as if it were the first sale of any merchandise to that individual. As part of that sales pitch, the customer deserves to know what they are buying. (Special diets abound; food allergies have to be taken

---

A Sample Retail Scenario—Something to Think About . . .

As a regular customer, I went into my local tea room one day, prepared to sit down to a delicious and perfectly brewed cup of tea. The owner greeted me weakly and I asked her if there were a new variety I should try today. She smiled wanly and said: "No, nothing new today, the same old thing." (Maybe she was having a bad day—these things happen from time to time, I thought to myself.) I gulped, and without missing a beat, said "Then I'll have my usual pot of Keemun Superior and a ginger scone with jam and butter."

What's wrong with this exchange? Well, many things. Despite any back-of-the-house difficulties or personal problems that day, the owner (and/or any well-trained staff member who represents the owner) should always engage the customer with an infectious, genuine-seeming enthusiasm for the product being sold. When asked by a customer for a recommendation of what to try, the savvy retailer should always have an answer that invites rather than repels or dampens the customers' enthusiasm. Either something like, "Have you tried our new China oolong?" or "Perhaps you might like to try the black tea flavored with red fruits" would have been more appropriate responses. Informing the customer about a new kind of scone or rich dessert would also have been in line. The owner should never underestimate the buying power or buying intentions of any customer who takes the effort to enter his store. To quote Ron Cardoos, a food retail industry consultant, "What is really happening here is that most of the time, it is the owners [who are] superimposing their shopping habits on their customers." The retailer is afraid to make a mistake by suggesting add-on sales to the customers, for fear of being rejected. Or the retailer is running scared when purchasing a new item to round out or enhance the shelf array. Thousands of dollars of profits are potentially lost in the process.

seriously.) Customers need to be aware of the ingredients that comprise a particular dish; if the salesperson does not have that information, it is his or her responsibility to find someone who does).

Each time a new or regular customer walks through your door, he or she has made a choice. In the mind of the customer, your operation is well-run if he or she can walk out the door with the positive feeling that the merchandise they purchased was priced well for its value and that the sales transaction went smoothly.

Regardless of price, foods that your customer considers delicious and time-saving (and as a bonus, healthful) are a bargain. These bargains are what will bring that customer back to you again and again.

CHAPTER NINE

BUILDING THE BUSINESS: MARKETING AND PROMOTION

SPENDING SOME MONEY TO MAKE MORE

You have opened your doors to customers without spending a nickel in advertising. The public has found you (remember you have chosen a highly visible and active area in which to locate) and word of mouth is beginning slowly. You need, however, to get more people into your store and ring up more sales to meet your projections. How will you accomplish this? Simply stated, look at your budget for advertising, promotions, and publicity, and then assign a portion of that budget to the following broad categories. Consider the following to extend your reach into the clientele that you have designated as your target audience:

1. Participating in major community events.
2. Joining organizations—chamber of commerce, business professional's associations, neighborhood retail merchants groups.
3. Participating in charitable work/events.
4. Cultivating relationships with the press—independently or through a professional publicity agent.
5. Developing and implementing an advertising campaign—check your budget for this and spend accordingly.

6. Executing a direct mailing of regularly produced newsletters. Use a purchased mailing list at first, and later augment it with the names you glean from your guest book, suggestion cards, questionnaires, and customers captured at the point of sale. This is discussed in more detail below.

7. Saturating the corporate community (businesses, schools, hospitals, government offices) in your area with flyers, menus, offerings of delivery free or at nominal charge.

A NEWSLETTER

As part of your overall marketing effort, a newsletter can provide at least three important benefits: spreading the word about your products, stimulating sales, and generally keeping in touch with customers. Producing a newsletter takes some work, but once the form is established it becomes easier. Each month or quarter your task is to insert relevant information about seasonal specials, events, products, or holiday themed promotions. Recipes and menu suggestions are always welcome parts of newsletters as well. Information about your staff's accomplishments, credentials, favorite dishes, or funniest stories all make great fodder for a newsletter. Just don't lose sight of the newsletter's real purpose, which is to introduce more people to your operation and keep your current customers informed of new developments in products and services that will cater to their lifestyle and capture a bit more of their disposable income in the process. Be sure to give prominent space to announcements for special in-store events like cooking demonstrations, guest chef's visits, cookbook author signings, and so on. See the examples in Exhibit 9-1.

If you wish to express *your* point of view as the owner about a particular cuisine or communicate information about your discoveries from recent food-related foreign travel or even a trade show (telling what you found there that will show up on your shelves shortly), this is the forum in which to do it.

It's also the place to allow your customers to sound off about a particular product or service you sell. Perhaps they have devised a use for a salad dressing or sauce you sell that you haven't even thought of. Highlight it and credit that customer (with prior permission, of course). Encourage staff submissions as well. Customers who can put a name or story with a face will seek out particular members of your staff. When customers build rapport with your employees, this translates into increased confidence in your store (and hence your products and services), which in turn builds sales.

EXHIBIT 9-1

NEWSLETTER SAMPLES

Newsletters, promotional mailings, menus, and other printed literature generated by a specialty food business can take many different forms. Some project a serious tone where information about products including food history is key: see the example of Corti Brothers' (Sacramento, CA) monthly mailing. Others are folksy or chatty in style: Zingerman's newspaper-like broadside. As a business owner, you can allow your imagination and enthusiasm free rein when pitching your products and services to your customer. In these examples, from operations both large and small, the personalized touch speaks volumes about the way these operators choose to do business.

CORTI BROTHERS

May, 1996

NEW, LIMITED PRODUCTION RED WINES; WONDERFUL FOODSTUFFS AND SOME WINE AND FOOD BOOKS

This newsletter has a wide range of lovely items: A very special lot of red wines heads the list, our aged Capital Vintage Marmalade and other fine comestibles, and some older wine books for the new collector.
Corti Brothers now has an 800 number to use when ordering.
The number is: (800) 509-FOOD (800-509-3663).

Darrell F. Corti

CORTI BROTHERS ANDERSON VALLEY CABERNET SAUVIGNON 1993

This wine represents one of the unique Cabernet microclimates of California. Anderson Valley in Mendocino County is home to a number of splendid wine producers, but producing Cabernet there is a bit problematical. Made by Jed Steele, a formidable winemaker producing wines under his Steele label and one of the Cabernet pioneers in the area, our first Corti Brothers Cabernet from this appellation was a 1974 from Edmeades winery made by Jed Steele. For this wine we commissioned a noted local artist, Bill Zacha, the founder and director of the Mendocino Art Center, to do a label which has only been used now four times for Cabernet Sauvignon from this region.

Anderson Valley was heavily planted to Cabernet in the late 1960's, early 1970's. The then viticultural opinion was that it was very "Bordeaux like" in its climate due to the proximity of the Pacific. There are now a little less than seven acres of Cabernet remaining in this narrow, 15 mile long valley around Boonville. Jed used to remark that there were probably only four good Cabernet vintages in a decade that could be made there. Corti Brothers offered the 1974, 1975, 1978, and now the 1993 vintage.

The Corti Brothers label depicts a unique Anderson Valley agricultural building, an apple dryer. The quote that surrounds the art work is from the English writer, Thomas Love Peacock. The label is the first, original, commissioned art label used for a California wine. Created for our first Anderson Valley Cabernet, it is only used for our bottlings of Anderson Valley Cabernet

1993 was one of the fine Cabernet vintages, with only a little rain coming at vintage end. Jed produced a lovely Cabernet and asked if I wanted to revive our Anderson Valley label. I immediately said yes. The wine has the ripe berry and almost chocolatey character of certain Cabernets with elegant, new oak in the background. Alcohol is 13% so that it is pretty much in the "modern" Bordeaux style. Very long in both flavor and finish, Corti Brothers Anderson Valley Cabernet is a special wine for cellaring.

Grocers and wine merchants since 1947.

PO BOX 191358 ✤ 5810 FOLSOM BOULEVARD ✤ SACRAMENTO CALIFORNIA 95819 ✤ TELEPHONE ✤ 916 736 3800 FAX ✤ 916 736 3807

Reprinted courtesy Corti Brothers.

Zingerman's Practical Produce

In Historic Kerrytown ¥Call us at 313.665.2558

Welcome to Great Chiles

Forget the more visible components of what we think of as Mexican cooking—beans, corn, rice, pork, fish, cilantro, avocados, tomatillos, garlic—all these are important elements of a wonderfully rich cuisine. But in the end, chiles are the key that turns the lock in making Mexican cooking authentic. To get the kind of flavor you'd find in a Mexican kitchen, there's no way around it: you've got to get to know your chiles.

A visit to most any outdoor Mexican market will make the point. You'll see a bigger variety of dried and fresh chiles on a single stand than you will in many Midwestern cities in this country. Two dozen different dried chiles, each type individually piled high in the kind of display you might see around here for popular produce like apples or oranges. They range from tiny, fire engine-red pequin chiles the size of a large pine nut, to deep-black, wrinkly-skinned dried anchos the size your hand. Then there might be a dozen more varieties, in the form of fresh chiles ranging in color from bright green to yellow, orange and red. A well-versed Mexican cook might go home with more types of chiles from the market than most of us see in a lifetime.

Taking the Chile Challenge

Those of us who are products of European eating backgrounds are at a distinct disadvantage when it comes to chiles—I guess you could say we're among the chile-challenged peoples of the world. Sure we've all had a hint of heat or the occasional hot jalapeño. But we really have hardly any experience dealing with the enormous variety and variability of chiles that Mexicans make a habit of as soon as they start eating solid food. Let's face facts: for most Midwesterners, choosing chiles can be as intimidating as making that first tentative move from a can of pre-ground Maxwell House to a bag of beautifully-roasted, varietal coffee beans. Here's a quick look at how something so seemingly simple could have reached such a stage of confusion:

5 Reasons Why It's Hard to Make Sense of Chiles

1) Many Varieties, Little Direction

It's not easy to pin the proper name on a chile. There are over 100 different chile cultivars, which readily cross-pollinate. To compound this already complicated scene different regions of the chile-growing world give different names to the same chile. Sometimes they give the same name to different chiles. It's getting me confused just writing it out. *Plus*, there are no U.S. regulations on what you can or can't call a chile, so almost any pepper can be marketed with almost any name, or just a generic "chili."

2) Same Names, Different Flavors

Even if you're able to identify that you've got the same chile cultivar being grown under the same chile name, you're still subject to the first rule of agriculture: a fruit or vegetable will taste different depending on the soil and climate of the area in which it was grown. For example, a poblano pepper from Chihuahua will not taste the same as one from southern California, which means you want to get to know your source, not just your nomenclature.

3) Pepper or Peppers?

Our American confusion between the stuff that comes out of the pepper shaker and the peppers that grow in the garden is an unsavory legacy left-over from the days of the Colombian Exchange. Looking for a route to India and a source for black pepper, Columbus named the spicy chiles he found in the Americas *pimiento*, drawing from *pimienta*, which in Spanish means "black pepper." Sixteenth century English agronomists aggravated the problem by using the direct translation from the Spanish and referred to chiles as *peppers*. Problem is that pepper (as in black) and peppers (as in chiles) have absolutely nothing botanically to do with each other. More importantly, they can't be used interchangeably in the kitchen.

4) Chiles vs. Chili vs. Chile

Even if you skip out of the pepper paradox and stick to words of native American origin you still run into trouble. "Chile" itself is an Aztec word referring to peppers, but it's also a country in South America as well as the state dish of Texas. The South American word for chile is *aji* which isn't likely to be confused with anything but I think we're about 500 years too late to try to get anyone to switch.

5) Is it Hot or Hot?

Then there's the heat problem. When we say a dish is hot in English, we have to specify whether we mean spicy hot, or just temperature hot. In Spanish, it's a lot easier since they have two different words: *picante*, which means "spicy," and *caliente*, which refers to temperature. (Unfortunately non-Spanish speakers confuse the two and come up with products like Salsa Caliente. Whoops!)

So how does a novice not get overwhelmed and just run back to the border? Well, the good news is that with a little bit of educational effort and a moderate amount of time in the kitchen, Midwesterners like me (and maybe you) can overcome our cultural disadvantages and get to know the depth, breadth and beauty of great chiles.

Midwestern Chile Masters

Rick and Deann Bayless are the owners of the Frontera Grill in Chicago, one of my favorite restaurants in the world. I've eaten there just about every time I go back to Chicago and I'd eat there a lot more often than that if it wasn't a four hour drive for dinner. Rick and Deann are actually ex-Ann Arborites—Rick received his Ph.D. in Linguistics from U of M, and in fact they used to live kitty corner to the Deli just before we started up in 1982. While we were opening Zingerman's, Rick and Deann were traveling all over Mexico learning and cataloging the authentic dishes and delights of Mexican food. When it comes to authentic Mexican cooking, Rick and Deann are two of the most knowledgeable people I've ever met. On top of which they're also two of the genuinely nicest people around.

If you've never been, the Frontera Grill will give you an entirely new perspective on Mexican food: it is to Mexican what an authentic Tuscan trattoria would be to a 1950's American spaghetti and meatballs joint. If you thought that Mexican meant a big plate of beans and rice piled next to things like cheese enchiladas or beef burritos, then it's guaranteed to be a real revelation.

The Frontera is about all sorts of wonderfully complex dishes with big, bold interesting flavors and colors, all of which stay true to their authentic Mexican roots. Things like pipians (sauces made from pumpkin seeds), soft tacos, corn tortillas wrapped around anything from duck to delicious melt-in-your-mouth beef, or authentic mole sauces made from a complex ingredient list that includes chiles and a hint of unsweetened chocolate.

Now that I've got you interested, I recommend that you pick up a copy of Rick's new book, *Rick Bayless' Mexican Kitchen*. It's filled with great recipes and good things to eat. Rick and Deann's earlier book, *Authentic Mexican*, is also highly recommended.

5 Reasons Why You Ought to Get to Know Good Chiles

1. Chiles are the Key to Authentic Mexican Flavor

Mexicans eat chiles, in one form or another, at almost every meal. Beyond all other ingredients, chiles are the key to authentic Mexican flavor.

2. Variety: the Spice of Chile Life

To limit yourself to using only one chile is like making cheddar the only cheese you eat: it's sort of one dimensional. Each chile contributes its own unique flavor to the dish in which it's used. Don't assume that one chile can innocently be substituted for another—anchos are as different from guajillos as English farmhouse cheddar is from Parmigiano Reggiano.

3. It's the Beat, Not the Heat

Although most of the attention chiles get in this country goes to their respective heat levels, in Mexico chiles are valued more for their flavors than for their fieriness. Heat levels can be induced with nothing more than a little cayenne pepper. But the flavor can come only from a good chile. One chooses an ancho not because of its mellowness in the heat department, but because of its hints of dried fruit and dark chocolate.

4. Where's the Vegetables?

Think about the standard plate of "Mexican" food you get in this country. Ever wonder where the vegetable was? To the casual observer it may appear that there aren't any. But don't worry, Mom, they're sort of "stealth vegetables"—you may not see them, but they're there. In Mexican cooking most of the vegetables are in the sauce. Mexican sauces are not the broth reductions or cream sauces we're used to. Rather, they're purées of vegetables, which usually include a generous helping of chiles. I should say too that in Mexican cooking, the sauce is the focal point of the food—it should be eaten in abundance. The chunks of meat, fish, or poultry are secondary. (To get the point across, when people ask for the "sauce on the side" at the Frontera Grill in Chicago, Rick and Deann Bayless serve the plate with sauce, garnish, et al, as is, and the meat on the side.)

5. There's Much More to Mexican Than ChiChi's

Just as Italian "cuisine" is actually made up of distinctively different regional styles of cooking and eating, so too is Mexican food a melange of different regional cuisines. Mexico comprises six major regions, each with its own distinctive dishes, its own style of serving, its own interesting mix of flavors, colors and aromas. Imagine Italian cooking without great olive oil, Parmigiano Reggiano, risotto, polenta, pesto, capers, and you'll get a glimpse of how much of real Mexican cooking we've been missing. Without walking into the world of authentic chiles you'll never get to enjoy the magical flavors of authentic Mexican food.

Ground Chiles

Most bottles with the name "chile powder" on supermarket shelves are really a *blend* of ground spices—ground chile of unknown origins and heat, salt, maybe some cumin or garlic powder. If that's what you want to sell, then let's call it "chile spice blend." In addition, the term is so general that it invites more questions than it answers. There are dozens of chiles out there and each one has its own flavor, aroma, character and heat level. Makes you wonder, doesn't it?

While I'm on the subject, I feel we ought to replace the word "powder" with "ground," which is more descriptive. In fact, I suggest that we stop using the generic term "chile," and instead fill in the kind of chile that is being ground. If you're grinding ancho chiles, then call it what it is: "Ground Ancho Chile." If we're grinding jalapeños, then call it "Ground Jalapeño Chile." And if someone grinds up leftovers, then call it "Ground Mixed Chiles." Point taken?

You can add ground chiles to soups, stews, sauces, or just about anything else. No soaking, no chopping, no muss, no fuss. Just a couple of spoonfuls, stir, and you're done.

I use ground chiles to rub onto fish or meat before cooking. I also like to mix ground chiles with a bit of sea salt and freshly ground pepper as a light coating for a salmon filet before broiling. If you like smokey flavors, rub ground chipotle onto a chicken breast or pork tenderloin and then saute in a bit of olive oil. Ground ancho chile with its mild, almost sweet, nutty flavor is a must for Mexican mole sauce. Enjoy the heat!

Why Buy Dry?

Despite our usual food prejudices, when it comes to chiles, fresh isn't necessarily the better buy. In fact, dried chiles are the single most important flavor contributor to authentic Mexican cooking. But because of their seeming strangeness to our "fresh produce" oriented eyes, I fear that we'll overlook them and miss out on some of the most flavorful food Mexico has to offer.

When you choose chiles for cooking, remember that dried and fresh are not two versions of the same thing. Like prunes and plums, the same sort of chile will taste different in its dried and fresh forms. For example, ancho chiles are "just" dried poblanos, but neither would ever be a suitable substitute for the other.

2 Jan-Feb 1997 ISSUE #139 Zingerman's News a guide to food fun & flavor

Reprinted courtesy Ari Weinzweig, Zingerman's.

> **Increasing the Customer Connection with a Newsletter**
> Distribute a newsletter or other throwaway handout about a cheese and wine pairing of the month; give a bio of a counterperson of the month; feature a particular line of mustards or olive oils and give history and uses; write about a seasonal specialty (fruit or vegetable) tied in with recipes, cookbooks, chefs as an opportunity for cross-merchandising.

A Calendar of Promotions

You can sit back and hope that customers find their way to your door, but a better idea is to set up a calendar of promotions tied to holidays or leading up to holidays, allowing at least a month before the season begins. Exhibit 9-2 shows an excellent example. This starts your customers thinking about upcoming occasions that require your products and services. In a newsletter or other promotional piece, throw out many more ideas than you intend to use to gauge your customers' interest level in each. Let your customers know about the versatility of your offerings and the extent of your creativity. Words and ink are cheap. You may be pleasantly surprised by the response, and you may stimulate the interest of a few early birds who book parties or contract for catered events around which you can plan the rest of your holiday business, led by the direction these orders take you.

In addition to regular seasonal or holiday-driven promotions, you can draw upon the following ideas to help you win the notice of press and public alike:

1. Hold a "Veritable Vinegar Extravaganza." Buy a few cases of aged balsamic vinegar. Send out invitations to your best customers for the bottle opening event. Plan a tasting dinner featuring that vinegar in each of the courses. Sell these dishes as part of your store's prepared foods array. This is one way to build your store's image and get you noticed.

2. Plan ahead to have fresh truffles for sale during the height of the fresh Italian truffle season, if only to send a message that you are serious about good food and the finer things in life. You may be surprised by how much attention this will bring your store.

3. During the summer berry season, throw a fresh berry festival. Prepare soups, salads, sauces, desserts, and ice cream using them. Everyone loves berries. Invite your customer's kids, provide inexpensive paper smocks, and let them help hull the strawberries or churn the ice cream.

EXHIBIT 9-2

CALENDAR OF MENUS

Building a loyal following for your store's prepared foods can be accomplished with a monthly calendar of menus, like the flyer shown below from The Black Cat, a gourmet foods store and cafe in Belleair Bluffs, FL. Keeping it simple is often the most effective approach to keeping customers informed about what's on your menu. Rather than using a static menu, try a rotating menu with a broad and varied range of offerings from which to choose. In this way, your customers will have more reasons to return to you more often. Developing a monthly calendar of offerings broken down into weekly menu cycles allows both the retailer and the customer to plan ahead. Furthermore, if you keep close track of what sells and what doesn't, you can easily plan succeeding months' calendars with confidence, keeping the winners and eliminating the losers. *Reprinted courtesy The Black Cat Gourmet-to-Go, Catering, and Cafe.*

THE BLACK CAT

FREE DELIVERY TO LOCAL BUSINESSES MONDAY—FRIDAY

TEL: 581-1122   FAX: 585-9897

JULY

DELIVERY ORDERS IN BY 10³⁰

$7⁵⁰ MINIMUM

	SOUP	QUICHE	SALAD ENTREE	BIG DEAL*	ENTREE
3 • 8	CORN CHOWDER • CHILLED MELON SOUP ★	CHICKEN PECAN TART	SPINACH FETA PASTA WITH FRESH FRUIT & ZUCCHINI BREAD $4⁷⁵	½ TEXICALI TUNA ON SOURDOUGH SOUP OR FRUIT & CHIPS $3⁹⁵	MARGARITA CHICKEN ★ • SUMMER SEAFOOD KBOB ★
10 • 15	SPLIT PEA • TOMATO ORANGE BISQUE ★	SEAFOOD	CHEF'S PASTA SALAD WITH FRENCH BREAD & FRESH FRUIT $4⁷⁵	½ HOBIE CAT SOUP OR FRUIT & CHIPS $3⁹⁵	STUFFED TURKEY BREAST WITH CRANBERRY RELISH ★ • VEGETARIAN LASAGNE
17 • 22	CINCINNATI CHILI • VICHYSSOISE	SPINACH	ORZO THE GREEK! WITH LEMON BREAD & FRESH FRUIT $4⁷⁵	½ CAT'S PJ'S SOUP OR FRUIT & CHIPS $3⁹⁵	SUN-DRIED TOMATO & CHEESE STUFFED CHICKEN BREAST • BEEF TENDERLOIN, MUSHROOM & ONION KBOB ★
24 • 29	SPANISH BEAN ★ • COOL SENEGALESE	SUN-DRIED TOMATO & FETA	NUTTY CHICKEN PASTA WITH CRANBERRY MUFFIN & FRESH FRUIT $4⁷⁵	½ BLTP SOUP OR FRUIT & CHIPS $3⁹⁵	STUFFED PORK LOIN WITH FRESH PEACH SALSA • CHICKEN & SHRIMP KBOBS ★

★ INDICATES LOWERED FAT   *M-F, NO SUBSTITUTIONS

4. Invite customers to get into the "Spear-It Asparagus Festival." Take your cues from European food festivals and do an asparagus festival where you feature four or five dishes each day made with asparagus (salads, pastas, soups, frittatas, stir fries). Other seasonal specialties such as artichokes and rhubarb also can become centerpieces of image-building events.

5. Draw upon relations with your best vendors to assist you in bringing in special seasonally available imported cheeses. Invite a cheese expert to give a talk. Build a menu around the product. Distribute recipe cards. Sample the product. Run a guess-the-weight-of-the-cheese contest and award a cheese dish of the month (to feed four) to the customer who comes closest to the exact weight of the wheel.

6. Offer a taste of history: Plan an in-store dinner, by invitation only, recreating a historic menu around President's Day or around Inauguration day, regardless of your political affiliation.

7. Invite some local dignitaries to work behind the counter at your store. Advertise this in the local papers.

> Michael Barefoot, owner of A Southern Season, Chapel Hill, NC, has a different view on promotions: "Do we really need to do this or would we be better off to promote special events less, and have a better quality product when the curtain goes up everyday?"

Designate some promotions as major, big deal, pull-out-all-the-stops events (perhaps two or three a year, depending on budgets, time, personnel, and interest). Also plan minipromotions, store tastings, markdown times, parking lot (or sidewalk) sales, get-rid-of-slower-moving-merchandise sales events throughout the year. Just put it all on a master calendar. Be conscious of other events in your area that may conflict with (or be complementary to) the dates of your events.

To pull off promotions successfully, you have to be sure that all of the logistics are planned out well in advance. If you have individuals on your staff whose strength is in detail-oriented catering, enlist them to orchestrate your store promotions (comp days or store scrip might serve as good incentives for these employees willing to work on their "days off"). Store promotions and catering each require some showmanship, and people who work well in the catering arm of your business are the most likely to shine at promotional events where they are given the opportunity to be creative.

What Kinds of Promotional Events Should You Plan?

According to Mike Margarites, a veteran specialty food consultant based in New York, there are three kinds of promotions:

1. Major sales promotions
2. Seasonal events
3. Store image builder

The first kind requires the most planning and the biggest budget. The other two require less planning, and therefore less lead time, and can offer help in off times when sales tend to be slower. (Of course, it's sometimes best to plan promotional events when sales are at their peak, such as holidays, as a way to increase dollar value of each sale.)

Now's the time to be just plain silly (after all, who owns the place?) Why not tie promotional events to tax time, your own birthday, or some local hero or anti-hero from your area's history? Celebrate the end of winter or the beginning of spring. Spotlight the arrival of a seasonal item or new line of shelf-stable products. Get some marketing support and sampling allowance from your suppliers. If you have an exclusive on an item (or line of items) or are the first in your area to carry it, then promote that. Above all, be creative and make your own traditions. There are really no rules here. Just bear in mind that the point of your promotions is not to spend more money than you can hope to bring in. Rather, your goal should be to sell more merchandise, bring new customers through the doors, and get some publicity from local press in the process.

Build the promotion around one product, or category of products, perhaps of like provenance—all things French, or Pacific Rim or Italian or British—take your pick (wines, cheeses, mustards, ethnic themed foods).

Can you rent props and hire celebrity look alikes for a Hollywood styled event? Can you bring in local music students to serenade shoppers with Viennese waltzes while you sample and sell Austrian products (strudels, cheeses, wines, wursts, etc.)? What about a mariachi band to turn up the heat on a salsa-spiced Mexican fiesta? The ideas are endless. Connect with tourist boards and local travel agents to get colorful backdrops and travel posters. Costumes add a festive touch. Rent them from local theater groups.

Work up a budget—what can you afford to spend on the props, publicity, printed matter, press releases, invited guests?

Getting the word out about your promotion, via your own newsletter and also through local media channels (newspapers, magazines, smaller local papers), is where you should put most of your dollars. Don't stint on the budget for additional help to set up, man, and take down the displays.

When the time comes for each promotional event, track sales by product category during this time (you may be doing this already). Jot down notes about any particularly successful (or unsuccessful) parts of the promotion to help plan future years' promotional events. You can learn a lot about your customers and their habits by tracking their purchasing behavior during promotional events.

Promotions need not always be big deal events. Sometimes, a spontaneous display of slow-moving merchandise can draw customers to a corner of your store that generally gets less attention. Good signage, recipe cards, and meal suggestions built around the particular item on sale all help to stimulate interest in a product that may have been the result of an overly zealous trade show purchase. As you learn more about what your customers like, you will experience fewer situations where markdowns become necessary. But if, despite your best efforts, a surplus of items in a particular category is crowding your shelf or stockroom space, price markdowns are a way to stimulate turnover and preserve profit. Markdowns should occur as soon as you detect customer resistance to the price you originally established for the item. Of course, the larger the markdown, the smaller the profit or the greater the loss.

Six Ways to Avoid the Dreaded Markdown

1. Sample the slow-moving product during peak hours on a regular basis, with the display staffed by a knowledgeable and persuasive person. Sampling when staffed can often lead to sales, while you can go broke if you use the free-for-all sampling approach. Feeding your customers for free can be costly, and it's an ineffective way to sell.
2. Make a statement with a large display of the item in a prominent spot in the store, appropriately supported with props and signage.
3. Include the item in cook's kits containing three or four major ingredients for a simple prepared dish, along with recipes for their use.
4. Spotlight the item in newsletters or other printed materials you distribute to the customers on your mailing list or in store.
5. Include the item in gift baskets at every opportunity where your profit is spread out over a larger number of items. (Use what's left as filler in baskets during the next gift-giving season.)
6. Last resort: Apply the "old wine in new bottles" adage and turn the item over to your prepared foods kitchen to incorporate in a dish and factor it into food costs.

PRESS AND PUBLICITY: PURSUING OTHER AVENUES TO GET INTO THE SPOTLIGHT

You're open a few months and business has been steadily picking up but you wish to make a greater impact on the corporate segment of your market area. Or you wish to reach the highly social movers and shakers in your community who haven't found you yet. Or you wish to become the contracted supplier of box dinners for the outdoor summer music festival in your town. Or you want to become the one stop of choice for those two career couples who don't have time to cook dinner three nights a week but wish to have a quality dining experience at home. How will you make any or all of the above happen?

Developing a good rapport with the local food writing and restaurant reviewing press would be a good place to start. If you have the budget, hire a public relations professional, one who comes to you highly recommended. Such a consultant can often provide the fastest link to the press. PR agents who are expert at working with food clients provide the best route to getting the story behind your store into the right hands. They may develop a campaign that will put samples of your products, press materials about you, and printed menus (like those in Exhibit 9-3) and other brochures and newsletters from your operation into the hands of influential members of the press. You have to be discreet, however, be patient while waiting for results, and be prepared to receive an onslaught of customers should your store become the focus of a newspaper or magazine feature. In light of the detail-laden nature of the business, it's best to allow a shakedown period of a few months before inviting anyone to scrutinize your offerings; you'll want to have all the wrinkles ironed out in your operation.

Getting and Keeping the Word Out There

This same individual can also help you develop an advertising campaign to fit your budget. Bear in mind, however, that advertising needs to be consistent and that getting results takes time (perhaps a year is a fair trial period). Repetition of your message is what gets customers in the door. Paid advertising is no substitute for good word of mouth, which is the slowest yet most effective method to spread the word about your business. Since people tend to associate with others of similar socioeconomic level, interests, and lifestyles, when they talk, the word about you spreads with laser-like accuracy to the audience you wish to reach.

More ideas: Take advantage of the tremendous press well-known chefs and restaurateurs are getting in the newspapers and other media. Tie in some of your menu items with specialties from these chefs, and cross-merchandise the foods

EXHIBIT 9-3

SAMPLE MENUS FROM TWO SPECIALTY FOOD RETAILERS

Through their design and graphics, menus can convey an image of your operation directly to your customers or the food press. Below are two examples, from *Flavors* (p.265) and from *Dino's Pasta Market* (p. 266), that might be used as models for their comprehensiveness and straight-forward style.

Reprinted courtesy Pamela Morgan, Flavors.

contorni (side dishes)

roasted sweet onions, in balsamic vinegar	5.99 lb.
grilled vegetables, with zucchini, yellow squash, eggplant and peppers	5.99 lb.
napoletano, crunchy eggplant, fresh mozzarella, ripe tomato slices and fresh basil, stacked in individual servings	5.99 lb.
marinated mushrooms, prepared with fresh mushrooms and herbs	4.99 lb.
baby artichokes, lightly roasted and drizzled with olive oil, minced garlic, italian parsley and white wine	6.99 lb.
caponata, with eggplant, tomatoes and capers	5.99 lb.
roasted garlic, with a touch of extra-virgin olive oil	4.99 lb.
portobello mushrooms, lightly grilled and dressed in a red wine vinaigrette	11.99 lb

secondi (entrees)

dino's meatloaf, dressed in a fresh tomato sauce	5.99 lb.
grilled boneless breast of chicken, marinated in mustard, garlic, parsley and a touch of chili	6.99 lb.
poached salmon, prepared in a white wine bath and served with a fresh dill sauce	14.99 lb.
toscana sausage & beans, prepared with fresh italian sausages	8.99 lb.
polenta lasagne, layered with wild mushrooms and bescamella	5.99 lb.
lasagne alla ferrarese, with a zesty ragu, parmigiano-reggiano and spinach pasta	5.99 lb.

pasta menu

flavors

egg	2.99 lb.	spinach	2.99 lb.
lemon	2.99 lb.	squid ink	3.99 lb.
beet	2.99 lb.	chili pepper	2.99 lb.
black truffle	3.99 lb.	whole wheat	2.99 lb.

daily specials

flat cuts	extruded shapes
linguine	angel hair
spaghetti alla chitarra	fusilli
tagliolini	penne
fettuccine	rigatoni
tagliatelle	radiatore
lasagne (cut to order)	rotelle
	conchiglie

ravioli

fontina cheese & truffle, in egg pasta	7.99 lb.
shrimp & chive, with egg whites and pepper, in egg and squid ink pasta	9.99 lb.
eggplant, with ricotta, parmigiano-reggiano, eggs, breadcrumbs, fresh thyme and italian parsley, in egg pasta	6.99 lb.
fresh spinach & ricotta cheese, with parmigiano-reggiano and a pinch of grated nutmeg in spinach pasta	5.99 lb.
pumpkin, with ricotta, parmigiano-reggiano and nutmeg, in a spinach pasta	5.99 lb.
roasted chicken, with eggs, parmigiano-reggiano, white wine, fresh herbs, and bay leaves, in a saffron pasta	7.99 lb.

fresh pasta sauce

chunky tomato, with fresh basil	4.99 lb.
bolognese, prepared with italian sausages	5.99 lb.
porcini mushroom, with roasted garlic in a light cream sauce	6.99 lb.
arrabbiata, with chunks of tomato, italian herbs and spices	4.99 lb.
pesto genovese, with fresh basil, pine nuts, parmigiano-reggiano and garlic	7.99 lb.
italian sausage, with fennel and tomatoes	5.99 lb.
alfredo, prepared with parmigiano-reggiano, cream and sweet butter	5.99 lb.

Reprinted courtesy Richard Heyman, Dino's Pasta Market.

with their cookbooks. Invite them into your stores to do a cooking demo (they can sell and sign some books as well). Build a themed promotion around a particular cuisine, adding shelf-stable items to your staples array in the process. If your featured cuisine is Asian, for example, bring in lines of sauces and condiments that are crucial here. By all means, read the food press in your area to get a glimpse at what food writers are talking about—stock your shelves with what is being written about. Be prepared for the next big wave or if your space and budget allow and you store concept says "comprehensive," be prepared for the next ripple, too.

JUSTIFYING PROMOTIONS

Any promotional plan you or your marketing agent implement needs to justify its expense. Build in some tracking mechanisms to check for effectiveness. Whether you use a tear-out coupon, frequent buyer card, an advertisement featuring an offer of free or deeply discounted merchandise, or simply an in-store entry blank that entitles the winner to some free food or services, you should be able to check whether or not your money is being well-spent. Set a timetable for tracking results, preferably on a biweekly basis for as long as the campaign is in effect. Then at the end of each two week period, compute the results of business that you can tie directly to the marketing effort. For the next campaign, adjust the strategy to pitch your marketing efforts in a slightly different way. Compare and contrast and think again whether this particular method is working or needs realigning.

OTHER PROMOTIONAL IDEAS

How do you intend to follow up on first time customers to keep them coming back? Good food and good service are frequently not enough to ensure repeat business. In a highly competitive business climate, you've got to find a way to stand out. You might institute a frequent customer rewards plan using some kind of punch card: buy nine sandwiches (or pounds of cheese or pâté) and get the tenth one free. You might offer a free loaf of hearth baked bread for limited time only as part of your opening promotion, redeemable with a coupon from your mailing piece. Birthday lunch could be on you. Are customers entering your store in response to a direct mail piece that you sent out to the neighboring communities? If so, capture their preferences with a brief, pointed questionnaire, like the one shown in Exhibit 9-4, and reward them with a discount or free product if they complete it and send it back or drop it by the next time they come in.

EXHIBIT 9-4

DINO'S QUESTIONNAIRE

Targeting your operations and product offerings to your audience is often made simpler with information that comes directly from your customers. In addition to talking with them on a one-to-one basis, a questionnaire may elicit some valuable responses. This one, from Dino's Pasta Market (Brentwood, CA), an Italian-themed takeout, was used in their opening promotions. For taking the time to fill it out, customers were rewarded with 10% off their next purchase. Tailor one to suit your particular operations, keeping in mind that it needs to be short, easy to fill out, and the customers need to get something in return for taking the time to respond.

10% off we want to get to know you!
Fill out these questions and return for a 10% discount on your next purchase.

NAME _____   EXPIRES _____

ADDRESS _____   PHONE (_____) _____

CITY/STATE _____   ZIP CODE _____

WHAT ARE YOUR 3 FAVORITE TAKE-OUT RESTAURANTS? _____

HOW MANY PEOPLE ARE IN YOUR HOUSEHOLD?_____ HOW OFTEN DO YOU COOK AT HOME? DAYS _____

WOULD YOU LIKE TO JOIN DINO'S BIRTHDAY CLUB? ☐   BIRTHDAY _____

WHAT TIME DO YOU USUALLY SHOP FOR DINNER? _____ IS YOUR REFRIGERATOR TYPICALLY EMPTY OR FULL?

WHAT ARE 3 THINGS YOU ALWAYS HAVE IN YOUR REFRIGERATOR? _____

WHEN COOKING, WHAT ONE THING ARE YOU'RE WILLING TO LEAVE THE HOUSE FOR TO FINISH PREPARING A MEAL?

HOW OFTEN DO YOU DRINK WINE WITH DINNER? _____

WHAT DO YOU THINK IS THE SEXIEST ITALIAN DISH? _____

Reprinted courtesy Richard Heyman, Dino's Pasta Market.

If you follow the guideline below each time you decide to execute a promotion, you will have a headstart to success with in-store promotions and publicity:

1. Decide on a plan.
2. Learn from the masters; read; attend seminars.
3. Consult your accountant or money manager regarding budget for marketing efforts.

4. Look to outside PR or marketing experts to plan and implement an effective marketing campaign; discuss your goals and evaluate the full range of possibilities before committing to a strategy.

5. Define your target audience and focus your efforts on them; attract and then sell to one customer at a time. This means that you focus your efforts on selling to the particular needs of each customer after he or she walks into the store. This will do more to boost your business than any other strategy. Focus on that customer and that customer only (through the efforts of your sales staff, of course) and the customer will leave your store having obtained all of what he or she came in for—and tell others about you to boot. One satisfied customer leads to many more individual satisfied customers. As Anne Lamott, the writer and writing teacher says about writing, it's "bird by bird," and then word by word. By extension, in retailing, building a business comes down to winning customer confidence and loyalty, one customer at a time.

CHAPTER TEN

WORKING TOWARD THE FUTURE: FINE-TUNING, GROWTH, AND EXPANSION

> **Time to Think/Time to Plan**
>
> A fixed percentage of your time, say 5%, must be allocated to the thinking time necessary for longer range planning, to keep ahead of the curve, to strengthen your customer base and consolidate your position in the community. Accept the reality that it's always going to be a push-pull between becoming enmeshed in daily routines and the more global, often more important planning that you need to be doing to move the business ahead to its next phase of growth. Unless you block out time on your calendar to do that kind of thinking and encourage a free interchange of ideas with others, you will stagnate and gradually erode the vitality of your business. You also will need to be able to get away from the business, as soon as you feel secure in the knowledge that the store is well taken care of, the fort is being watched by capable, well-trained staff. Don't put off getting away from the business. From afar, you may be able to see your business from a different and refreshing perspective. To keep your footing in a rapidly changing landscape of product and services, you must be able to allot time and money to attend out of town trade shows and conferences.

You're a year or two down the road and the business is running smoothly. You've reached your sales projections by dint of hard work, good forecasting, stringent cost controls, and good customer service, based on a comprehensive staff training program. What's more, your investors are pleased with the return on their investment. You're making good on your bank loan and you're itching to take the business to its next step. What are your options? A second location? A franchise? A manufacturing plant to produce signature items from your product line?

First, you need to examine the market. What areas are experiencing growth right now—stores? mail order? home-meal replacement? private labeling? If you were to open another store, where might you consider doing so? Would you encounter the same demographics in another spot to support your current concept? What about start-up costs? Would the new location carry with it higher overhead costs and would you therefore need to restructure the revenue centers to accommodate a new setup? How would you restructure your current P & L's to accommodate a new reality? Or in another location, would you need to downscale prices and change your offerings somewhat to appeal to that area's prevailing demographics? Is there more competition than when you opened the first store?

Next, you need to ask yourself all the same questions as when you assessed going into business in the first place, but this time there are a few more questions to add to the list. Unless you can be cloned, being responsible for two or more places at the same time presents some difficulties. Are you ready to shuttle back and forth between locations? Do you have a management team that can grow with you? Have you discussed the possibilities of expansion with them? Could any of them potentially be partners in the new venture? You also need to think about time. Are you ready to give up any free time you may have had to launch and then oversee the operations of a new location? Another issue is whether you are willing to relinquish more control over the day-to-day operations of the store. Furthermore, your managers' salaries are inching their way up, and with increased responsibility and greater oversight over the new location, they will need to go even higher. Can the business afford a higher percentage of operational dollars going into salaried labor?

Third, you need to think about the funding for the expansion. Are you in a strong enough position financially to turn to your investors and interest them in upping their stake of the business? Could you conceivably buy them out and go it alone? On the strength of your profit and loss statements and operational history, might you be able to approach the bank for a larger loan and extend your line of credit in anticipation of major expansion? Or is your concept ready to franchise? Are you interested in seeking venture capital to take the business national? Can the business concept be simplified, reduced to a formula, so that you can duplicate it elsewhere, keeping consistency of quality a priority and good service a necessary correlative? Is there space adjacent to your current store (or down the block) into which you might expand, allowing you to increase your offerings or add or expand the seating area for on-premises eating?

Consider, too, whether you might have the makings of a winner on your hands in the form of a signature product or line of products upon which you have been largely building your reputation. Can you take these star sellers to a manufacturer who can produce in large batches what you have been doing on a smaller scale in your kitchen? With your reputation growing locally, are you emboldened enough by your retailing success to launch a private label series of products and launch a regional or even national distribution of it? As in the case of your single unit store, producing product is only the start. Packaging, labeling, marketing, gaining reliable wide distribution and supporting the product(s) with point of sale promotional materials all need to be factored into the picture. *All* of the human and monetary costs must be considered before plunging into the wholesale manufacturing business. Exhibit 10-1 shows a questionnaire used by a specialty food retailer considering such an expansion into wholesale food production and marketing.

From a production perspective, considering the economies of scale that may result from centralizing some or all of your preparations, does it make financial sense to invest in building a commissary facility in a lower-rent district with easy access to your market area to handle the production for each of your locations? All of this takes time-consuming research just like the first time. Just because you have done it before doesn't guarantee that you can simply sail onto the next sea. You have more at stake now that you already have a business.

Framing all of the above considerations is the answer to the question: "*Is big necessarily better?*" With multiple locations, you may need to spin your wheels harder and faster to yield the same or even lesser profits for a time. Will the new location create a drain on the established location in many ways? Just how will your current location suffer as a result of your attentions being focused on the new one? Human resources? Cash flow? Capitalization? Product line? Consistency of service and quality of foods?

Can you spare any of your key personnel at your current location and move them to the new store for the initial start-up period? Again, you need to look deeply into what makes you happy about being in business in the first place. Is it the sense of accomplishment, the money, the recognition, the power? The hands-on involvement (which will, in all likelihood, be reduced with increased managerial responsibilities as your build your "empire")? Does your adrenaline feed on working in a high pressure position? Is burnout around the corner? Perhaps now the answers will be different, the circumstances changed since business #1 began.

EXHIBIT 10-1

CUSTOMER SURVEY

This is a survey you might use as a model to gauge the viability of a move into large-scale manufacturing. For a modest investment in time and dollars, you can assess whether to commit more dollars to developing that arm of your business by sending it to other retail businesses in your market area.

Bean Bag

Great Food for Healthy Bodies

Due to the terrific enthusiasm friends and customers have shown for Bean Bag's prepared meals, we are developing a new line of healthfully prepared and packaged food for wholesale distribution. We would most appreciate a few moments of your time in completing this survey.

Please indicate your household size: _____ Children _____ Adults _____

Please indicate your profession _____

How many days per week do you eat lunch on the job? _____

How much do you spend weekly on food in restaurants or from takeout? _____

What percentage of this is purchased ready-to-eat from stores? _____

Do you currently purchase Bean Bag meals? _____ If so, how many per week? _____

On a scale of 1 (least important) to 5 (most important), please rate the importance of each of the following with regard to your meals:

____ Calories	____ Cholesterol content	____ Spicy
____ Fat content	____ Vegetarian	____ Kosher
____ Protein content	____ Organic	____ Environment-friendly

Do you have any specific dietary concerns?

_____

_____

Which of our products would you be interested in purchasing in individual containers or in bulk packaging?

____ Vegetable burgers	____ Grain or pasta salads	____ Muffins
____ Turkey burgers	____ Steamed vegetables	____ Cakes
____ Stuffed turkey rolls	____ Brown rice rolls	____ Cookies

Other (please specify) _____

Where would you like to be able to purchase Bean Bag products?

____ Local delis	____ Health food stores	____ Supermarkets
____ Specialty food stores	____ Health clubs	____ By Delivery

Thank you for completing this survey. Please fax to: _____ or mail it to: _____

THE EVALUATION PROCESS

The business planning process outlined in this book is a step-by-step approach that guides you through the start-up process in a logical way. At every major juncture, you and your team can take the information you have culled from a particular activity (i.e., writing a mission statement, conducting a feasibility study or a marketing study, writing the business plan, calculating the capital needed, or taking a first stab at your sales and expense projections) and make a "go" or "no go" decision based on the findings. The evaluation process is incremental and ongoing, both throughout the business planning phase and later, when you're up and running. At that later time, such evaluation is also crucial to help understand where you stand and, perhaps, whether to expand. It is the key to making effective and timely decisions about your business at all points in its life cycle.

Evaluating information and results and coming to careful conclusions and decisions takes your most precious commodity—time. It is imperative to go slowly and to be patient and reflective in order to arrive at an honest review of the findings. With careful evaluation you will have clearer basis on which to move forward. Furthermore, the evaluation process is intimately bound up with the need for effective communication, of which listening is the most crucial part—listening to yourself as you communicate your "take" on what your findings show, listening to the objective truth, and listening to others (your partners, your employees, your consultants). It's pointless to go through the process of first undertaking a feasibility study and then writing a business plan, for example, if you don't intend to act on the basis of the key findings and adjust your vision and direction in light of them. Careful listening and honesty aren't easy, however. They often require you to change your vision or your plan of action. The good news is that in most cases you will be making changes *for the better*—that is, you will find that less start-up is needed, that higher profits can be realized sooner, that you should not take a jump that is too big for you at the time, that you can train your staff more effectively, plan a better menu, and so on.

ADDING UP THE SCORE

People are generally more comfortable with absolutes than gray areas, but when performing an evaluation of your business, too many variables are involved to make it a mathematical exercise. It's not as straightforward as getting a passing grade for a difficult college course and then moving on to the next class in that subject. Getting a green light to proceed with the opening or expansion of a business does not happen based on a score of "right" answers. The answers lie in considering the potential of your resources and your business' position and timing in four categories of evaluation (see below). It lies in a culmination of the findings, an honest response to them, and a logical plan of action moving forward.

THE "SWOR" TEAM

One tool for establishing the structure of the evaluation process is a simple grid that separates the findings from your work into four major categories—strengths, weaknesses, opportunities, and risks: SWOR. It can be a powerful tool when used as the catalyst for your team discussions. Use this approach to determine a "go" or "no go" based on a discussion of your findings using the following four touchstones as catalysts to your thinking.

1. **Team**—Who are the members? What are their areas of expertise? What is their time availability? What is their level of commitment to the project? Who else do you need to join your team to make this venture (either a start-up or expansion) move forward? Do you have the resources to attract and sign on that person/those people?

2. **Financial Position**—What resources do you now have? What do you need to move forward? Can you acquire more resources? How will this be done? How much time will it take? What are the alternate forms of resources available?

3. **Market**—What are the current and future trends? What is going out of style? What are people willing to pay for similar products and services? If you're already in operation, where are you now in the market? What's needed to move forward?

4. **Operations**—What is your business now? What is your current production capacity? What do you need to increase capacity to meet demand of new or desired market? Will you increase with your own current facility or need to expand? What will this cost to undertake? How long will it take to build and set up efficiently?

With these in mind, you can then perform an evaluation of any stage of the business planning process. Take a situation or an idea and think through each of the above four areas applying the SWOR grid to each and ending up with a visual mind map that will facilitate clear and objective thinking and lead you to the brink of the decision-making process. After applying the grid to each of the above four, you are ready to sit down and evaluate the results.

Here is an example of how to fill in the blanks on the four-quadrant grid.

The situation: You find a location that at first glance looks ideal to build your new store. It is large, nicely laid out to build a kitchen and have ample space for merchandising and, perhaps, a small café. However, the rent is about double what you initially expected to pay. Should you move forward or not?

Strengths

Downtown location with lots of foot traffic

Owner willing to help with build-out (i.e., ventilation)

No other store like it (little competition) in general area

Weaknesses

New building, not yet fully occupied

Will need to use union labor to build (higher cost)

It might take me twice as long to raise the money to build here

Opportunities

Would be the first store of its kind in immediate area

I could generate enough business to hire more staff, assemble a great team (i.e., chef/manager)

I could get the word out to a much larger audience in this location/ operation than I can now

Risks

Rent is double what we originally projected

Would need to hire more staff than originally planned

This would be a much larger market than I am now used to

Analyze the findings in terms of these four touchstones, and see how they stack up on the grid. Seeing these results visually will often help you assess the results objectively. Seeing more significant entries in the two quadrants labeled Weaknesses and Risks, for example, might indicate that you should move away from that original idea, and might guide you to take a look at more viable alternatives.

The SWOR system distills the facts into a chart where you apply your resources to the situation and then make a "go" or "no go" decision to move forward. In the example above, only you (the operator) would be able to know whether you could raise more money or hire a good team to meet the needs of this potentially great location. Until you have looked at the options carefully and logically, however, you cannot expect to make an *informed* decision. Therefore, a "go" decision might indicate only that you need to take the next step in a series of steps. In the case we've been looking at, the next step might be a commitment to do extensive financial projections for this potential location, projections that will

let you see just how much business it will take to justify a larger space than originally planned, along with its more expensive rent and bigger payroll.

Another approach to SWOR could be this: strengths and weaknesses relate to
how the concept and your team's expertise match up to what you have discovered
about the market and the area in which you desire to open your business. Do you
have the resources to take this to the next step, whatever the next step is?
Opportunities and risks focus on the money needed and potential money to be
earned. The evaluation process uses the information you have worked hard to
amass (via a feasibility or marketing study or by periodically reviewing the state
of your business' overall health over a given period of time) and analyzes the
findings or the current situation based on information contained in the answers
to the questions under each of the four touchstones above.

Putting the pieces of a business together is somewhat like creating a painting: a
balanced composition (read "healthy business") takes into account all of the effects
of the various components, making choices about which are reasonable, which
provide the most opportunity, and which are unreasonable or too risky to include.
This means, for example, that if the rent in a particular area seems a little (or a lot)
high, but the volume of potential customers is great (i.e., main downtown commercial district), then the risk of high rent may be worth taking. Furthermore, if the
rent is high but the foot traffic is also very high *and* there are no other businesses
like yours meeting the determined needs of those customers, then the cost of that
high rent just got even more reasonable. The trick here is to use the evaluation
process to prove that you have a good idea, that there is a good (or great) market for
your idea to be made into a business, that you have a unique and appealing way to
bring the concept to fruition, that you can capitalize it fully, and that you can be
profitable, based on the findings from your studies. *How* you carry it all off in the
end will be based on your original vision tempered by what you have discovered
from the feasibility study and business plan writing processes. For example, when
other stores come into the area where you are located, you might choose to offer an
office delivery service that is state-of-the-art, thereby establishing regular customers
who get more than the average set of needs met by *your* business, which will give
you a competitive edge.

After all is said and done, after all the technical finesse has been learned and
applied to make your business successful (effective organization, accurate financial projections, continual staff training, creative design, clever merchandising,
and, let us not forget, cooking and selling good food), a lot of what takes a business to expansion, as it was the first time around, are decisions made simply by
evaluating your strengths and weaknesses in an honest and objective way. It's
analytic and not technical, but don't let this confuse or enrage you.

The first key to success is remembering where you are starting from: Are you creating this new business because you love what you do or because you are trying to get away from something (such as a first store that needs your attention)? The second key is planning logically, taking information from each step, analyzing it, and making decisions to move forward that are realistic for your capabilities and resources. Using the evaluation tools will minimize your risk and enhance your opportunities every step of the way. Remember why you started your business in the first place. If running your business is taking you further and further away from the reasons you opened in the first place, then it is time to reassess your role and your goals and rethink how much satisfaction you are deriving from the day-to-day operations. You always have the option to switch roles in your business; if you began in the kitchen, maybe you need to consider returning to it. If your strength lay in the front of the house role, and you have been spending more time supervising cooks and production personnel, then maybe it's time to make provisions to return to the arena where you are best suited to apply your skills. But remember, above all, that if you are equipped with objectivity, patience, and the ability for attentive listening, you are more likely to have fun with your business as it is operating and growing throughout its life. Be flexible, stay open minded, tune into what your employees and customers are saying, and keep your ear to the ground ready to pick up on the next trend. Success can be yours; reach high but remain grounded in good common sense. Trust your instincts. If you never swerve from offering quality products backed up by caring service, success will follow.

A P P E N D I X

EMPLOYEE AGREEMENTS

EXHIBIT A-1

EMPLOYEE NONCOMPETE AGREEMENTS

Several years down the line after your business is in full flower, you may be faced with the departure of a key staff member (perhaps your chef, manager, or other) who has plans to open a business similar to yours. You have no recourse unless that person agrees to sign one of the following agreements. Underlying their willingness to do so, of course, is your willingness to continue to make it worth their while to remain in your employ. That may include offering them a stake in your business. Even given those realities, there is still no guarantee that any individual, no matter how committed to you as an employer, will be content with his or her status as an employee. Greater ambitions and a wish to be one's own boss often lead the most devoted and capable employees down their own entrepreneurial path. That's life. Nonetheless, here are two forms which you might use as models for such noncompete agreements.

Employee Noncompete Agreement (Specific Radius)

In consideration of my being employed by _____ (company), I, the undersigned, hereby agree that upon the termination of my employment and notwithstanding the cause of termination, I shall not compete with the business of the Company or its successors or assigns, and shall not directly or indirectly, as an owner, officer, director, employee, consultant, or stockholder, engage in the business of _____ or a business substantially similar or competitive to the business of the Company.

281

This noncompete agreement shall extend only for a radius of __ miles from the present location of the Company, and shall be in full force and effect for _____ years, commencing with the date of employment termination.

Employee Signature _____ Date _____

Witness Signature _____ Date _____

Employee Noncompete Agreement (General)

For good consideration, and in consideration of my being employed by _____ (Company), I, the undersigned, hereby agree that upon my termination of employment and notwithstanding the cause of termination, I shall not compete with the business of the Company, or its successors or assigns.

The term "not compete" as used in this agreement means that I shall not directly or indirectly, as an owner, officer, director, employee, consultant, stockholder, or partner:

1. Solicit orders for any product or service competitive with the Company.
2. Accept employment with or be employed by a firm engaged in selling products or services competitive with the products or services of the Company.
3. Contact, for the purpose of soliciting their business, any customer or account that existed during the course of my employment with the company.

This agreement shall remain in full force and effect for ___ year(s) commencing with the date on which my employment with the company will have been terminated and notwithstanding the reason for termination or the party terminating.

Employee Signature _____ Date _____

Signature subscribed and affirmed, or sworn to, before me in the county of _____ State of _____

Date _____

E X H I B I T   A - 2

EMPLOYEE CONFIDENTIALITY AGREEMENT

You may build your reputation on a single signature item without which your store would not be your store. Therefore, it pays to put as many safeguards in place as possible to protect the exclusivity of your stock-in-trade by asking all of your staff members to sign an employee confidentiality agreement. In the specialty food arena, particularly where you are producing an array of prepared foods, sweets, or other foods in house, your uniqueness is based on your own version of a classic dish. Consider the fact that what sets your brownie apart from the rest on the market are the macadamia nuts and nut liqueur you use as flavoring. Would you want one of your bakers to divulge that information to his or her friend who works in a neighboring business? It's doubtful. You stand a better chance of preventing a hard-won formula from getting into the hands of the competition by insisting that your staff sign an agreement similar to what follows, even if you believe in your heart of hearts that you can't truly enforce the terms of such an agreement. Putting your employees on notice about your commitment to remaining unique in the marketplace is a message worth conveying. Such an agreement should help to accomplish this.

Employee Confidentiality Agreement

I, _____ am an employee of the _____ Company. As part of my duties I may be exposed to or have access to certain trade secrets and knowledge of ingredients used in the production of company products. I hereby certify that all knowledge or information I gain from the company about those trade secrets or product ingredients, including all patented or unpatented inventions, designs, know-how, technical data or information, specifications, blueprints, transparencies, test data, additions, or modifications which are to me as strictly confidential will be held in strict confidence and trust by me. I will not reveal, or disclose the trade secrets or information on secret ingredients to any other person, firm, corporation, company, or other entity now or at any time in the future, unless my employer instructs me to do so. This secrecy protection will continue even if I no longer am employed by this company. I understand that if I reveal these trade secrets to unauthorized persons, I personally may be subject to penalties and lawsuits for injunctive relief and money damages as well as possible criminal charges.

Employee Signature _____ Date _____

Witness Signature _____ Date _____

EXHIBIT A-3

NONDISCLOSURE/NONCOMPETE AGREEMENT

Before opening your business, you may be putting on your payroll key personnel (head chef, store manager, etc.) to help with the start-up work that needs to be done. You also may be in earnest conversations with these individuals with an eye to hiring them. In either case, they will therefore be privy to important information about your plans for the business. Considering the key nature of their involvement, it may be desirable to have them sign an agreement which enjoins them from sharing that information with other ongoing businesses who can benefit from copying your ideas, presentation, or overall concept before you have had a chance to open. You might also consider devising a similar form to help protect you during the growth stages of your business.

Nondisclosure/Noncompete Agreement During Initial Start-up Phase

I, _____, have been invited to review extremely confidential and valuable information. I realize this information has been gathered at considerable expense to others and has been shared with me due to my possible involvement. I agree not to share or use this information with any parties without written consent from _____, or to use it for myself to enter into a competitive venture.

Employee (or Prospective Employee) Signature _____
Date _____

Signature Subscribed and Affirmed, or Sworn to, Before me in the County of
_____

State of _____

Date _____

~

RESOURCES

The following individuals, organizations, publications, and other sources can help the start-up entrepreneur to find information needed to make crucial decisions about launching a business. Doing extensive research before you take any costly first steps is crucial. The better informed you are about the industry you are contemplating, the higher your chances for success.

Professional Associations

American Business Women's Association
9100 Ward Parkway
Kansas City, MO 64114

Food Marketing Institute (FMI)
800 Connecticut Avenue
Washington, DC 20006-2701
202-429-8298
Source for publications, training materials

International Dairy/Deli/Bakery Association
PO Box 5528
Madison, WI 53705
608-238-7908

National Association for the Self-Employed
PO Box 612067
Dallas, TX 75261-2067

National Association for the Specialty Food Trade (NASFT)
120 Wall Street
New York, NY 10005

National Association of Women Business Owners
1413 K Street, NW, Suite 637
Washington, DC 20005

National Federation of Independent Business
53 Century Boulevard, Suite 300
Nashville, TN 37214

National Retail Federation
Liberty Place
325 7th Street, NW, Suite 1000
Washington, DC 20004
202-783-7971

National Small Business United
1155 15th Street
Washington, DC 20005

Retailer's Bakery Association
14239 Park Center Dr.
Laurel, MD 20707
301-725-2149

Small Business Foundation of America
1155 15th Street
Washington, DC 20005

Women in Franchising
53 West Jackson Boulevard, Suite 205
Chicago, IL 60604

Culinary Organizations

American Culinary Federation
10 San Bartola Drive
St. Augustine, FL 32086
800-624-9458

American Institute of Wine and Food
1550 Bryant Street, Suite 700
San Francisco, CA 94103
415-255-3000

International Association of Culinary Professionals
304 West Liberty, Suite 201
Louisville, KY 40202-3011
502-581-9786

James Beard Foundation
167 West 12th Street
New York, NY 10011
800-36-BEARD

Magazines

American Demographics
Business Week
CNBC How to Succeed in Business
Entrepreneur
Entrepreneurial Edge—Edward Lowe Foundation, founder of Kitty Litter
Fancy Food
Food Arts—for trends, chef profiles, restaurant layouts, in-depth articles on upscale foods and wines
Forbes
Fortune
Gourmet News
Gourmet Retailer
inc.
Nation's Business—US Chamber of Commerce
Nation's Restaurant News—good reportage on trends
Progressive Grocer—store profiles
Success
Supermarket Business

Web Sites

The following Web sites offer up-to-the-minute information on many areas of interest to the gourmet to go entrepreneur.

www.accessil.com/aisb/home/htm
The American Institute of Small Business offers information about seminars, workshops, and networking.

www.businessfinance.com
America's First Business Funding Directory provides information on potential funding sources.

www.census.gov
Provides data about jobs, housing, crime, income, transportation, recreation, and more, by city, county, and state. A good starting point for research on your market area.

www.dol.gov/dol/asp/public/programs/handbook/contents.htm
The Labor Department maintains a site that includes employment and small-business information.

EGG@aol.com
Food news, recipes, and other information for professionals and amateurs alike.

www.FoodNet.com
A site serving culinary professionals.

www.law.indiana.edu/law/v-lib/states.html
Provides links to state-specific law information useful for setting employee policies.

www.lowe.org
The Edward Lowe Foundation maintains this site, which includes smallbizNet and Entrpreneurial Edge Online, to provide news about venture capitalists, small-business legislation, and links to other online sources.

www.membership.com/aswe
Women entrepreneurs can turn to the American Society of Women Entrepreneurs and WomenBiz.

www.moneyhunter.com
Provides tips on sources of capital.

www.sbaonline.gov
A resource for SBA information on loan programs.

www.scn.org/civic/score-online
The Service Corps of Retired Executives (SCORE), a group of volunteers, provides personal counseling on business issues through your local Small Business Administration.

www.stat-usa.gov
The U.S. Department of Commerce provides a wide range of business and economic statistics on their site.

New web sites are constantly being created. Read the business pages of the major metropolitan newspapers for updates and information.

Database Searches

Obtaining current information about specialty food retailing via on-line searches is one avenue of approach. The following are good places to start. You will find that one search will lead to another.

America Online
8619 Westwood Center Drive
Vienna, VA 22182-2285
800-927-6364

Compuserve Information Service, Inc.
PO Box 20212
Columbus, OH 43220
800-848-8199

Dialog Information Services, Inc.
Knight Ridder Information, Inc.
2440 El Camino Real
Mountain View, CA 94040
800-334-2564
This service provides focused database searches for a fee. Culled from trade journals, this information may be helpful in gaining insight into particular industry trends, both national and regional.

Dow Jones News/Retrieval
Dow Jones and Company
PO Box 300
Princeton, NJ 08543-0300
800-522-3567

Federal Database Finder
Edited by Sharon Zarozny
Published by Information USA, Inc.
Chevy Chase, MD 20814

Foods AdLibra
612-540-2720
This is one of many on-line search services who will do the reading for you, digesting all the major trends and zeroing in on specific hot products or dishes about which you should be aware.

Newsnet
945 Haverford Road
Bryn Mawr, PA 19010
800-345-1301

Demographic Data

American Demographics, Inc.
PO Box 68
Ithaca, NY 14851
800-828-1133

Demographics USA
355 Park Avenue South
New York, NY 10010
800-266-4714

Books, Data Products, and Other Business Reference Sources

American Profile System
Donnelly Marketing
1515 Summer Street
Stanford, CT 06905
203-353-7000

Bureau of the Census
US Department of Commerce
Washington, DC 20233
301-763-7662
301-763-1580

Bureau of Labor Statistics
Division of Information Services
441 G Street, NW
Washington, DC 20212
202-523-1239

E & P Market Guide
Editor and Publisher Company
575 Lexington Avenue
New York, NY 10022
212-675-4380

A Guide to Consumer Markets
The Conference Board, Inc.
Information Services
845 Third Avenue
New York, NY 10022
212-759-0900

S & MM's Survey of Buying Power, Parts 1 and 2
Sales and Marketing Management
355 Park Avenue South
New York, NY 10010
212-592-6300

Sourcebook of Demographics and Buying Power for Every Zip Code in the USA
CACI, Inc.
℅ Find SVP
500 Fifth Avenue
New York, NY 10110
800-346-3787
212-354-2424

Tough Times—Tough Tactics, The Tenant's Guide to Leasing Commercial Real Estate
is available in a *Retail and Restaurant Edition* and an *Office Edition*
Andrew M. Johnson, Managing Director of Johnson Commercial Brokerage, 1994
800-270-4848

Key Entrepreneurial Sources

Statistical Abstract of the United States
US Department of Commerce
Washington, DC 20233
202-482-2000
Provides data on a wide range of subjects: population, housing, manufacturers, businesses, mineral industries, agriculture, transportation, and government. Information is available on national figures, as well as city, county, state, and regional. Catalogs are available.

Entrepreneur Educational Sources

The Association of Collegiate Entrepreneurs (ACE)
Wichita State University
Box 40A
Wichita, KS 67208
316-689-3000
A national organization of student and future entrepreneurs with chapters at leading business schools around the country.

The Association of MBA Executives (AMBA)
277 Commerce Street
East Haven, CT 06512
203-467-8870
A 20,000-member network for business school graduates. Publishes a bimonthly magazine entitled *MBA Executive*. Membership is $55 per year; $25 for students.

Center for Entrepreneurial Management Inc.
180 Varick Street
17th Floor
New York, NY 10014
212-633-0060
Nonprofit membership association of entrepreneurs and CEOs.

Entrepreneurship Education
by Karl H. Vesper, available from
UCLA, Anderson School of Management
Attn: Cindy Adams
Room 4284
405 Hilgard Avenue
Los Angeles, CA 90024-1481
310-825-2985
Course descriptions, alphabetically by school, plus name of person most recently known to be associated with the course. A good way for teachers of entrepreneurship to exchange information.

International Council for Small Business
St. Louis University
3674 Lindell Boulevard
St. Louis, MO 63100
314-977-3896
or
Ryerson Polytechnic Institute
350 Victoria Street
Toronto, Ontario
Canada M5B2K3
Raymond Kao, President
A research foundation that focuses on academic development of entrepreneurial and small business applications. Sponsors an annual international entrepreneurship conference and publishes a quarterly journal.

Junior Colleges or Community Colleges
The National Small Business Training Network, established and maintained through
a grant from the Small Business Administration, is a network of 186 2-year colleges in
47 states that concentrate on providing business training. Contact your local college
or SBA office for information.

MIT Enterprise Forum
Massachusetts Institute of Technology
MIT Alumni Association
77 Massachusetts Avenue
Cambridge, MA 02139
617-253-8200

Business Plans that Win $$$, published by the MIT Enterprise Forum
To contact them locally:
MIT Enterprise Forum of New York
MIT Alumni Center of New York
50 East 41 Street
New York, NY 10017
212-532-8181
An opportunity for companies seeking advice or assistance to present their case
before a panel of experts. The panel offers constructive advice after reviewing the
entrepreneur's business plan. There are MIT Forums in a dozen locations throughout
the country. Additionally, the Enterprise Forum publishes a monthly newsletter.

National Association for the Self-Employed
PO Box 612067
DFW Airport, TX 75261-2067
800-232-6273
The self-employed members of this association have access to a business consultant
hotline. Group health and disability insurance is also available.

National Business Incubation Association
One President Street
Athens, OH 45701
614-593-4331
Provides information on the benefits of business incubation and offers training in the
management and development of incubators.

National Federation of Independent Business
53 Century B, Suite 300
Nashville, TN 37214
615-872-5800
Represents the interest of independent and small businesses to US and state legislative bodies.

Howard Solganik
5531 Far Hills Avenue
Dayton, OH 45429
513-438-1666
Consultant to supermarkets and the food service industry; runs seminars for store operators, provides specialized consulting and marketing services.

Zingtrain
421 Detroit Street
Ann Arbor, MI 10158
Contact: Maggie Bayless
This company offers three-day training sessions on retail store operations, staff motivation and other issues pertinent to the specialty food retailer, based at Zingerman's Deli in Ann Arbor, MI (See Zingerman's mission statement, excerpts from newsletter, and house organ for staff elsewhere in this book.)

Entrepreneur Reference Books

Starting a Business, Selling a Business
Business Basics
Pueblo, CA 81009

Catalog of Catalogs, 1997: *The Complete Mail Order Directory*
Edward L. Palder
Woodbine House
This is a survival guide and success kit for small business owners on how to launch and grow a business. It's packed full of entrepreneurial guidelines, tips, and new resources. Library resource book.

Entrepreneur's Handbook, 1994 Edition
Richard Buskirk
Premier Entrepreneur Programs, Inc.
3551 S. Monaco Parkway, Suite 254
Denver, CO 80237
This book is a comprehensive review of the field of entrepreneurship and features a practical "how-to approach," which includes all aspects of playing the entrepreneurial game. It is used as a classroom text as well as a working guide for aspiring entrepreneurs.

New Venture Creation: Entrepreneurship for the 21st Century
Jeffry A. Timmons
Richard D. Irwin, Inc., 1995
Homewood, IL 60430
This book presents an overall view of entrepreneurship that treats it as the meeting of an opportunity, an individual, and the environment. It features cases, concepts, and new research findings and is designed as a classroom text with reference sources for entrepreneurs.

Entrepreneurship
Robert Ronstadt
South Western Publishing Company, 1996
800-543-0487
This book includes a text, cases, and notes designed primarily for classroom use. It contains some practical information for the entrepreneur. The cases, which tend to be quite lengthy, provide the entrepreneur with special insight to solutions that confront entrepreneurs in starting as well as growing enterprises.

Entrepreneurship, Intrapreneurship, and Venture Capital
Robert D. Hisrich
Lexington Books
Jossey-Bass, Inc.
800-956-7739
This book provides blueprints for stimulating innovation and the entrepreneurial spirit, for attracting seed and venture capital to support the development of new ideas, and for bringing innovations to the marketplace. It incorporates a section on internal venturing for major corporations.

New Business Ventures and the Entrepreneur
Howard H. Stevenson, Michael J. Roberts, and H. Irving Grousbeck
Richard D. Irwin, Inc., 1993
Homewood, IL 60430
800-634-3961
This book features interesting entrepreneurial cases and technical notes on all aspects of entrepreneurship, tracing the process from the initial stage through business operations to the harvest of results. It includes sample business plans, prospectuses, leases, laws, and legal opinions.

The Entrepreneur's Master Planning Guide
John A. Welsh and Jerry A. White
Prentice-Hall, Inc.
Englewood Cliffs, NJ 07631
This book discusses the components of building a business from the concept stage to developing a competitive marketing strategy to financing under changing economic conditions. It specializes in explaining how the entrepreneur prepares and uses cash flow to ensure a successful venture.

Investing in Private Companies
Arthur Lipper and George Ryan
Dow Jones/Irwin
Homewood, IL 60430
This book takes a practical approach, written from the experience gained by author Lipper as a result of investing in many different types of new ventures. It is written from the investor's viewpoint, yet gives much insight to the entrepreneur seeking financing to drive his/her venture.

Big Profits from Small Companies
Steven B. Popell
Lomas Publishing Company
Mountain View, CA
This book focuses on becoming a better manager of an entrepreneurial company. It presents reasons why companies fail and provides guidelines and techniques for marketing management, financial management, profit management, and bank relations.

How to Prepare and Present a Business Plan
Joseph R. Mancuso
Simon and Schuster, 1990
800-223-2336
This book provides a practical workbook approach explaining what to include in a business plan, how a business plan is analyzed by investors, and how to present it to financial decision-makers.

Anatomy of a Business Plan and *Automate Your Business Plan* software
Linda Pinson, small business educator and software developer
Out of Your Mind . . . and into the Marketplace
Tustin, CA 92781
714-544-0248 or 800-419-1513

Business Plans that Win $$$: Lessons from the MIT Enterprise Forum
Stanley R. Rich and David E. Gumpert
HarperCollins Publishers, 1987
New York, NY 10022
This book is a summary of the experiences gained from the MIT Enterprise Forums, which furnish the entrepreneur with practical advice for developing, writing, and presenting the business plan to obtain financing for growing businesses.

Playing Hardball with Soft Skills
Steven J. Bennett
Bantam Books
New York, NY
This paperback offers a pragmatic approach to marketing new business ideas. Practical but imaginative methods for developing success from "soft skills" in this technical age are stressed.

Innovation and Entrepreneurship: Practice and Principles
Peter F. Drucker
Harper Business, 1993
New York, NY
800-242-7737
This book presents both innovation and entrepreneurship as a practice and discipline that can and should be organized. It uses case examples and explains what established businesses, public-service institutions, and new ventures have to know, learn, and do.

Encyclopedia of Entrepreneurship
C. Kent, D. Sexton, and K. H. Vesper, Eds.
Prentice-Hall, Inc.
Englewood Cliffs, NJ
This book is a collection of research articles by academicians on the entrepreneurial process and suggestions for further research.

Encyclopedia of Small Business Resources
David E. Gumpert and Jeffry Timmons
Harper & Row
New York, NY
This book presents a topical listing of sources for information, consulting help, and capital for new and small enterprises. It is a helpful entrepreneurial resource source.

Experiences in Entrepreneurship and Small Business Management
Donald L. Sexton and Philip M. VanAuken
Prentice-Hall, Inc.
Englewood Cliffs, NJ
This book is primarily a case book in small business management, designed for use in most entrepreneurship and small business courses.

Entrepreneurship for the Eighties
Gordon Baty
Prentice-Hall, Inc.
Englewood Cliffs, NJ
This book provides the entrepreneur with a practical walk-through of how to start a new business.

The Entrepreneur's Planning Handbook, 1994 Edition
Richard H. Buskirk
Creative Management Unlimited, Inc.
3551 S. Monaco Parkway, Suite 254
Denver, CO 80237
303-761-3119
The *Planning Handbook* is a step-by-step guide on business and operational planning. Over 200 questions help you research and write a professional business plan.

Raising Venture Capital and the Entrepreneur
Leonard A. Batterson
Prentice-Hall, Inc.
Englewood Cliffs, NJ
This book specializes in explaining how to secure financing from venture capital funds. It provides resource lists of all different types of venture capital organizations, including a book list, venture capital directory, incubator directory, and deal-doing lawyer directory.

"How to Read a Financial Report"
Merrill Lynch, Pierce, Fenner & Smith, Inc.
Merrill Lynch Response Center
PO Box 20200
New Brunswick, NJ 08968-0200
800-637-7455 (ext. 1745)
If you are not an accountant and you find that annual reports are "over your head," this booklet (Code 10006-0197) can help you grasp the facts contained in such reports to become a better informed investor. It can be obtained free of charge by contacting their regional offices.

The Successful Business Library
The Oasis Press
300 North Valley Drive
Grants Pass, OR 97526
541-479-9464 or to order 800-228-2275
A series of practical "how to books" provides the basic information needed to start and operate a new business venture. Listed below are some of the books most helpful to the entrepreneur. They can be obtained at most local bookstores or through the 800 number.
Starting and Operating a Business Series (available for all states including Washington, DC)
The Essential Corporation Handbook
The Buyer's Guide to Business Insurance
The Successful Business Plan: Secrets & Strategies
Start Your Business: A Beginner's Guide
Financial Management Techniques for Small Business
The Business Environmental Handbook

Entrepreneurship and Management
Clifford M. Baumback and Joseph R. Mancuso
Prentice Hall, Inc.
Englewood Cliffs, NJ
This book is oriented toward the entrepreneur and new business formation. It contains 36 selected articles by well-known writers in the field.

Entrepreneurial Megabucks
A. David Silver
John Wiley & Sons
New York, NY
Lists 100 of the greatest entrepreneurs in the last 25 years who generated over $100 billion.

The Entrepreneur's Guide to Capital
Jennifer Lindsay
Probus Publishing
Chicago, IL
This book offers techniques for capitalizing and refinancing new and growing businesses. It contains references that business owners need to properly finance their enterprises.

Who's Who in Venture Capital
A. David Silver
John Wiley & Sons
New York, NY
This book is a directory of venture capitalists and venture capital funds; it contains biographical data on 1,100 venture capitalists. It can aid the entrepreneur in matching business plans to the proper venture capitalists.

Intrapreneuring
Gifford Pinchot, III
HarperCollins, 1986
New York, NY
800-331-3761
This book is designed for internal corporate entrepreneurs who are given the freedom and incentive to create and market new business ideas for their own profit and for the company. It presents techniques for developing entrepreneurial talents within the corporate structure.

The Complete Book of Corporate Forms
Ted Nicholas
Enterprise Publishing, Inc.
Wilmington, DE
This collection of over 150 simplified basic forms for incorporation also contains instructions for their use. It simplifies corporate law, although specifics may vary from state to state.

Buying and Selling a Business: A Step-by-Step Guide
Robert F. Kleuger
John Wiley & Sons, 1988
New York, NY
This treatment of problems encountered in buying and selling a business gives procedures for mergers and acquisitions. Ready-to-use forms, checklists, worksheets, sample correspondence, contracts, and agreements are included.

Basic Book of Business Agreements
Arnold S. Goldstein
Enterprise Publishing, Inc.
Wilmington, DE
This book contains ready-to-use agreements, contracts, letters, and forms covering most routine business agreements. Instructions for using these documents are included.

Program for Writing Winning Business Plans
Creative Management Unlimited
3551 S. Monaco Parkway, Suite 254
Denver, CO 80237
303-761-3119
This is an easy-to-follow guideline for writing a business plan. It covers product evaluation, marketing, competition, organization, financing, and other essential elements of a business plan.

Small Business Sourcebook
Gale Research, 1992
835 Penobscot Building
Detroit, MI 48226-4094
800-877-4253
An easy-to-use directory that identifies where to find general business help and includes special sections covering 163 specific types of small businesses and where to find advice and assistance. This is an excellent resource on where to begin research on starting a new business.

Sample Business Plans
Creative Management Unlimited
3551 S. Monaco Parkway, Suite 254
Denver, CO 80237
303-761-3119
This book is a collection of selected business plans to use as models while preparing one. It includes retail, service, manufacturing, and product business plans.

Creating Effective Boards for Private Enterprise
John L. Ward
Jossey-Bass, 1991
This book suggests ways to create an effective board of directors.

Growing a Business
Paul Hawken
Simon & Schuster, 1988
This book provides an overall view of starting and operating a business.

Honest Business
Michael Phillips and Salli Rasberry
Random House, 1981
800-726-0600
This book provides the idea that there is more than one way to run a company and there are many ways to measure success.

Start Up: An Entrepreneur's Guide to Launching and Managing a New Venture
Rock Beach Press, 1989
716-442-0888
This book offers an overall start-up plan for new businesses.

Ultra-Preneuring
James B. Arkebauer
McGraw-Hill, 1993
New York, NY
800-2-MCGRAW
This book describes how to take a venture from start-up to harvest in three years or less.

Financial Sources

Capitalbase: Over 10,000 Sources for Start-Up or Expanding Business Software by Datamerge, Inc., 1994

Data Merge, Inc.
4521 East Virginia Avenue, Suite 201
Denver, CO 80222
Contact: John Bach
303-320-8361

Provides databases of financial sources for small businesses and entrepreneurs. Also provides packages for business plans and loan proposals, national and international.

Cash Flow Problem Solver: Common Problems and Practical Solutions
Bryan Milling
Sourcebooks, 1991
800-432-7444
This book offers suggestions on financing for the person who is intimidated by numbers.

Commercial Finance Association
225 W. 34th Street
New York, NY 10122
212-594-3490
International trade association for the financial services industry.

The Ernst & Young Guide to Financing for Growth, 1994
Daniel R. Garner, Robert R. Owen and Robert P. Conway
John Wiley & Sons
New York, NY
This book is an entrepreneur's overall guide to financing.

Financing Sources Databank: Find Millions in Financing in Five Minutes or Less, 1994
DataMerge, Inc.
4521 East Virginia Avenue, Suite 201
Denver, CO 80222
303-320-8361
This software offers an assortment of financing alternatives.

Keeping What's Yours: Proven Asset Protection Strategies for Everything from
Handling Creditors to Becoming Legally Judgment-Proof
Brett K. Kates
Dearborn Trade, 1994
312-836-4400
This book suggests many ideas for the overall functions of financing for the small business.

Money Sources for Small Business: How You Can Find Private, State, Federal, and
Corporate Financing
William Alarid
Puma Publishing, 1991
800-255-5730
This book lists alternative methods of financing.

National Association of Trade Exchanges
27801 Euclid Avenue, Suite 610
Euclid, OH 44132
This association provides business owners with information on barter exchanges in their area. These exchanges have a network of businesses who barter goods and services. They usually charge an annual membership fee and collect 10 to 15% of each trade.

Planning and Financing the New Venture
Jeffry A. Timmons
Brick House Publishing, 1990
Amherst, NH
800-446-8642
Covers the practicalities of planning start-up, finding money and negotiating the deal.

Government & Business Resources

Chamber of Commerce USA
1615 H Street, NW
Washington, DC 20062
202-659-6000
Provides data on all forms of business nationwide. Ask for sources of state information and state industrial directories. Local chambers can supply information for a specific region.

Consumer Information
Superintendent of Documents
US Government Printing Office
Washington, DC 20402
202-783-3238
Comprehensive lists of publications are available from the Government Printing Office.

Consumer Information Catalog
Consumer Resource Handbook
US Office of Consumer Affairs
Consumer Information Center
Pueblo, CO 81009
Identifies the major federal agencies and US corporations.

The Directory of Federal and State Business Assistance
National Technical Information Service
US Department of Commerce
Springfield, VA 22161
703-487-4650
This publication lists more than 180 federal and 500 state business assistance programs and provides information on funding, assistance finding, free management consulting, and more.

Directory of State and Federal Funds
Pilot Books
103 Cooper Street
Babylon, NY 11702
519-422-2225
Provides information on financial assistance available through federal and state agencies and enables the entrepreneur to determine the possible sources and programs to fit specific needs in a concise manner.

The Entrepreneur's Guide to Doing Business with the Federal Government
Charles R. Bevers with Linda G. Christie and Lynn R. Price
Prentice-Hall, Inc.
Englewood Cliffs, NJ
This book offers many ideas for entrepreneurs interested in pursuing procurement opportunities with the federal government.

Gale Research, Inc.
835 Penobscot Building
Detroit, MI 48226
800-877-4253
Publishes *Small Business Source*, which lists state and federal government programs.

General Services Administration
18th & F Streets, NW
Washington, DC 20405
202-472-1082
202-566-1231 (Public Information)
703-557-7901 (Procuring Information)
202-535-7662 (Freedom of Information)
Assistance in locating the proper government agency or bureau to render help.

Gibbs Publishing
Box 1120
Vacaville, CA 95696
707-448-0270
Publishes a list of federal loans and grants.

Information U.S.A.
Matthew Lesko
Viking Penguin, 1986
This volume contains names, addresses, and phone numbers for a wide variety of government data experts, and an exhaustive listing of government publications, available free or at low cost.

Internal Revenue Service
Taxpayer Service Division
111 Constitution Avenue, NW
Washington, DC 20224
202-622-5000
Provides a publication list addressing the tax issues of concern to entrepreneurs.

Library of Congress
10 First Street, SE
Washington, DC 20540
202-707-5522 (National Reference Service)
202-707-7564 (Photo Duplication Service)
The Library of Congress in Washington, DC is the largest library in the world. The library's Reference Service can be of great help in locating information you are trying to find. If the requested information is not too extensive, the staff can relay it over the phone. If the needed information is too in-depth, you will be referred to a private researcher who charges a fee. Another excellent source is the Library's photo duplication service, which will find material and send you photocopies. Turnaround time can run six to eight weeks.

National Association of Development Agencies
4301 N. Fairfax Drive #860
Arlington, VA 22203
703-812-9000
SBA loan programs that promote small business expansion for fixed asset financing.

National Association of Small Business Investment Companies (SBIC)
1199 N. Fairfax Street, Suite 200
Alexandria, VA 22314
703-683-1601
Firms, sponsored by the SBA, that provide loans to small business.

National Association of State Development Agencies
750 First Street, NE #710
Washington, DC 20002
202-898-1302
Publishes *Directory of Incentives for Business Investment and Development in the United States.*

National Institute of Standards and Technology
Building 411, Room A115
Gaithersburg, MD 20899-0001
301-975-5500
Promotes US economic growth through technology, measurement, and standards.

Procurement Automated Source System (PASS)
Procurement Assistance
Small Business Administration
1441 L Street, NW
Room 628
Washington, DC 20416
202-653-6938
The SBA facilitates small businesses in procurement opportunities through the Office of Procurement & Technical Assistance. The PASS organization brings together federal agencies, major contractors, and small businesses.

Roadmap
Office of Business Liaison
Room H5898C
US Department of Commerce
Washington, DC 20230
202-377-3176
This program can assist you in answering questions regarding government policies, programs, or services. It can also help you locate published materials on a variety of topics.

Service Corps of Retired Executives (SCORE)
409 Third Street, SW
Washington, DC 20416
202-205-6600
800-827-5722 (Answer Desk)
SCORE provides free individual counseling, courses, conferences, and workshops. The answer desk provides information on all government agencies. Check your local SBA for SCORE services.

Small Business Administration
1441 L Street, NW
Washington, DC 20416
202-205-7701
Internet address: www.sbaonline.com
Services include: Women's business advice; veteran affairs; disaster, financial, management, minority, and small business assistance; statistical data; export advice. Check with your local SBA also.

Small Business Administration Publications
PO Box 15434
Fort Worth, TX 76119
817-355-1933 or 817-885-6500
The SBA offers free and low-cost booklets to help you plan your budgets, personnel policies, and business plans. A publications list is available.

Small Business Innovation Research Program (SBIR)
Office of Innovation, Research & Technology
Small Business Administration
1441 L Street, NW
Washington, DC 20416
Provides seed money grants to serve as research and development funds. Administration is controlled by governmental agencies.

US Government Printing Office
Superintendent of Documents
Washington, DC 20402
202-783-3228
The US government is the largest publisher in the world. Typically documents are concise and very readable. There are a variety of publications on topics ranging from starting a business to securing funding. Consult *The Monthly Catalog of US Government Publications* or order its *Subject Bibliography Index*. You could also contact one of their Government Depository Libraries or GPO Bookstores located in most major cities.

Washington Researchers
2612 P Street, NW
Washington, DC 20007
202-333-3499
A collection of books, tapes, and directories to provide information on available government services and programs.

Library Sources

The following books are considered to be industry standards and are available in most libraries.

The Almanac of Business and Industrial Financial Ratios
Leo Troy
Prentice-Hall, 1996
Lists total receipts and 22 ratios for industries.

City and State Directories in Print
Gale Research
835 Penobscot Building
Detroit, MI 48226-4094
800-223-GALE
Business and industrial directories, buyers' guides, association membership lists, and other directories whose coverage is limited single locations.

Do-It-Yourself Market Research, 1989
George E. Breen and Albert B. Blackenship
McGraw-Hill
New York, NY

Rent-a-Researcher
Some libraries now offer these programs at a reasonable price for those individuals who have gotten as far as they can on their own.

RMA's Annual Statement Studies
Provides information on the four sizes of businesses in every major industry. Includes income statements and financial ratios.

Securities Data Publishing, Inc.
40 W. 57th Street, 11th Floor
New York, NY 10019
212-765-5311
Publisher of business reference books.

State and County Business Patterns
Lists local businesses' sales and annual payroll as well as other information available for each state and county.

Thomas Register
Thomas Publishing
800-647-1908
Lists industry manufacturers, addresses, and volumes of business. It is a three-volume set of useful manufacturers' information. Library resource book.

Standard & Poor's Industry Surveys
US Industrial Outlook
Standard & Poor's Corp.
25 Broadway
New York, NY 10004

Company Information

Contacts Influential
Ward's Business Directory
Gale Research, Inc.
835 Penobscot Building
Detroit, MI 48226-4094
800-877-4253

Demographic Data

County Business Patterns
County and City Extra
Lifestyle Market Analyst
Sourcebook of Zip Code Demographics
Sourcebook of Country Demographics

Periodicals and Other Publications

Business Start-Ups
Entrepreneur Media, Inc.
2392 Morse Avenue
Irvine, CA 92714
714-261-2325

Entrepreneur
2392 Morse Avenue
Irvine, CA 92714
714-261-2325

The Funk & Scott Index
F&S is a leading guide to published articles about industries and about company activities and developments, including new products, technology, forecast, company analysis, etc. Most libraries have this index.

Harvard Business Review
Harvard University
Graduate School of Business
Soldiers Field
Boston, MA 02163
617-495-6182

Home Office Computing
Scholastic, Inc.
411 Lafayette St.
New York, NY 10003
212-505-4220

In Business
Magna Publications, Inc.
2718 Dryden Drive
Madison, WI 53704-3086
608-249-2455

Inc.
Technology Publishing, Inc.
670 West End Avenue
New York, NY 10025

Money
Subsidiary of Time, Inc.
Time and Life Building
Rockefeller Center
New York, NY 10029-1393
800-633-9970

Success
Success Unlimited, Inc.
401 N. Wabash Avenue, Suite 530
Chicago, IL 60611
312-828-9500

Ulrich International Periodicals Directory
Gale Directory of Publications
Standard Periodical Directory
Newsletters in Print
Oxbridge Directory of Newsletters
These are periodicals and newsletters covering thousands of different subjects. The directories identify tens of thousands of magazines, newsletters, newspapers, journals, and other periodicals. Practically all libraries have one or more of these directories.

Wall Street Journal
Editorial and Publication Headquarters
200 Liberty Street
New York, NY 10281

Wall Street Journal Index
An index to articles published in the *Wall Street Journal* and *Barron's*. There are two parts: a subject index and a company name index. This index is available in nearly all libraries.

Yellow Pages
One of the cheapest, quickest sources of information for the entrepreneur. A good source for researching your competition.

National Trade and Professional Associations

Trade associations are membership organizations specializing in a particular line of business—like the Menswear Retailing Association. They offer beneficial sources of information and assistance. For a complete list of associations, refer to the *Encyclopedia of Associations, Vol. 1*. It, and the other directories listed below, should be available at your local library.

American Society of Association Executives
1575 Eye Street, NW
Washington DC 20005-1168
202-626-2723
Call or write this association of associations to find those that deal with your area.

Business Publication Rates and Data
Standard Rate and Data Service
5201 Old Orchard Road
Skokie, IL 60077
Names and addresses of business periodicals are listed by name of magazine and business fields. Library resource book.

Directory of Conventions and Successful Meetings
New York, NY
This publication lists conventions and professional conference held around the country and can be found at larger libraries.

Encyclopedia of Associations, Vol. 1
National Organizations of the United States
Gale Research Company
Book Tower
Detroit, MI 48226
Offers detailed information and addresses of trade associations. Library resource book.

The IMS Ayer Directory of Newspapers, Magazines, and Trade Associations
Ayer Press
West Washington Square
Philadelphia, PA 19106
Lists names and addresses of business publications and trade associations. Library resource book.

National Trade and Professional Associations of the United States
Columbia Books
777 14th Street, NW
Washington, DC 20005
Lists in alphabetical order 6,300 national trade associations, labor unions, and professional societies.

Trade Show Information

There are three major publication sources for trade shows: *Trade Show Week Data Book*, 800-521-8100; *Trade Show and Exhibit Schedules*, 800-253-6708; and *Trade Shows Worldwide*, 800-877-4253. You should be able to find these publications in your local library.

Trade Show Bureau
1660 Lincoln Street, Suite 2080
Denver, CO 80264
303-860-7626
This national bureau is the industry's resource center, providing information about the latest industry trends, successful practices, and hot topics of interest. An extensive catalog of publications assists entrepreneurs with exhibiting at trade shows.

National Association of Small Business Investment Companies
1199 N. Fairfax Street, Suite 200
Alexandria, VA 22314
703-683-1601
Trade association for its industry.

INDEX